Race Versus Class

The New Affirmative Action Debate

For my friend, Mentor, and Colleague with much love and admiration.

Edited by
Carol M. Swain

*Carol
10/1/96*

University Press of America, Inc.
Lanham • New York • London

Copyright © 1996 by
University Press of America,® Inc.
4720 Boston Way
Lanham, Maryland 20706

3 Henrietta Street
London, WC2E 8LU England

Library of Congress Cataloging-in-Publication Data

Races versus class : the new affirmative action debate / edited by Carol
M. Swain.
p.   cm.
1. Civil rights--United States. 2. Affirmative action programs--
United States. 3. United States--Race relations. 4. Social classes--
United States. I. Swain, Carol M. (Carol Miller)
JC599.U5R23   1996   323.1'73 --dc20   96-21837   CIP

ISBN 0-7618-0412-9 (cloth: alk. ppr.)
ISBN 0-7618-0413-7 (pbk: alk. ppr.)

Contents

iv

Tables and Figures

Chapter 3

Chapter 4

vi

Preface

After profoundly shaping the character of America's major public and private institutions for more than twenty-five years, affirmative action now finds itself under formidable attack from those who question the use of group preferences as a means of countering past discrimination. Indeed, many cite the Republican party's relentless assault on preferential treatment as a major factor in its stunning electoral success in the fall of 1994. Whatever the merits of the arguments on either side, one thing is clear—affirmative action is currently provoking a national debate that is more open, more contentious, and more polarized than at any other time in the policy's history.

The essays in this volume address important aspects of the affirmative action controversy. Most were written in conjunction with a student-led Task Force on Affirmative Action during the spring semester of 1995 that was sponsored by Princeton University's Woodrow Wilson School of Public and International Affairs. The task force's theme—"Redesigning Affirmative Action Policies for the 1990s"—was originally proposed by Professor Carol M. Swain, who served as organizer and faculty leader. Task force members met for three hours each week and heard a variety of speakers on the issue. Those who addressed the task force included Derrick Bell, New York University Law School; Wilbur Hicks, Princeton University ombudsman; Randall Kennedy, Harvard Law School; Nancy King, Vanderbilt Law School; Andrew Koppelman, Politics Department, Princeton University; Glenn Loury, Economics Department, Boston University; Joann Mitchell, associate provost and special assistant to the president, Princeton University; Karen Nagasaki, National Asian Pacific American Legal Consortium; and Russell Nieli, Politics Department, Princeton University.

Although task force members came to the topic from different perspectives, there was considerable agreement on several important points. Members were agreed, for example, that a polarized racial climate had developed in the United States in recent years, particularly regarding affirmative action, and that this climate had prevented the development of a healthy, informed, and constructive national dialogue. Many came to believe, further, that the issue of affirmative action was an unusually complex one that often called for varying and highly

vii

nuanced responses to the circumstances at hand. Support for certain affirmative action policies in certain areas under certain specified conditions should not be taken to imply wholesale support for all such policies everywhere. And in the current polarized climate, it was clear that both supporters and opponents of affirmative action had been driven to take extreme positions that thwarted the search for a more moderate, consensus-building middle ground.

Task force members also generally viewed current affirmative action policy as insufficiently targeted at the poor and disadvantaged members of the minority groups it was intended to benefit. Many members believed that the policy should either be redesigned specifically to target poor blacks, poor Hispanics, and the disadvantaged members of other minorities or be converted into a more general means-tested program that would seek to benefit the poor and disadvantaged of all races and ethnic groups. The latter solution, it was felt, would be not only better suited to aid those most in need but more likely to enjoy public support than current policies.

Another common perception concerned the need for more extensive empirical data on the effects of affirmative action initiatives. There is a vacuum of information concerning those who receive preferential treatment under affirmative action, and it is often not known how many people benefit from specific policies, their socioeconomic background or other pertinent characteristics, or what would happen if race-based preferences were replaced by a race-neutral scheme. The highly politicized nature of the current debate seems responsible for this dearth of objective data.

Finally, almost all members of the task force agreed that whatever changes may occur in affirmative action policies in the near future, there will be a continuing need for rigorous and aggressive enforcement of existing antidiscrimination laws. Prejudice against minorities and women is not a thing of the past, and government at all levels will have an important role to play in ensuring nondiscrimination in employment and other areas of American life.

Of the nine essays in this volume, all but one (by Frederick Vars) was written by a task force member. Chapter 1, by Carol Swain, offers a general survey of the history and development of race-based affirmative action policies from their inception in the late 1960s. She traces the shift from color-blind equal opportunity policies to race- and ethnicity-based affirmative action policies, and gives an account of the major Supreme Court decisions that deal with race-conscious public policies in the areas of employment, education, voting, and contracting set-asides. Swain, like many other members of the task force, suggests that in the wake of continuing public hostility, the wisest course to follow in regard to aiding disadvantaged minorities may be to replace race- and ethnicity-based public programs with those based either primarily or exclusively on need.

In Chapter 2, April Chou delves into the many difficulties and complexities involved in sorting out the U.S. population according to race. Chou stresses the socially constructed nature of all racial and ethnic categories and both the arbitrariness and the poor fit of the current classificatory scheme. She concludes with a number of suggestions for change.

Fredrick Vars, in Chapter 3, presents the findings of a survey he conducted that sought to measure attitudes regarding distributive and compensatory justice. Vars found that compensatory schemes enjoy considerable support when they are narrowly tailored to compensate actual victims of wrongdoing, but that this support falls off sharply when the beneficiary category is expanded to include large numbers of people who have not suffered personal loss. Support for compensatory policies increases, moreover, when the party that is required to make restitution to the victims of discrimination is perceived as an actual victimizer rather than a noninvolved third party.

In Chapter 4, Ricshawn Adkins takes a closer look at polls that have been taken to gauge public opinion on affirmative action and concludes that survey results on this topic are heavily influenced by question wording. She explains how polling results can be easily manipulated by parties with ideological interests at stake, and recommends a clearer definition of terms—particularly the term "affirmative action"—as a way of clearing up some of the confusion and ambiguity that exist in regard to the public's attitude toward race-based policies.

Justin McCrary considers the moral and philosophical issues surrounding race-conscious public policies in Chapter 5. McCrary explores various possible justifications for such policies and concludes that they are probably on firmest ground when defended as a means of compensating for past injuries (compensatory justice) rather than as a means of redistributing current wealth (distributive justice). As redistributive programs, today's affirmative action policies are deeply flawed, he believes, because they tend to benefit the more privileged members of the disadvantaged groups while often visiting their greatest harm upon the less privileged members of the relatively better-off groups.

In Chapter 6, Jessica Malman focuses on race-exclusive scholarships for college undergraduates. She concludes that such scholarships can be an important factor in attracting more blacks to predominantly white campuses, but suggests that the disadvantages of such policies are severe and may outweigh any positive good they do. Race-exclusive scholarships are generally won by middle-class blacks from educationally enriched home environments and do little to help poor blacks from more deprived circumstances. Moreover, such aid programs tend to exacerbate racial tensions on campus because many whites feel they are unjust and bitterly resent those who benefit. Malman thinks that race-exclusive scholarships should be replaced with scholarships for the disadvantaged, but rather than advocating that the qualifications for these awards become completely color-blind, she believes that race could be taken into account as one important criterion of disadvantage.

Jonathan Goldman, in Chapter 7, similarly adopts the view that affirmative action programs—at least those in higher education—should be based on relative disadvantage, with race included as a critical determining element. He develops the outlines of a ranking scheme he calls Fresh Start, which would allow consideration of race, gender, and socioeconomic status in awarding educational benefits to needy students. Goldman's Fresh Start approach is predicated on the central belief that education is the way out of poverty in America and should be the central focus of public policy concern.

Cindy Kam takes up the issue of residential segregation in Chapter 8. She presents considerable evidence demonstrating that housing discrimination continues to plague black Americans, and that aggressive government policies are needed to eradicate it. Government measures, she says, must go beyond merely reacting to individual complaints and should focus on disrupting the many commercial and informational networks that help to perpetuate racial exclusion in the housing market. Only in this way can the current racial and social isolation that afflicts so many African Americans in the United States be overcome.

In Chapter 9, Priya Rajan examines the Head Start program and suggests that it might serve as a model of a politically feasible mechanism to fulfill many affirmative action goals. Head Start has benefited many of the poor black and Hispanic children who have participated in it, and although studies have shown a "fade out" in terms of the ability of Head Start participants to sustain their improved cognitive development in elementary school, this, Rajan believes, merely demonstrates the need for follow-up programs aimed at those in the most disadvantaged circumstances. Improving the educational opportunities of the poor, she concludes, will help to raise the general level of competence in minority communities and allow more minorities to compete successfully for the rewards of American society.

This volume thus provides an overview of some of the more salient topics in the affirmative action debate. If anything can be said to characterize these chapters, it is a nonideological pragmatism that is free from the anger, guilt, and mutual recriminations that have poisoned many exchanges in the past. A new generation that is not burdened with the psychological and ideological baggage of the past gives voice in these pages to a new vision, a public policy future that looks toward practical results and the need to consider widely shared public attitudes concerning basic fairness and justice. It is hoped by all the contributors that these essays will point the way to a new "fresh start" in addressing the pressing problems in the areas of race and poverty that currently threaten the overall health and vitality of America's increasingly multiethnic—and increasingly polarized—society.

Acknowledgments

We would like to express our appreciation to the following people for their generous contributions to the success of this project: Ian Blasco, Alicia Gutierrez, Jill Nishi and Chris Schussler-Fiorenza. In addition, Reggie Cohen, Justin Estrin, Elizabeth Gretz, and Russell Nieli provided us with invaluable assistance with the editing, production, and proofreading of this volume. We are also indebted to Mr. J. Sherrerd for his generous financial support and for Mr. David Hillman for indexing this volume.

The Task Force on Affirmative Action
Woodrow Wilson School, Princeton University

Chapter 1

Affirmative Action Revisited

Carol M. Swain

A ffirmative action refers to a range of governmental and private initiatives that offer preferential treatment to members of designated racial or ethnic minority groups (or to other groups thought to be disadvantaged), usually as a means of compensating them for the effects of past and present discrimination. In the United States the groups covered by affirmative action include Asians, blacks, Hispanics, Native Americans, and white women. Among the areas covered are hiring, promotions, admissions to colleges and universities, government contracting, the disbursement of scholarships and grants, legislative districting, and jury selection.

Survey data indicate that most white Americans oppose affirmative action programs and consider them unfair to their group. Strong opposition to the policy was first noted in a 1977 Gallup poll which asked the following question:

> Some people say that to make up for past discrimination, women and members of minority groups should be given preferential

treatment in getting jobs and places in college. Others say that ability, as determined by test scores, should be the main consideration. Which point comes closest to how you feel on this matter?[1]

Eighty-three percent of white Americans responded that ability, as determined by test scores, rather than preferential treatment based on minority status or gender, should be the main consideration in employment and college admissions decisions. African Americans, too, show great ambivalence on the issue of preferential treatment.[2] In the same Gallup poll, for instance, 64 percent of non-whites believed ability as determined by test scores should be the main focus of employment and college admissions decisions rather than preferential treatment.

Despite their misgivings, however, African Americans are far more supportive than white Americans of affirmative action programs, and generally see a greater need for governmental policies of various sorts to assist the poor and disadvantaged.[3] Such racial differences can be seen, for instance, in a poll taken in 1988. When asked whether "blacks and other minorities should receive preference in hiring to makeup for past inequalities," 85 percent of whites disagreed with the idea (only 10 percent supported it), 64 percent of Hispanics disagreed (31 percent supported it), while a near-majority of blacks—a full 48 percent—*supported* the idea (44 percent opposed it). A majority of each of the three groups, however, opposed preferential treatment in college admissions.[4] Similarly, a 1991 *Newsweek* poll showed 72 percent of whites opposed to preferential treatment in hiring (only 19 percent favored the idea), while blacks were more evenly split, 48 percent against to 42 percent in favor.[5] Similar patterns have been shown in more recent polls.[6]

Although many Americans hold strong opinions on the subject, few, it would seem, have accurate information about what affirmative action policies are, how they work, or what they were meant to accomplish.[7] To some, affirmative action is simply the hiring of unqualified minorities or the admissions to colleges and universities of ill-prepared black students ahead of higher-achieving and better qualified whites. A young college-educated white woman, for instance, recently explained in a focus group her understanding of affirmative action in the following words:

If you are the hiring boss and one applicant is black and one of them is white, . . . you have to select the quota, . . . you have to fill that quota and hire the black.[8]

A white male agreed:

[Employers] will not take . . . white males when they have to take black, Hispanic, and Chinese . . . otherwise, they're going to be called racist. The government has put this policy in [place and] . . . rammed [it] down our throats, this [policy of] affirmative action.[9]

Some whites have understood the policies to mean that once hired, blacks could not be fired even with cause. As we shall see, the actual truth of the matter is more complicated than that suggested by some of these critics.

The Path from Equal Opportunity to Preferential Treatment

Equal Opportunity

When the civil rights movement began to achieve national prominence in the mid-1950s, African-American leaders such as the Reverend Martin Luther King, Jr., did not demand reparations for slavery or preferential treatment for minorities, but sought, rather, equal rights with whites and an end to discrimination. Decades earlier, the 1919 platform of the NAACP had similarly sought as its main goal equality of rights under the law and an equal opportunity for black Americans to partake of the many rewards and responsibilities of American public life. The NAACP platform proclaimed at that time its dedication to the following nine equal opportunity principles:

1. A vote for every Negro man and woman on the same terms as for white men and women.

2. An equal chance to acquire the kind of education that will enable the Negro everywhere wisely to use his vote.

3. A fair trial in the courts for all crimes of which he is accused by judges in whose election he has participated without discrimination because of race.

4. A right [for members of his race] to sit on the jury which passes judgment on him.

5. Defense against lynching and burning at the hands of mobs.

6. Equal service on railroad and other public carriers. This to mean sleeping car service, Pullman service, at the same cost and upon the same terms as other passengers.

7. Equal right to the use of public parks, libraries, and other community services for which he is taxed.

8. An equal chance for a livelihood in public and private employment.

9. The abolition of color-hyphenation and the substitution of straight Americanism. . . . [10]

Similar goals would later be sought by the Southern Christian Leadership Conference (SCLC) that was founded by King in 1957. The SCLC worked assiduously for equal rights and the full integration of black citizens into the wider American society.

Prior to the passage of comprehensive civil rights legislation in the late 50's and 60's, blacks in the South had been systematically denied such simple pleasures and amenities as the right to eat at a lunch counter, to sleep in a hotel, to eat in a restaurant, to use public restrooms, and to vote without personal risks—rights which white Americans had always taken for granted. The civil rights leaders of the 50's and 60's demanded no more from America than as a nation it live up to its ideal of equal rights under the law as that ideal had been embodied in both the Declaration of Independence and the post-Civil War amendments to the U.S. Constitution.

Two pieces of civil rights legislation passed in 1957 and 1960 represented modest breakthroughs for African Americans in their struggle for equal rights. With support from President Dwight Eisenhower, and under pressure from black leaders, Congress passed the 1957 Civil Rights Act which created a civil rights commission and authorized the Justice Department to initiate actions to counter irregularities in federal elections. A second civil rights bill in 1960 called for the use of federal referees to oversee voting procedures and to insure the preservation of state voting records. Like the 1957 act, the 1960 bill was designed to help prevent the intimidation of black voters in federal elections.

The concept of "affirmative action," which was taken over from labor law, did not become firmly associated with civil rights enforcement until 1961, the year President Kennedy issued Executive Order 10925. Kennedy's order directed all federal contractors to take "affirmative action" (the concept was not formally defined) to ensure nondiscrimination in hiring, promotions, and all other areas of private employment. While this represented considerable progress over the 1957 and 1960 bills, it did not address many of the major concerns of the NAACP including discrimination in public accommodations, in housing, in government employment, or discrimination in that sector of the private economy involving firms that did not have contracts with the federal government.

Continued pressure from the NAACP and civil rights leaders, however, in conjunction with the urban riots in the summer of 1963, and the increased white-initiated violence in the South during the same period (which shocked millions of Americans when it was displayed in all its brutality on national television), convinced President Kennedy to take stronger action than his previous Executive Order. In the summer of 1963 Kennedy appealed to Congress to pass legislation giving all Americans equal rights and equal access to public accommodations and jobs in what some at the time hailed as "the civil rights bill of the century."

Support for such legislation among northern liberals was greatly enhanced by the ugly defiance of federal law on the part of a number of prominent southern politicians including perhaps most notoriously Alabama Governor George Wallace. The latter had stood in the doorway of the University of Alabama in June of 1963, blocking the entry of two black students, as he defiantly proclaimed to the American public his determination to preserve the Jim Crow system as it had long existed in the South by whatever means necessary: "I draw the line in the dust and toss the gauntlet before the feet of tyranny, and I say, Segregation now! Segregation tomorrow! Segregation forever!"[11]

The proposed legislation, however, was too drastic for a Congress that was still to a considerable extent controlled by southern Democrats. It took the combination of the sympathy generated by Kennedy's assassination in November of 1963, the formidable legislative skills of President Lyndon B. Johnson, and the pleas and reassurances of Majority Whip Hubert Humphrey (D-Minn.) to persuade Congress to pass a comprehensive civil rights act.

Because the term discrimination was left undefined in the civil rights bill that stood before Congress in 1964, opponents of the legislation feared that it would, in fact, lead to quotas in employment. For instance, Senator James Eastland (D-Miss.), had argued:

> The bill would discriminate against white people . . . I know what will happen if there is a choice between hiring a white man or hiring a Negro both having equal qualifications. I know who will get the job. It will not be the white man.[12]

Largely as a result of these fears, the 1964 Civil Rights Bill was amended explicitly to ban quota hiring.

However, the arguments of the bill's critics were discredited in the minds of many by the fact that they were most often advanced by segregationist Democrats from the South. A broad coalition of northern Democrats and moderate Republicans were able to unite in an effective coalition that would eventually ensure the bill's passage. On June 10, 1964, after months of wrangling, supporters of the bill were finally successful in invoking cloture to break a southern filibuster that had lasted for 82 days and filled 63,000 pages of the *Congressional Record*.[13] The debate over the bill had been the longest debate in the Senate's history.

Passage of the Civil Rights Act of 1964 was a major victory for African Americans and their supporters. In addition to its employment provisions, the legislation barred discrimination in public accommodations such as lodging, public conveyances, theaters, and restaurants, and it authorized the government to withhold federal funds from schools that had not desegregated in compliance with the 1954 *Brown v. Board of Education*[14] decision. The Act was truly comprehensive in scope and contained the following eleven sections:

Title I.	Voting Rights
Title II.	Injunctive Relief Against Discrimination in Public Accommodations
Title III.	Desegregation of Public Facilities
Title IV.	Desegregation of Public Education
Title V.	Commission on Civil Rights
Title VI.	Nondiscrimination in Federally Assisted Programs
Title VII.	Equal Employment Opportunity

Title VIII.   Registration and Voting Statistics
Title IX.   Intervention and Procedure After Removal of
              Civil Rights Cases
Title X.   Establishment of Community Relations
Title XI.   Miscellaneous

Of these eleven sections, Title VI and Title VII are most important for enhancing our understanding of the connection between civil rights enforcement and affirmative action. Title VI covered nondiscrimination in federally-assisted programs and Title VII covered employment discrimination in all large and medium-sized private businesses. Congress created the Equal Employment Opportunity Commission (EEOC) to monitor Title VII violations, and a year later the Labor Department established the Office of Federal Contract Compliance (OFCC, subsequently reorganized and renamed the Office of Federal Contract Compliance Programs, OFCCP), which was charged with regulating federal grants, loans, and contracts. The original legislation, however, gave the EEOC no power to enforce its dictates.

Far from promoting preferential treatment or quota hiring, as some believe, what Title VII originally required was simply that employers and admissions officers stop discriminating, and make special efforts to reach out to members of previously excluded groups. If this was done in an acceptable manner, then businesses were considered in compliance with the law. By the mid-1960s, employers were displaying equal opportunity notices and great strides were being made in bringing qualified blacks into businesses and into educational institutions from which they had previously been excluded because of past discriminatory practices.

The language of the 1964 Civil Rights Act stated that no distinctions were to be made in the right to vote, in provision of public services, and in the right to public and private employment on the basis of race, color, religion, or national origin. A similar color-blind principle was embodied in both the Open Housing Act of 1968, which made it a crime to refuse to sell or rent a dwelling to any individual on account of that individual's race, ethnicity, or religion, and in the 1965 Voting Rights Act, which gave the attorney general the authority under specific circumstances to suspend the use of literacy tests—tests which had long been used in the South as a means of discriminating against black voters.

The Shift To Preferential Treatment

As Nathan Glazer has pointed out, in the debates over the 1964 Civil Rights Bill it was said repeatedly that no distinctions were to be made on the basis of "race, color, or national origin." Then, paradoxically, only a couple of years after the bill's passage, America began an extensive effort to document the race, color, and national origins of just about every student, employee, and recipient of a government grant or contract, and to restructure its public policies to take these factors into account.[15] According to Glazer, America moved from a system of color-blindness and nondiscrimination to a policy of "affirmative discrimination" characterized by statistical goals and quotas. Hugh Davis Graham, who has written the most comprehensive history of federal civil rights policy from the Kennedy years through the 1970s, argues with some cogency that the net effect of this shift from color-blindness to color-consciousness was to strengthen the economic and political base of the minority community while at the same time weakening its moral claims and its public support among the white majority.[16]

Both Presidents Johnson and Nixon, we can now see in retrospect, were instrumental in moving the country away from policies of strict neutrality in regard to the treatment of minorities and women towards policies of preferential treatment whose goals would be equal (or proportional) results rather than equal opportunity. Johnson's War on Poverty, for instance, can be seen in this context as a kind of affirmative action program designed to empower underprivileged minorities and poor whites. On the specific issue of blacks Johnson set the stage for more aggressive, results-oriented affirmative action policy in a commencement address at Howard University given in June of 1965. It was in his Howard address that Johnson first introduced the powerful image of a shackled runner, which would later influence much of the subsequent debate on the affirmative action issue:

> You do not take a man who, for years, has been hobbled by chains, liberate him, bring him to the starting line of a race saying, "You are free to compete with all the others," and still believe you have been fair. . . . This is the next and more profound stage of the battle for civil rights. We seek not just freedom of opportunity; not just legal equity but human ability; not just equality as a right and theory, but equality as a right and result.[17]

Also in 1965, Johnson issued Executive Order 11246, which reaffirmed support for Kennedy's 1961 order linking civil rights enforcement with affirmative action requirements (though as in Kennedy's earlier order, the concept of affirmative action was not specifically defined). The summer of 1963 brought the first of many urban riots to America's central cities. These were often seen at the time as an expression of frustration at the slow pace of racial change. In 1964 a riot broke out in Harlem, and in 1965 a much larger and bloodier clash occurred in the Watts section of Los Angeles. These culminated in what was called the "long hot summer" of 1967, which brought riots to over 100 cities, and resulted in almost 2,000 injuries, 13,000 arrests, and at least 83 deaths, as inner-city black youths burned down many of their own neighborhoods.[18] Detroit, Cincinnati and Newark were among the major troubled areas. In response to the riots, President Johnson issued Executive Order 11365 establishing a National Advisory Commission on Civil Disorders, which came to be known as the Kerner Commission after its chairman, Otto Kerner, then Governor of Illinois.

The Kerner Commission was composed largely of white and black moderates and was directed to answer three basic questions: What happened? Why did it happen? What can be done to prevent it from happening again? The Commission's report would attribute most of the problems in the black ghetto to racism among whites. Its summary conclusion read in part:

> This is our basic conclusion: our nation is moving towards two societies, one black, one white—separate and unequal. Reaction to last summer's disorders has quickened the movement and deepened the divisions. . . . What white Americans have never fully understood—but what the Negro can never forget—is that white society is deeply implicated in the ghetto. White institutions created it, white institutions maintain it, and white society condones it.[19]

Following the issuance of the Kerner Commission Report, Congress passed a number of anti-riot bills, but after the assassination of Martin Luther King, Jr. in the spring of 1968, more urban riots occurred with outbreaks in at least 100 cities. Washington, D.C., Chicago and Baltimore were among the hardest hit areas. Historian Herman Belz has persuasively argued that racial preferences were adopted largely as a result of the riots of this period and the impact they had on high-ranking government policy planners and officials. The latter, he says, came to believe that a simple policy of race-neutrality was no longer sufficient to address the deep racial divisions and inequalities that beset American society. Affirmative action, according to Belz, was "defended by government policy makers [at this time] as a transitional step towards the ultimate goal of a color-blind society and as a necessary means of enforcing equal opportunity laws."[20]

The most aggressive governmental affirmative action came paradoxically in the early 1970s, during the conservative Nixon administration, when the Department of Labor issued an implementing regulation that in effect amended Johnson's Executive Order 11246 by extending the quota-like features of the earlier Philadelphia Plan to all private contractors doing business with the federal government. Contractors were now required to establish target "goals and timetables" for the hiring of "underutilized" minority group members and women, and to display "good faith efforts" to meet these hiring goals and timetables. While not a rigid quota system, the "goals and timetables" requirement was nevertheless a result-oriented group approach to employment policy that critics would charge operated in practice little different than a quota system. The new regulations read in part:

> [Affirmative Action] is a set of specific and results-oriented procedures in which a contractor commits himself to apply . . . good faith effort. The objective of these procedures plus such efforts is equal employment opportunity. . . . An acceptable affirmative action program must include an analysis of areas within which the contractor is deficient in the utilization of minority groups and women, and further, goals and time-tables to which contractors' good faith efforts must be directed to correct deficiencies and thus, to increase materially the utilization of minorities and women, at all levels and in all segments of his workforce where deficiencies exist.[21]

The "goals and timetables" approach to job discrimination that was embodied in this new regulation was very similar to the "disparate impact" theory of employment discrimination that was adopted by the U.S. Supreme Court in the important case of *Griggs v. Duke Power Co.* (1971). "Disparate impact" is a technical term in employment discrimination law that refers to a situation where a given hiring practice—a requirement, for instance, of a high school or college diploma in a job for which it is not strictly necessary—while racially neutral on its face, may disproportionately exclude members of minority groups or women. "Disparate impact" thus views discrimination in terms of statistical racial disparities or disproportionate group outcomes that may result from practices within institutions that were not necessarily intended to be discriminatory.

Explaining the Shift

The shift from color-blind policies of racial neutrality to color-conscious policies of racial preference, has often been viewed, as suggested, as a direct response on the part of certain elites in the federal government to the urban riots of the mid 1960's. This view, while not the whole story, contains a very important element of truth. It was the traumatic experience of the riots of this period that convinced many high ranking government bureaucrats and officials of the need to do more to help the disadvantaged members of minority groups—and particularly disadvantaged blacks—than was being done by existing equal opportunity laws. To move the poorer and less educated members of the African-American community into the mainstream of American life, it was believed, was a goal so important to the domestic peace and social stability of America that it required going beyond simple non-discrimination policies. However admirable in other ways, such policies came to be viewed by many liberals as working at too slow a pace to satisfy the legitimate demands of America's disadvantaged minorities, who were no longer willing to accept peaceably and quietly the subordinate social and economic position that they had traditionally occupied. To give minorities a stake in the American system, many white policy-makers came to believe, it was necessary to accelerate the pace of their social, economic, and educational advancement. A large, stable black middle-class and upper- working-class, according to this view, was the best social insurance against future social turmoil.

Besides such considerations of social utility, many of those who supported affirmative action policies in the late 1960s justified them on the basis of simple justice. The decades of slavery, segregation, and oppression, many argued, had created an historical entitlement to just compensation on the part of those who had been the victims of such practices, and preferential treatment, whether in employment, education, or other areas of American life, came to be seen as a means of making up for this past deprivation. Like the return of stolen goods, giving preference to minorities, particularly blacks, was viewed by affirmative action supporters as simply returning to them what was only rightfully theirs. The dictates of compensatory justice demanded no less.

In addition to the issues of social utility and social justice, many of the early supporters of affirmative action in the federal government seem to have been swayed by arguments that racism and the kind of favoritism embodied in Old Boy Networks were so ingrained in American culture, that only numerically-based hiring goals closely monitored by the federal government could ensure fairness to minority members and women. Affirmative action was thus seen as a practical necessity to avoid continued discrimination and the kind of foot-dragging and concealment of discriminatory activities that many believed would persist in the absence of extraordinary enforcement measures.

Two other factors which must be taken into account in trying to explain the shift from color-blindness to color-consciousness that occurred in the late 60's were the influence of clientele groups and the political considerations of the Nixon Administration. What social scientists sometimes call "clientele control," in which interest groups come to dominate the programs and agencies that handle the policies affecting them, seems to have been an important factor shaping federal civil rights policies during this period. The establishment of contract-compliance offices in federal agencies, and the creation of affirmative action positions in government as well as private industry created a situation in which groups representing the interests of blacks, Hispanics, and women were able to gain considerable influence over the formation of public policy. The combination of a receptive white liberal political establishment and an aggressively importuning array of clientele groups appears to have been a major cause of the rapid movement away from the older color-blind and gender-blind ideals that had dominated the civil rights movement in the period before the riots.[22]

Political considerations of the Nixon Administration may also have contributed to this process. Some have speculated that the Nixon Administration's approval of the Philadelphia Plan, which involved the direct imposition of hiring quotas in the building trades industry, and its extension of numerically-based hiring goals to all federal contractors through the Office of Federal Contract Compliance, may have been motivated in part by a desire to sow dissention among core Democratic groups. Whether this was Nixon's intention or not, affirmative action policy during this period most certainly did weaken the already fragile black-Jewish relationship and drove a wedge between blacks and labor unions.[23] Suspicion of the motives of the Nixon Administration would seem to be called for on this matter since Nixon himself had shown little inclination in the past to support black causes or to stand up for civil rights. Nixon had, after all, run for election in 1968 on a tough law-and-order platform that many interpreted as an appeal to the white backlash vote against black progress. While in office during his first term, he opposed the 1971 extension of the Voting Rights Act, and he fought vigorously throughout his years as President to block busing for school integration.[24] If his administration's embrace of affirmative action appears to skeptical outsiders as a Machiavellian ploy, there is certainly good reason for this.

The Role of the Supreme Court

Employment Discrimination

While the shift from color-blind to color-conscious civil rights policies which took place during the late 60's was largely the result of decisions made in the executive branch of the federal government—particularly in some of the more important federal regulatory agencies such as the Department of Labor, and the Department of Health, Education and Welfare—the Supreme Court would play a crucial, if somewhat more ambiguous, role in the period which followed in legitimating some of these policy changes. Mention has already been made of the crucial decision of the Court in the case of *Griggs v. Duke Power Co.* (1971).[25] In this early employment discrimination case the Court ruled unanimously that under Title VII of the 1964 Civil Rights Act any screening device which produced unequal consequences for different races—i.e. "disparate" in the sense of "disproportionate" group impact—would be held to constitute invidious employment discrimination unless the screening device were shown to be clearly job-related. Four years after *Griggs* the Court reaffirmed its support for the disparate impact approach in *Albemarle Paper Company v. Moody* (1975), a case in which employers sought to protect themselves against discrimination charges by hiring enough minorities to counteract any statistical charges of racial imbalance.[26]

Nevertheless, a year later in *Washington v. Davis* (1976) the Court refused to extend the theory of disparate impact developed in Title VII cases to discrimination cases arising under the equal protection provisions of the U.S. Constitution. The Court held that to establish a *constitutional* claim of unequal treatment (as opposed to a statutory claim of discrimination under Title VII) there had to be a showing of intent to discriminate, not simply a showing of disparate impact.[27] The case in question involved unsuccessful applicants for positions of policemen in the District of Columbia, who charged that the police department's use of a written test was discriminatory because blacks had a disproportionally high failure rate. At the time the case was brought before the federal courts, Title VII, which would later be extended in its reach, did not cover municipal employees.

In 1989 the Court, reflecting the influence of the Reagan appointees, shifted the burden of proof in disparate impact cases from businesses to plaintiffs, thus making it more difficult to sustain an employment discrimination claim under Title VII. The switch occurred in its ruling in *Ward's Cove Packing Co. v. Atonio* (1989), and *Price Waterhouse v. Hopkins* (1989).[28] The Court in *Ward's Cove* ruled that "a simple statistical comparison of racial percentages between skilled and unskilled jobs was insufficient to make a *prima facie* case" of employment discrimination.[29] In *Price Waterhouse* the Court shifted the burden even further by requiring the plaintiff to prove that "employment practices substantially depended on illegitimate criteria."[30] However, the 1991 Civil Rights Act, which was passed by a Democratic congress—and with some reluctance signed into law by President Bush—overturned *Ward's Cove* by limiting the ability of employers to use "business necessity" as a defense against discrimination claims under Title VII. It also overruled the Court's decision in another case, *Patterson v. McLean Credit Union* (1989), where the Court had invalidated a black woman's attempt to seek relief from racial harassment under the 1866 Civil Rights Act.

Charges of "reverse discrimination" became common during the 1970s as more and more corporations and private businesses, often under pressure from federal enforcement agencies, began more aggressive hiring of minorities and women. The question of whether Title VII of the Civil Rights Act also protected whites against discrimination arose in *McDonald v. Sante Fe Transportation Company* (1976).[31] The case involved a situation in which a company fired two white employees who had been charged with theft, while retaining a black employee who had been similarly charged. The Court ruled unanimously that whites as well as blacks are protected from racial discrimination under the anti-discrimination provisions of Title VII.

Despite this ruling, a number of subsequent court decisions would hold that Title VII permitted the preferential treatment of minorities and women in hiring and promotion decisions (but not in decisions affecting layoffs) if such treatment were part of an affirmative action plan designed to increase the employment of previously excluded or under-represented groups. Perhaps the most important of these decisions was that in the case of *United Steelworkers of America v. Weber* (1976). The *Weber* case involved a white blue-collar worker (Brian F. Weber) who was refused admission to an on-the-job training program at the Kaiser Aluminum Company plant at which he worked, although he had higher seniority than some of the minority workers who were accepted. In an attempt to increase minority representation in its workforce, Kaiser Aluminum had developed two seniority lists, one for whites and one for blacks, and it filled its vacancies by selecting persons from the top of each list.[32] Weber filed suit, claiming that the 1964 Civil Rights Act specifically prohibited this kind of racial quota. While winning at the district court level, Weber lost in the Supreme Court, which claimed that Title VII, though not *requiring* race-conscious affirmative action preferences in employment, nevertheless *permitted* them if the purpose was to increase the employment of groups previously discriminated against. "It would be ironic indeed," Justice Brennan wrote in the majority decision, "if a law triggered by a nation's concern over centuries of racial injustice and intended to improve the lot of those who had 'been excluded from the American dream for so long' constituted the first legislative prohibition of all voluntary, private, race-conscious efforts to abolish traditional patterns of racial segregation and hierarchy."

Quota-like employment practices were also upheld by the Court in *Local 28 Sheet Metal Workers International Association v. Equal Employment Opportunity Commission* (1986), where in a 5-4 decision a lower court ruling was allowed to stand that imposed a race-based quota requirement on a labor union.[33] Similarly, in *United States v. Paradise* (1987), the Court in another 5-4 decision affirmed the constitutionality of a quota system involving the hiring of state police.[34] Gender-based preferences would also be upheld under Title VII in the important case of *Johnson v. Transportation Agency, Santa Clara County* (1987). In these cases, Herman Belz has argued, "the Court acknowledged that affirmative action is a prospective policy based on the idea of group rights that aims at achieving racial and gender balance, under the idea of proportional representation that is inherent in the disparate impact theory."[35]

The Court's support for affirmative action, however, was quite fragile as shown by the many 5-4 decisions, and restrictions were placed on affirmative action programs in a number of areas. In *Firefighters Local Union No. 1794 v. Stotts* (1984), for instance, the Court considered the validity of a district court order modifying the arrangements of a consent decree for hiring and promoting black firefighters in Memphis. The decree attempted to protect newly hired black workers from the layoff policy of "last hired, first fired" by ruling that the use of the seniority system was illegitimate. The Supreme Court found the district court in violation of Title VII and modified the consent decree.[36] A similar action occurred in *Wygant v. Jackson Board of Education* (1986), where the Court ruled that an affirmative action plan that protected black teachers while laying off white teachers with more seniority violated Title VII.[37]

Set-Asides

One form of affirmative action preference that became very popular among state and municipal governments in the second half of the 1970s was the minority contracting set-aside. Set-aside programs usually involve the reservation of a fixed proportion of public contracting dollars that by law must be spent on the purchase of goods and services provided by minority-owned businesses. Like preferences in hiring, set-asides have been enormously controversial and cries of "reverse discrimination" abound.

The Supreme Court first took up the issue of set-asides in the case of *Fullilove v. Klutznick* (1980), which dealt with a challenge to a provision of a federal law passed during the Carter administration that required 10 percent of the federal funds allocated to state and local governments for public works projects to be used to purchase goods and services from companies owned by members of six specified minority groups.[38] The Court held in this case that the federal set-aside law did not violate the equal protection provisions of the federal Constitution on the grounds that the set-aside provision was a legitimate remedy for the present competitive disadvantages of minority firms resulting from past illegal discrimination.

Nine years later, however, in *Richmond City v. J.A. Croson Co.* (1989), the Court took a different course on set-asides, this time the set-aside provision being that of a local municipality (Richmond,

Virginia) rather than the Federal government.[39] Again reflecting the influence of the Reagan-era appointees, the Court held that racial classifications within state and local set-aside programs were inherently suspect and were to be subject to the most searching standard of constitutional review ("strict scrutiny") under the equal protection provisions of the Fourteenth Amendment. By a 6-3 vote, the Court invalidated the Richmond City Council's set-aside plan that had required contractors to subcontract at least 30 percent of the dollar value of contracts to minority-owned businesses.

The following year, however, in *Metro Broadcasting Inc. v. Federal Communications Commission* (1990), the Court ruled constitutional a policy developed by the Federal Communications Commission that granted preferences in the purchase of broadcast licenses to minority-controlled firms.[40] In a 5-4 decision the Court held that the race-based classification in this case was "benign" in intent, and as such should not be subject to the "strict scrutiny" standard of constitutional review. An intermediate level of scrutiny, rather than strict scrutiny, was held to be the appropriate level of review in such cases. The interest in enhancing broadcast diversity was an important enough state objective in this case, the Court majority declared, to validate the state's use of an otherwise suspect racial classification.

Five years later, however, in *Adarand Contractors Inc. v. Pena* (1995), the Court ruled that however benign in its intent, affirmative action programs that draw racial classifications, even those at the federal level, *are* subject to strict scrutiny.[41] To critics, at least, it seemed that the Court had abruptly turned its back on settled law, particularly in regard to its earlier decisions affirming racial preferences at the federal level in *Metro Broadcasting* and *Fullilove*. Conservative critics of affirmative action, however, were elated with the decision, and Justice Clarence Thomas, the only black on the Court and a long-time foe of racial preferences of all kinds, issued a concurring opinion defending the color-blind principle of racial justice: "That these programs may have been motivated, in part, by good intentions," Thomas wrote, "cannot provide refuge from the principle that under our Constitution, the government may not make distinctions on the basis of race. As far as the Constitution is concerned, it is irrelevant whether a government's racial classifications are drawn by those who wish to oppress a race or by those who have a sincere desire to help those thought to be disadvantaged."

Education

Equally important—and equally controversial—were the court cases dealing with affirmative action in higher education. Beginning in the late 1960's many universities and professional schools began admitting minority students, particularly African Americans and Hispanics, with substantially lower grades and lower scores on standardized tests than white students. Many of these white students charged "reverse discrimination" and some brought suit in federal court claiming that affirmative action in higher education was a violation of Title VI of the 1964 Civil Rights Act, as well as of the equal protection provisions of the U. S. Constitution.

The first reverse discrimination case in higher education to come before the Court was that of *DeFunis v. Odegaard* (1974).[42] This was a case involving a white applicant, Marco DeFunis, who had applied for admission to the law school of the University of Washington. DeFunis's application for admission had originally been rejected despite the fact that lower-scoring minority students had been admitted under a special admissions procedure that sorted the applicants into two separate, race-based applicant pools, with a much less rigorous standard being applied to the minority group than to the non-minority group. While the Supreme Court initially accepted the case, and heard oral arguments, it finally decided to declare the case moot since DeFunis, who had been accepted to the University of Washington law school by order of a lower court, was nearing completion of his studies, and thus the decision in the case would have had no effect upon him. *DeFunis* was an important case, however, because of a dissenting opinion against the decision to moot by Justice William O. Douglas. Although generally considered the Court's leading liberal theorist, Douglas in his dissent offered a ringing denunciation of race-conscious admissions policies. Despite their benign intent, Douglas claimed, such policies were stigmatizing to minority groups by suggesting that minorities "cannot make it on their individual merit." That, he said, "is a stamp of inferiority that a state is not permitted to place on any lawyer."

Two years after the decision to moot in *DeFunis* the Court again took up the issue of special preferences in higher education in the case of *Regents of the University of California v. Bakke* (1978).[43] The Bakke case dealt with the unsuccessful application for admissions to the medical school of the University of California at Davis of a white applicant, Alan P. Bakke. Bakke, a thirty-two year old mechanical engineer, had twice sought admission to the Davis medical school and was each time rejected despite the fact that his college grade-point- average and his score on the Medical College Admission Test were substantially higher than those of most of the minority group members who were accepted by the school. Because Davis filled sixteen of its one-hundred entering slots through a special admissions program open only to minorities, Bakke claimed that he was a victim of reverse discrimination. Minority applicants, his lawyers pointed out, were permitted to compete for all of the one-hundred seats in the entering class, while whites could only compete for the eighty-four "regular" seats specifically open to them. In a long-awaited decision written by Justice Lewis Powell, the Court struck down the preferential admissions program at Davis as incompatible with the Fourteenth Amendment's Equal Protection Clause, and ordered Bakke admitted. However, while ruling against Davis's explicit racial quota system, Powell declared in his opinion that admissions officers in institutions such as the Davis medical school could take race into account as one of many "plus" factors designed to enhance the diversity of a school's student body.[44]

The *Bakke* case was in many ways the most publicized of any of the affirmative action cases to come before the U.S. Supreme Court, and probably generated more heated commentary than any other case. It dealt with an issue that was even more contentious than affirmative action in employment, and one which drove the deepest wedge between traditionally liberal Jewish groups (most of which supported Bakke's position), and black groups (most of which supported the position of the U.C.-Davis Medical School). Justice Powell's decision was seen in many quarters as a Solomonic compromise, with something good in it for each side. To the disappointment of affirmative action critics, however, the decision had little effect in changing the affirmative action policies at most universities and professional schools. These continued to recruit and admit minority students, particularly black and Hispanic students, with considerably lower grades and test scores than white students. Such policies were vigorously defended by affirmative action supporters on the grounds that more minority students enhanced the diversity and enriched the overall atmosphere in institutions of higher learning.

Voting Rights and Redistricting

The Fifteenth Amendment to the U.S. Constitution was specifically passed to guarantee to the freed slaves the right to vote on the same terms as other American citizens. Nevertheless, in the decades following the withdrawal of federal troops from the South in 1877 systematic efforts were made in most Southern states to deny the franchise to former African slaves and their descendants. Through a host of stratagems and subterfuges, ranging from grandfather clauses, to poll taxes, to sheer physical intimidation and terror, the white-dominated governments of the South successfully kept most blacks away from the polls well into the 1960s. Before the passage of the 1965 Voting Rights Act, less than 40 percent of voting-age blacks in the South were registered to vote. The 1965 act, however, which provided for the use of federal registrars to register voters in areas where voting registration was very low, had a dramatic impact in increasing the total number of black voters in America, particularly in the South. The increase in the number of black elected officials in the U.S. was even more dramatic, rising from less than one-hundred in the early 1960s, to over eight-hundred a decade later.[45]

As in the case of affirmative action policy in education and employment, the voting rights arena is plagued by controversies which the Supreme Court has had to address on numerous occasions over the past thirty years. Many of these controversies stem from a fundamental philosophical disagreement over whether federal voting rights legislation, in conjunction with the Fifteenth Amendment, should merely try to insure access to the ballot for all citizens in a racially neutral manner, or whether such legislation should also be concerned with the way in which electoral districting and other structural features of the electoral process affect the relative ability of minority voters to elect minority candidates to office. Proponents of the latter view say that federal oversight is required to insure that white majorities in state or local legislatures do not use their power to dilute the effective voting strength of black and Hispanic minorities through such devises as gerrymandered reapportionment, at-large voting schemes, or the use of multi-member districts under winner-take-all election rules. Critics of this view say that for the federal government and the courts to be concerned with the racial outcomes of elections and the relative electoral strength of different racial and ethnic groups is to apply a group-entitlement approach to questions of civil rights which is fundamentally at odds with the basic American system of government in which only individual rights are recognized.[46]

Judicial decisions in this area have often been plagued by inconsistency over time, mixed messages, and confusion, and the Supreme Court has never seemed sure about how to define just what the electoral exclusion of blacks precisely means. One decision that was fairly clear and that the Court has not retreated from over the years was delivered in the case of *Gaston County v. U.S.* (1969).[47] This was a case involving a state's use of a literacy test that, while fair on its face, had the effect of excluding many African Americans from the franchise. The Court ruled that since blacks had long been unjustly confined to segregated and inferior school systems, the use of a literacy test which many of them would not be able to pass was a denial of their fundamental constitutional right to vote.[48]

One of the most important early cases decided under the 1965 Voting Rights Act was that of *Allen v. State Board of Education* (1969).[49] Under the Voting Rights Act, Section 5, jurisdictions which were covered by the act because of their prior record of excluding large numbers of citizens from voting were required to attain preapproval ("preclearance") from the Justice Department for any changes in their voting practices or procedures. What constituted a voting practice or procedure was not clearly defined, and in *Allen* the Court interpreted the wording of the statute very broadly so that it would include the redrawing of district lines, the substitution of at-large elections for ward-based districts, and a number of other practices that were sometimes used by states and localities to dilute the voting strength of minorities. The case was viewed by black civil rights advocates as a tremendous victory.

Another important protective ruling for minorities occurred in *Beer v. New Orleans* (1976).[50] This case was to set a no-retrogression standard that interpreted the 1965 Voting Rights Act as prohibiting changes in electoral practices such as districting that would leave minorities worse off in their ability to elect a minority candidate. An important effect of this ruling has been to protect black incumbents from being redistricted out of seats in states losing a portion of their congressional representation. A violation of the no-retrogression standard would be said to occur if a redistricting plan substantially reduced the percentage of black voters in an historically black district.

A setback for voting rights advocates came four years after *Beer*, however, in the case of *Mobile v. Bolden* (1980), when the court made racist *intention* the test of electoral exclusion rather than discriminatory *effects*.[51] The case involved a challenge to an at-large electoral voting scheme in Mobile, Alabama, which had produced an all-white Mobile City Commission, despite a population that was 40 percent black. Although the black plaintiffs in the case had won at the lower court levels, the U.S. Supreme Court reversed and held that a showing of discriminatory purpose, not merely discriminatory effects, was necessary to establish a voting discrimination claim under both Section 2 of the Voting Rights Act, as well as under the Fourteenth and Fifteenth Amendments to the federal Constitution. The *Mobile* decision created a storm of protest within the liberal civil rights community, and two years later Congress amended the Voting Rights Act to include a "totality of circumstances" test of racial discrimination that would take into account discriminatory effects, not simply discriminatory purpose.

Much of the aggressive drawing of legislative districting to ensure the election of black elected officials came after the 1986 case of *Thornburg v. Gingles* (1986), in which the Justices interpreted the law in a manner that leaned toward proportional representation.[52] The Court in *Gingles* devised a complex, three-pronged test for discrimination that focused on the local situation, on the openness of the political process to minorities, and on the ability of minorities to elect representatives of their choice. After the redistricting that followed the 1990 decennial census, thirteen black- and five Hispanic-dominated congressional districts were created in accordance with the map-maker's understanding of the law.

As late as 1993, the Court seemed to reaffirm its position in *Gingles*, when, in *Voinovich v. Quilter* (1993), it upheld an Ohio redistricting plan that concentrated black voters in state legislative districts to insure the election of black candidates even though there was no evidence of prior discrimination or the inability of minority members to elect candidates of their choice.[53] Writing for the Court majority, Sandra Day O'Connor said that states could create any districts they desired as long as black voting strength was not diluted.

In another 1993 case, however, the Court appeared to rethink its position in *Gingles* and *Voinovich* when it used a challenge by white voters to the constitutionality of North Carolina's Twelfth congressional district to question all race-conscious redistricting. In *Shaw v. Reno* (1993), the Court gave white voters the standing to bring voting discrimination suits before the federal courts, and it sent the North Carolina case back to the state, where it was heard by a three-judge federal panel.[54] Although agreeing that the Twelfth district was a product of racial gerrymandering, the three-judge federal panel allowed it to stand as a necessary remedy for North Carolina's past history of racial exclusion. The judges found it significant that although blacks constituted 22 percent of the state's population, they had been unable to elect a single black representative since 1901, when George White was forced out of office at the beginning of the Jim Crow era.

Three court rulings in 1994 and 1995 seemed to signal an even clearer retreat from the position the Court had taken in *Gingles* and *Voinovich*. In *Johnson v. DeGrandy* (1994), Florida Republicans, Hispanics, and blacks charged that the state legislature was failing to create the maximum number of Hispanic districts.[55] Instead of the existing nine Hispanic districts, the plaintiffs argued, eleven districts could be drawn from the total of twenty. The question before the Court was whether the Voting Rights Act requires states to create the maximum possible number of districts in which minorities form a majority as was thought to be the case after *Gingles*. Delivering the opinion of the Court, Justice David Souter rejected the view that the Voting Rights Act required maximizing the total number of minority representatives and declared that Florida's districting scheme involved no violation of Section 2 of the Voting Rights Act. It was seen as significant that despite discrimination and racial bloc voting, minority voters formed voting majorities in a number of districts that were roughly proportional to their percentages in the voting-age population.

The second case, *Holder v. Hall* (1994), involved a rural Georgia county that since 1912 had been governed by a single commissioner.[56] African-American voters constituted 22 percent of the county and had never elected a black to the commissioner post. As a consequence, advocates of black voting rights sought to enlarge the existing commission from a one-member to a five-member body, with districts drawn to ensure that at least one black commissioner would be elected. In a 5–4 decision, the Court ruled that the current size of a governing body cannot be subject to a vote dilution claim under Section 2 of the Voting Rights Act. The *Holder* decision has been seen as greatly restricting the ability of plaintiffs to use the Voting Rights Act to guarantee equal or proportionate racial outcomes.

The third case signaling a retreat from *Gingles* and *Voinovich* was *Miller v. Johnson* (1995), a case involving charges of racial gerrymandering in the state of Georgia.[57] In a 5–4 decision, the Court ruled it unconstitutional to use the race of voters as a "predominate" factor in drawing legislative district lines. After the Georgia legislature was unable to agree to a redrawing of its district lines, the Court gave the authority to a three-judge panel which redrew the state's congressional district lines in such a way that two of the newer black-majority districts were obliterated and only the original black-majority district remained. The new plan, however, created a number of black-influenced districts.

Although it is nearly impossible to predict how the Court will rule on some of its pending cases, its more recent decisions in the voting rights area seem to suggest a retreat from race-conscious affirmative action. The crucial swing vote is held by Justice O'Connor, who has not as yet made her position on voting rights and affirmative action fully clear. Legal scholar Jeffrey Rosen chides her for creating confusion by stating in *Shaw* that oddly shaped districts may violate the constitutional rights of whites without giving states guidelines as to what types of districts are acceptable. After providing the crucial fifth vote in *Miller*, O'Connor wrote in a concurring opinion that most existing congressional districts are not at risk. But which one's are and which one's are not is not clear, nor is the criteria by which to decide. Rosen concludes his assessment of O'Connor in the following words: "there is nothing moderate or restrained about Justice O'Connor's jurisprudence. Rather than being guided by consistent legal rules, lawyers and judges must try to read her mind before they can be confident about what the law requires. This increases Justice O'Connor's authority, but it undermines the stability of the law."[58]

There may be less at stake in the recent voting rights cases than many imagine, however. While the retreat from the Court position in *Gingles* and *Voinovich* was denounced by many civil rights advocates, even if the Court had approved of race-conscious districting in *Miller* and not taken on *Shaw*, the strategy of enhancing black voter strength by grouping together black voters in the same districts has nearly been exhausted. Today there are few places where African Americans are concentrated enough to create many additional black districts. It is also worth noting that before the race-conscious redistricting of the 1990s, 40 percent of the blacks in Congress were elected from districts where African Americans were less than 50 percent of the voting-age population. In the 104rd Congress eleven black incumbents represent districts where blacks are a minority of the population. Eight others administer districts where less than 55 percent of the voting-age population is black.[59] Clearly many black candidates are able to attract some level of white support. These numbers, moreover, understate the ability of black candidates to draw white support as black registration and turnout rates are traditionally lower than whites, and some districts which have a black majority voting-age population, have a white majority electorate turning out on election day. Their black representatives, nevertheless, are easily reelected.

Affirmative Action: Pro and Con

Neither race-conscious policies designed to improve the life-situation of African Americans nor the controversies provoked by such policies were new to the 1960s. Many of the themes surrounding the contemporary affirmative action debate, in fact, can be traced back as far as the immediate post-Civil War period, when Congress established the Freedman's Bureau to aid the newly emancipated slaves. To justify vetoing the Freedman's Bureau, Johnson advanced the argument of reverse discrimination. "The Congress of the United States," he asserted,

. . . has never founded schools for any class of its own people. . . . It has never deemed itself authorized to expend the public money for rent or purchase of homes for the thousands, not to say millions of the white race who are honestly toiling from day to day for their subsistence. A system for the support of indigent persons was never contemplated by the authors of the Constitution; nor can any good reason be advanced why as a permanent establishment it should be founded for one class or color of our people more than the other.[60]

Johnson's veto was overriden by Congress. Concern about reverse discrimination was also evident in Senator Eastland's earlier quotation about the damage that civil rights legislation might wreak on white Americans.

Arguments in Favor

As in Johnson's day, supporters of race-conscious programs designed to help African Americans adjust to the demands of American life will defend such programs on the grounds that the long historical oppression of black people (as well as of women and other minorities)

have left them without the resources necessary to succeed in our highly competitive society. Supporters of affirmative action can point to statistics which show wide disparities between the socio-economic condition of blacks and other minorities relative to that of whites, and to the gross underrepresentation of African Americans in many leading professions (e.g. law, engineering, medicine, journalism).[61] The black unemployment rate, they will point out, is often double and sometimes triple that of whites, and even when minorities are employed, their median income is appreciably lower than whites.[62] This is the case despite aggressive affirmative action policies in many areas of employment and college admissions. In the absence of such policies, affirmative action supporters argue, the plight of minorities would be even more bleak.

Harvard Law Professor Randall Kennedy, for instance, says that the adoption of race-neutral policies for admissions to the elite institutions of higher learning in America would lead to the near absence of minorities from those institutions. "Without affirmative action," Kennedy argues, "continued access for black applicants to college and professional education would be drastically narrowed."[63] Affirmative action supporters like Kennedy who make dire predictions about the harmful consequences of abandoning race-conscious educational policies can point to distressing statistics to back up what they say. Of the nearly 100,000 blacks who took the Scholastic Achievement Test (SAT) in 1992, for instance, only 109 scored over 700 on the verbal section, and only 430 scored above 700 on the math section.[64] On most standardized tests, in fact, blacks perform significantly less well than whites, and this holds true at every socio-economic level. Even black children from affluent families do not do outstandingly well on such tests—black children from families with annual incomes over $50,000, for instance, average no higher on the SAT than Asians and whites with family incomes in the $10,000 to $20,000 range.[65]

In defense of admitting minority applicants with below- average standardized test scores, supporters of affirmative action often point out that few people complain about giving special preference in college admissions to the offspring of alumni, who benefit from affirmative action on the basis of their lineage. If it is all right to give special preference to campus legacies on the basis of their family relationships, then to give similar consideration to previously oppressed racial and ethnic groups, many argue, can hardly be considered unfair.

The situation in medical schools is of particular concern to many affirmative action supporters, since the number of blacks in medical schools has shown a precipitous decline in recent years. This, it is argued, has contributed to the shortage of medical personnel in inner-city areas where minority doctors have traditionally been far more likely to practice than whites.[66]

The situation in the corporate employment world, affirmative action supporters point out, is only marginally better than that in higher education and the professions. Once again they have the statistics to back up their claims. Despite more than two decades of affirmative action, women and blacks lag significantly behind white men when it comes to jobs and promotions. While constituting roughly 42 percent of the labor market, white males hold almost 100 percent of senior management positions in Fortune 500 companies.[67] And while white women hold 40 percent of middle management jobs, black women hold only 5 percent, and black men only 4 percent.[68] Some observers, such as sociologist Andrew Hacker, say that the situation in the employment world is significantly harder for black men than for black women. Given a choice between a black man and a black woman, they contend, most employers will opt for the black woman because they view her as easier to assimilate and easier to handle.[69] Law Professor Derrick Bell points out that white women have received by far the highest percentage of jobs under affirmative action programs, and even white men, he says, have benefitted from the widespread advertising of jobs and the objective selection procedures used for hiring and admissions under affirmative action programs.[70] Bell does not believe that affirmative action policies have done much to help black people, though rather than ending them, he would rather see them genuinely implemented and expanded so that they really do serve the interests of blacks.

While the greatest beneficiaries of affirmative action policies have been white women, supporters of affirmative action point out that this has not always been the case.[71] During the 1970s, for instance, Jennie Farley observed that affirmative action did little if anything to help women. Farley cites a study that compares the gender and race composition of companies that were visited by contract compliance officers and those that were not. The study suggested that affirmative action was actually helping *men*—especially white men—but having an adverse effect on women. Other studies of university administrative posts where there was a professed commitment to hiring women showed little actual progress in the mid-1970s.[72] Only because of more aggressive enforcement of affirmative action requirements in the Carter years, some affirmative action supporters argue, did the proportion of women in certain key sectors of the workforce improve. To retreat from affirmative action policy, they claim, would set the clock back and threaten the hard-won advances women and minorities have made in the employment arena over the past twenty years.

When presented with data on racial and gender disparities in employment, top executives invariably attribute the low numbers of women and minorities to a lack of qualified applicants. Affirmative action supporters, however, usually reject such a claim, and argue that these numbers reflect the lack of mentoring opportunities for blacks and women, and the fact that members of these groups have to combat stereotypes that are not applied to white males. Labor statistics indicate that women and blacks, while making considerable progress in certain fields, are still disproportionately concentrated at the lower rungs of many occupational ladders.[73]

Many supporters of affirmative action deny that there exist agreed upon standards of merit that can be fairly and objectively applied in making employment decisions. Merit, says Randall Kennedy, is always politically defined, and is therefore "a malleable concept, determined not by immanent, preexisting standards but rather by the perceived needs of society."[74] If what society needs is more blacks and more women in positions of authority, many affirmative action supporters contend, then it is legitimate to consider being black or being a women as part of a job-candidate's merit. Affirmative action supporters are particularly hostile to the idea that merit can be gauged by scores on standardized tests.

One area that affirmative action supporters insist requires the consideration of racial minority status as part of a job-candidate's "merit" is the area of law enforcement. Given the hostility that exists in many minority neighborhoods against the white-dominated criminal justice system, it is only prudent, many hold, to hire police personnel of the same race or same ethnicity as the population that is being policed. Affirmative action policies have been responsible for the expansion in the number of black police officers, it is claimed, and this has been very beneficial to minority communities. Black police, says Andrew Hacker, simply have a better understanding of black people, both criminal and law-abiding, than do white police, who are often influenced by racist stereotypes. In black communities white police, says Hacker, "cannot catch the clues that distinguish law-abiding young men from those who are up to no good."[75]

Other arguments in favor of affirmative action focus on the need for diversity in both the workplace and on college campuses. In a multi-racial, multi-ethnic society, it is contended, all students and all workers benefit from personal contact with members of different racial, ethnic, religious and gender groups. Such personal exposure, it is said, helps to break down debilitating stereotypes and shows that talent in various fields is not monopolized by the members of any one group.

Closely related to the diversity-enhancement argument is the claim that minorities and women need same-race or same-gender role models before they can aspire to positions of power. In the absence of such role models, it is contended, many blacks, Hispanics, and women will feel that certain jobs are "white male jobs" that are not open to them or that they could never successfully perform. Even employment in private industry, supporters of this view maintain, has an important social function which goes well beyond the technical aspects of the work itself. Raising the aspirations of the members of formerly disadvantaged minority groups, it is said, is a social goal of such tremendous importance, that it is imperative to require employers to pay careful attention to the racial and gender composition of their workforce.

A final argument in favor of affirmative action stresses its nature as a compensatory device. Black people never got the forty acres and a mule that was promised them after the Civil War, many argue, and affirmative action is no more than a late—and very meager—attempt to pay them back for the centuries of unrequited toil and oppression which they have faced throughout their long sojourn in America. Those who make this argument sometimes point out that as a compensatory device, affirmative action should not be faulted for its failure to rescue the most disadvantaged blacks from a life of poverty and despair. Affirmative action, they contend, was never meant to be an anti-poverty program, and if many who benefit from it today are middle-class blacks, this is no more unfair than any case where heirs receive debts owed to their deceased parents or grandparents. All African-Americans, it is asserted, have been disadvantaged in some way by the effects of racism both past and present.[76]

Arguments Against

Critics of affirmative action charge that policies of racial, ethnic, and gender preference are contrary to core American values regarding fairness, equality, and respect for the worth of individuals.[77] These values, they say, find expression in our constitution, which guarantees equal treatment to all American citizens as individual persons, not as members of racial, ethnic, or gender groups. The wording of the Fourteenth Amendment and its equal protection provisions is very significant in this regard, affirmative action opponents insist, as it speaks only of persons and personal rights, not of groups or group rights: "No state shall make or enforce any law which shall abridge the privileges or immunities of citizens of the United States; nor shall any state deprive any person of life, liberty, or property without due process of law; nor deny to any person within its jurisdictions the equal protection of the laws." Clarence Thomas, shortly before he became a Supreme Court Justice, expressed this view very forcefully:

> I don't believe in quotas. America was founded on a philosophy of individual rights, not group rights. I believe in compensation for actual [victims of discrimination but] not for people whose only claim to victimization is that they are members of a historically oppressed group.[78]

Affirmative action is also attacked for conferring benefits primarily on the better-off members of the beneficiary groups, while treating all white males who are not of Spanish origin as privileged individuals who can legitimately be held liable for compensatory damages to all women and minorities.[79] Many black critics of race-conscious policies have sounded this theme, and have criticized affirmative action for driving a wedge between poor whites and poor blacks, while doing little to help the "truly disadvantaged" in America's urban ghettos.

Black sociologist William Julius Wilson has been among the more influential proponents of this view. The real problem of the inner-city black poor, as Wilson sees it, is due to a deteriorating employment picture resulting from a combination of automation, de-industrialization, and the relocation of American industry offshore and to the Sunbelt. Many poor blacks have been hurt by these developments just as many poor whites have, Wilson says, and the problems they cause can only be adequately addressed by an aggressive full-employment policy. "Economic dislocation," Wilson writes, "is more central to the plight of the black poor than is the problem of purely racial discrimination."[80]

In diverting attention away from the real source of ghetto problems, and in helping mainly better-off blacks while alienating many whites, affirmative action policies, Wilson believes, have been of little or no benefit to America's truly disadvantaged.

Striking a similar note, Robert Woodson, president of the National Center for Neighborhood Enterprise, criticizes affirmative action policy for not targeting the poorest segment of the minority populations. "My own children and the children of most members of the Congressional Black Caucus," Woodson told a congressional committee, "have better prospects for a successful future than many children, white, black, or brown, who live in impoverished communities. It should come as no surprise that when preferential treatment is offered without regard to economic circumstances, those who have the most training and resources will be the best equipped to take advantage of any opportunities offered."[81]

Another criticism of affirmative action concerns the psychological impact it may have on members of the beneficiary group. Affirmative action, according to its critics, demeans, degrades, and stigmatizes the members of the groups that benefit from it by suggesting that they are inferior to white males and incapable of competing with them. Yale Law Professor Stephen Carter has developed some of these themes at considerable length in his widely read book, *Reflections of an Affirmative Action Baby*. Affirmative action policies, Carter contends, set up a dichotomy in which employers and admissions officers make an invidious distinction between the "best" candidate and the "best black." Although not opposing all forms of racial preference, Carter believes that these program inevitably make the accomplishment of all blacks suspect, even those who are well qualified and high achievers.[82]

In a manner similar to Carter, former Princeton President William Bowen has drawn attention to the potentially harmful side-effects of race-conscious admissions policies. Although a staunch supporter of such policies, Bowen has warned of the potential harm that can flow from their misuse or misinterpretation. Commenting on the Bakke controversy during the late 70s, Bowen acknowledged that

> One of the discouraging by-products of much of the recent discussion stimulated by the Bakke case is that it seems to have encouraged a certain tendency to assume that all, or nearly all, minority students are less well qualified academically than all, or nearly all, white students. This is not so, and it is unfair to individuals and harmful to our understanding of the real issues to think that it is so.[83]

Black economist Thomas Sowell offers similar observations but claims that the effect of preferentialist policies in college admissions is even more harmful than that suggested by Carter or Bowen because they cause a "mismatch" between students and the colleges and universities they attend. Minority students who are sufficiently qualified to attend the less competitive institutions of higher learning are admitted into much more competitive ones, Sowell charges, where they are ill-prepared to deal with the intellectual demands thrust upon them. As a result of preferentialist admissions policies, minority students who might have succeeded at a state college, he says, find themselves floundering at elite institutions. [84]

Sowell makes another argument that is common to affirmative action critics. Racial preferences, Sowell says, almost always breed hatred and resentment among the members of the non-beneficiary groups, who see such policies as fundamentally unfair. This tendency, according to Sowell, is not only true in the United States, but can be seen worldwide wherever preferentialist policies are instituted. The net result of such policies, he says, is often an increase in inter-group enmities, which in many places around the world have led to violence or even civil war. [85]

A final argument against affirmative action concerns its effect on the structure of incentives for work and achievement. Black economist Glenn Loury, a prominent critic of preferentialist policies, says that affirmative action preferences "may alter the terms on which employers and workers interact with each other so as to perpetuate, rather than eliminate, existing disparities in productivity between minority and majority populations." [86] If workers believe that they will be favored by affirmative action, Loury argues, they will have less incentive to work hard and upgrade their skills: "they may invest less because . . . it has become easier for them to get high level positions." [87]

Affirmative Action Today

Affirmative action policies are undergoing their most vigorous challenge since they first appeared on the public scene more than thirty years ago. In the minds of many Americans these policies have gotten out of hand, and instead of focusing on outreach and non-discrimination as originally conceived, they have become synonymous with quotas, reverse discrimination, and naked racial preference. [88]

A number of polls and surveys in recent years have documented the depths of dislike that many Americans feel towards these policies.

Political scientists Paul Sniderman and Thomas Piazza, for instance, found in a national survey that the mere mention of affirmative action can create hostility among whites towards blacks.[89] Sniderman and Piazza randomly divided people into two groups and asked one group whether they agreed with certain negative characterizations of blacks, including the contention that blacks are irresponsible and lazy. Only a relatively small proportion of the respondents in the first group agreed with these characterizations—for instance, only 26 percent of those in this first group agreed with the "irresponsible and lazy" characterization. Sniderman and Piazza asked the second group the same question but preceded the question with a prior question on affirmative action preferences:

> In a nearby state, an effort is being made to increase dramatically the number of blacks working in state government. This means that a large number of jobs will be reserved for blacks, even if their scores on merit exams are lower than those whites who are turned down for the job. Do you favor or oppose this policy?[90]

The group asked the affirmative action question before being asked whether they agreed with certain negative characterizations of blacks, Sniderman and Piazza found, was much more likely to accept such negative characterizations. Instead of 26 percent agreeing with the lazy-and-irresponsible label, 43 percent of respondents in this second group agreed with such a characterization.[91] Explaining this huge difference in the proportion of respondents holding negative images of blacks, Sniderman and Piazza concluded that "affirmative action is so intensely disliked that it has led some whites to dislike blacks."[92]

Opposition to affirmative action may be affecting Americans in other ways. In 1994, for the first time in the seven years that the question has been asked, a majority of white Americans (51 percent) agreed with the statement: "We have gone too far in pushing equal rights in this country."[93]

Anti-affirmative action sentiments were perhaps most visible in the 1990 senatorial race between the black Democrat Harvey Gantt and the Republican incumbent.Jesse Helms.[94] During the last week of the campaign, while trailing Gantt in the polls, Helms aired a series of anti-affirmative action TV commercials that were very likely responsible for his victory in the race. The one that got the most attention nationally featured the hands of a white male crumbling a job application, with the voice-over stating that while the white applicant needed the job, it was given to a lesser qualified minority because of a racial preference. The announcer accuses Harvey Gantt and Massachusetts Senator Ted Kennedy of favoring racial quotas. A second Helms advertisement showed a broadcasting station that Gantt had purchased through a federal set-aside program, which Gantt sold some weeks later to a white businessman at a huge profit. The voice-over explains how the minority community was outraged by the sale, but that the deal made Gantt a millionaire. Postelection voter surveys attributed Gantt's defeat to increased turnout among whites spurred to vote by Helm's anti-affirmative action advertisements.[95]

The frustration of whites over affirmative action programs was also given credit for former Klansman David Duke's ability to win 55 percent of the white vote in Louisiana's 1991 gubernatorial race. Three years earlier Duke won 44 percent of the vote in his senatorial campaign. According to political analyst Gary Esolen, Duke's message was always the same:

> Why do reporters and politicians pick on me and say hateful things about me when anyone can see I'm a nice guy and reasonable fellow? Besides, even if I did say and do extreme things once or twice that's all over with now.
>
> The real reason they pick on me is that they are afraid of my message on the issues, which is that affirmative action has gone too far and become racism in the reverse, the black underclass is dragging us down, we can't afford welfare, and it's time white people had some rights again.[96]

Polling data suggest that Duke's anti-affirmative action message resonated very well among whites in Louisiana.[97]

Anti-affirmative action sentiments may also account, at least in part, for the 1994 Republican capture of the House of Representatives. A postelection poll showed that a clear majority of white males, constituting 42 percent of the electorate, voted for the Republicans. Newspaper and television reports repeatedly found these men to be angry over minority preferences and declining wages.[98]

Riding the wave of the post-1994 affirmative action backlash, California Governor Pete Wilson, who had earlier in his career supported many affirmative action measures, convinced a majority of the members of the Board of Regents of the University of California to ban all racial, gender, and ethnic preferences in both admissions and employment at all UC campuses. A development of even greater national significance that emerged around the same time was the California Civil Rights Initiative (CCRI), the brainchild of two California academics, Glynn Custred and Thomas Wood. The CCRI is a ballot initiative scheduled for a public referendum in November of 1996, which, if passed, would ban all forms of preferential treatment in government-supported state programs.[99] Because California has long been a trendsetter, how its voters react to the CCRI may well affect affirmative action policies throughout the nation.

President Clinton may have given white Americans some cause for concern about his position on affirmative action. When Clinton campaigned for office in 1993, he presented himself as a "New Democrat." As a founding member of the conservative-to-moderate Democratic Leadership Council, he was expected to be sympathetic to the concerns of middle class whites no less than to those of minorities. Soon after taking office, however, his administration issued a directive endorsing race-based scholarship programs that the Bush administration had challenged in favor of need- and merit-based awards. In addition, the Clinton Justice Department's Civil Rights Division, led by Deval Patrick, an African American, abruptly changed course in a case involving teacher layoffs. A New Jersey school board had made a decision to lay off a white teacher instead of a black teacher of roughly the same education and seniority levels, although black teachers were not underrepresented in that school system. While the Bush administration's Justice Department sided with the white teacher, the Clinton Justice Department, in an unusual switch, supported the school board. These highly publicized reversals seemed to contradict President Clinton's claims of being a New Democrat. After ordering a review of affirmative action policy in February 1995, and after close consultation with the Congressional Black Caucus, Clinton reaffirmed his support for the policy in July of that year. In a widely televised speech that was praised by civil rights groups Clinton said that affirmative action should be amended but not ended.

The Republicans, however, have taken on the issue of minority preferences in governmental programs with great fervor. In the spring of 1995, the Republican-controlled Congress voted to kill the controversial tax break for companies that sold broadcast licenses and cable stations to minorities, the same program that benefitted Gantt. Some of the early Republican presidential candidates, moreover, including Senator Bob Dole (R-KS.), Senator Phil Gramm (R-Texas), former Tennessee Governor Lamar Alexander, and California Governor Pete Wilson eagerly staked out high profile anti-affirmative action positions, even though for some, including the front-runner Dole, this represented a considerable change from their earlier positions. Dole, the Majority Leader, introduced a bill in the Senate in the summer of 1995 (Senate Bill 1085), which would terminate all race, gender, and ethnic preferences in federal programs, while Representative Charles T. Canady (R-Fla.) introduced a similar bill into the house (House Bill 2128). Canady's bill, however, would allow preferences for the economically disadvantaged if administered without regard to race or gender. "For too many citizens," Dole announced in introducing his bill, "our country is no longer the land of opportunity but a pie chart where jobs and other benefits are often awarded not because of hard work or merit but because or someone's biology."[100]

Redirecting Affirmative Action

Defenders of affirmative action see much of the backlash against such policies as having little relationship to the actual harm the policies have done to non-minorities, which they contend is very small. "Affirmative action has become a scapegoat for the anxieties of the white middle class," writes political commentator Michael Kinsley. "Some of those anxieties are justified; some are self-indulgent fantasies. But the actual role of affirmative action in denying opportunities to white people is small compared with its role in the public imagination and public debate."[101]

Whether Kinsley is right on this matter or not, it is clear that to gain widespread public support among the white majority, affirmative action must be changed and perhaps re-created in a different form. There is certainly much confusion about how the programs originated and what they were designed to address. Affirmative action was originally adopted to provide equal opportunity to minorities and to combat past and present discrimination. Discrimination seems to call for a remedy different from what is needed to assist the poor and disadvantaged. The solution for discrimination may be nothing more than the vigorous enforcement of existing anti-discrimination laws rather than preferential treatment. If Americans are serious about fairness, then a way must be found to ensure adequate funding of antidiscrimination agencies such as the EEOC or to support the creation of new enforcement agencies. Voluntary compliance from businesses and agencies would be increased if the government funded more testers—blacks, whites and Hispanics with identical qualifications and resumes who apply for jobs, housing, and loans, and have their experiences recorded by race. Such data can help agencies identify businesses and industries where discrimination continues.

Increased civil penalties for violating the anti-discrimination laws can also make a difference by making discrimination unprofitable to those tempted to violate the law. It does not seem unreasonable to triple the punitive damages normally incurred on companies and agencies found guilty of discrimination. Successful lawsuits can serve to put individuals and companies on alert that not only is discrimination illegal; it is costly, and will not be tolerated by our society.

Americans are far more sympathetic to outreach programs that open doors for women and minorities than they are to policies that appear to give preferential treatment to these same groups. Policies which encourage "affirmative action" at the recruitment stage of employment or university admissions resonate well with public sentiment on this issue in a way that quotas and the use of race or gender as "plus" factors do not. Currently, the public views situations in which deserving whites appear to lose out to less prepared minorities as unjust. Cases like that of Cheryl Hopwood, a white women from a disadvantaged background who was denied admission to the University of Texas Law School in 1994 despite grades and test scores above many of the blacks and Mexican Americans admitted, inflamed some Americans.[102]

The best course of action for those who want to assist the "truly disadvantaged" among America's minority poor may well be class-based affirmative action rather than race-based. Even conservatives such as Antonin Scalia and the authors of *The Bell Curve* have come out in support of means-tested programs designed to assist the genuinely disadvantaged on a race-neutral basis. "It may well be," Scalia has written, "that many, or even most, of those benefitted by such programs would be members of minority races that the existing [affirmative action] programs favor. I would not care if *all* of them were. The unacceptable vice is simply selecting or rejecting *on the basis of race*."[103] Even affirmative action opponents Charles Murray and Richard Herrnstein profess support for admissions policies in colleges and universities that favor the disadvantaged. What *The Bell Curve* authors say they find most disturbing is the fact that the low-scoring offspring of privileged blacks are allowed to displace higher-scoring poor whites from places like Appalachia.[104]

Perhaps the Head Start program can be taken as a model of such a means-tested policy. The vast majority of the beneficiaries of Head Start are poor black and Hispanic children, yet the program continues to receive widespread support among middle class whites. It does so because those who are benefitted are benefitted not on the basis of their race or ethnicity but on the basis of their individual need. While the current situation could change, it appears that race-based preferences are no longer acceptable either to a majority of the public, to a majority of the members of Congress, or to a majority of the justices on the U.S. Supreme Court. Given such a state of affairs, need-based affirmative action seems to be the only viable strategy remaining for those concerned about the plight of the minority poor. William Julius Wilson may have accurately gauged the future of affirmative action when he stated in 1987 that programs to aid the black ghetto underclass should be of a nature "to which the more advantaged groups of all races and class backgrounds can positively relate."[105] Head Start, and other programs patterned after it, can meet Wilson's criterion in a way that quotas and other race-based public policies currently do not. This is certainly a crucial advantage in a consensus-oriented democracy such as our own, and never more so, perhaps, than in an area as volatile as race.

Notes

1. National poll conducted March 25-27, 1977, *The Gallup Index*, June 1977, Report no. 143.
2. African-American leaders differ from the African-American public. In response to a similar question asking whether preferential treatment or ability should be used in obtaining jobs and college placement, 77 percent of African-American leaders supported preferential treatment, while only 23 percent of the black public did. See Linda Lichter, "Who Speaks for Black America?" *Public Opinion Quarterly*, August/September 1985, p. 43.
3. Everett C. Ladd, "People, Opinion, and Polls: Affirmative Action, Welfare, and the Individual," *The Public Perspective*, April-May 1995, Report of the Roper Center, pp. 37-40.
4. *The Polling Report*, August 22, 1988, cited in Hugh Graham, *The Civil Rights Era: Origins and Development of a National Policy* (New York: Oxford University Press), p. 565, n. 43.
5. William Schneider,"In Job Quota Debate, Advantage GOP," *National Journal*, June 8, 1991, p. 1374.
6. Ladd, "People, Opinions and Polls," pp. 23-42
7. Tori DeAngelis, "Ignorance Plagues Affirmative Action," *Psychology and Society*, 26, no. 5 (May 1995).
8. Focus group, New York, N.Y., May 8, 1995.
9. Ibid.
10. NAACP, *Annual Report*, 1920, cited in Albert P. Blaustein, *Civil Rights and the American Negro* (New York: Washington Square Press, 1969), p. 338.
11. Graham, *The Civil Rights Era*, p. 75.
12. Senator James Eastland, quoted in Nicholas Lemann, "Taking Affirmative Action Apart," *New York Times Magazine*, June 11, 1995, p. 40.
13. Graham, *The Civil Rights Era*, p. 151.
14. *Brown v. Board of Education*, 347 U.S. 483 (1954).
15. Nathan Glazer, *Affirmative Discrimination: Ethnic Inequality and Public Policy* (New York: Basic Books, 1975).
16. Hugh Graham, "Origins of Affirmative Action: Civil Rights and the Regulatory State," *Annals, AAPSS*, September 1992, p. 60.
17. President Lyndon B. Johnson, June 4, 1965, Howard University commencement address, Washington, D.C.
18. *Report of the Advisory Committee on Civil Disorders* (New York: Bantam Books, 1968), "Patterns of Disorder," chap. 2.
19. Ibid., pp. 1-13.
20. Herman Belz, *Equality: A Quarter-Century of Affirmative Action Transformed* (New Brunswick, N.J.: Transition Books, 1991), p. 234.
21. Quoted in Paul Seabury, "HEW and the Universities," *Commentary*, February 1972, p. 39.

22. Lemann, "Taking Affirmative Action Apart," p. 54.
23. LeMann, "Taking Affirmative Action Apart," p. 54; Thomas Sowell, "Affirmative Action Reconsidered," *The Public Interest*, Winter 1976, cited in Barry Gross, *Reverse Discrimination* (New York: Prometheus Books, 1977), p. 113.
24. Rowland Evans and Robert Novak, *Nixon in the White House* (New York: Random House, 1975).
25. *Griggs v. Duke Power*, 401 U.S. 424 (1971).
26. *Albemarle Paper Company v. Moody*, 422 U.S. 405 (1975).
27. *Washington v. Davis*, 426 U.S. 229 (1976).
28. *Price Waterhouse v. Hopkins*, 490 U.S. 228 (1989); *Ward Cove's Packing Company v. Atonio*, 490 U.S. 642 (1989).
29. Kermit L. Hall, ed., *The Oxford Companion to the Supreme Court of the United States* (New York: Oxford University Press, 1992), p. 21.
30. Hall, *The Oxford Companion*, Ibid., p. 351.
31. *McDonald v. Sante Fe Trail Transportation Company*, 427 U.S. 273 (1976).
32. Carl Cohen, "Why Racial Preference Is Illegal and Immoral," *Commentary*, June 1979, p. 41.
33. *Local 28 Sheet Metal Workers International Association v. Equal Employment Opportunity Commission*, 478 U.S. 501 (1986).
34. *United States v. Paradise* 107 U.S. 1053 (1987).
35. Herman Belz, in Hall, *The Oxford Companion*, p. 21.
36. *Firefighters Local Union No 1794 v. Stotts*, 467 U.S. 563 (1984).
37. *Wygant v. Jackson Board of Education*, 476 U.S. 267 (1986).
38. *Fullilove v. Klutznick*, 448 U.S. 448 (1980).
39. *Richmond v. J. A. Croson Co.*, 488 U.S. 469 (1989).
40. *Metro Broadcasting Inc. v. Federal Communications Commission*, 497 U.S. 547 (1990).
41. *Adarand Contractors Inc. v. Pena*, 115 S. Ct. 2097 (1995).
42. Ronald Dworkin, "DeFunis v. Sweatt," in Marshall Cohen, Thomas Nagel, and Thomas Scanlon, eds., *Equality and Preferential Treatment*, (Princeton: Princeton University Press, 1977), pp. 63-83.
43. *DeFunis v. Odegaard*, 416 U.S. 312 (1974); *United Steelworkers of America v. Weber*, 443 U.S. 193 (1979); *Regents of the University of California v. Bakke*, 438 U.S. 265 (1978).
44. Nathan Glazer, "Why Bakke Won't End Reverse Discrimination," *Commentary*, September 1978; see also Thomas Sowell, "Bakke and the Backlash," *Washington Star*, July 8, 1978 (reprinted in Sowell, *Pink and Brown People*, Stanford, Calif.: Hoover Press, 1981, pp. 113-114).
45. See the discussion in Peter Eisinger et al., *American Politics* (Boston: Little, Brown and Company, 1978), pp. 432-436.
46. For two contrasting views on this issue see Frank P. Parker, *Black Votes Count* (Chapel Hill: University of North Carolina Press, 1990), and Abigail Thernstrom, *Whose Vote Counts?: Affirmative Action and Minority Voting Rights* (Cambridge, Mass.: Harvard University Press, 1987).

47. *Gaston County v. United States*, 395 U.S. 285 (1969).
48. Hall, *The Oxford Companion*, p. 19.
49. *Allen v. State Board of Education*, 393 U.S. 544 (1969).
50. *Beer v. United States*, 425 U.S. 139 (1976).
51. *Mobile v. Bolden*, 446 U.S. 55 (1980).
52. *Thornburg v. Gingles*, 478 U.S. 30 (1986).
53. *Voinovich v. Quilter*, 507 U.S. 500 (1993).
54. *Shaw v. Reno*, 113 S. Ct. 2816 (1983).
55. *Johnson v. DeGrandy*, 512 U.S. 775 (1994).
56. *Holder v. Hall*, 512 U.S. 687 (1994).
57. *Miller v. Johnson*, 515 U.S. 762 (1995).
58. Jeffrey Rosen, *New York Times*, December 26, 1995.
59. Carol M. Swain, *Black Faces, Black Interests: The Representation of African Americans in Congress*, enlarged edition, Cambridge, Mass.: Harvard University Press, 1995), chap. 11.
60. Richardson, *Messages and Papers of the Presidents, vol. II*, pp. 398-405, cited in Blaustein, *Civil Rights and the American Negro*, pp. 215-216.
61. Andrew Hacker, *Two Nations: Black and White, Separate, Hostile, Unequal* (New York: Ballantine Books, 1992), chap. 7.
62. Gerald David Jaynes and Robin M. Williams, eds., *A Common Destiny: Blacks and American Society* (Washington, D.C.: National Academy Press, 1989), chap. 6.
63. Randall Kennedy, "Persuasion and Distrust," in Russell Nieli, ed., *Racial Preference and Racial Justice*, (Washington, D.C.: Ethics and Public Policy Center), p. 48.
64. Theodore Cross, "Suppose There Was No Affirmative Action at the Most Prestigious Colleges and Graduate Schools?" *Journal of Blacks in Higher Education* (Spring 1994): 49.
65. Hacker, *Two Nations*, p. 146.
66. Lemann, "Taking Affirmative Action Apart," p. 66.
67. Peter Kilborn, "Women and Minorities Still Face 'Glass Ceiling,'" *New York Times*, March 16, 1995.
68. Ibid.
69. Hacker, *Two Nations*, p. 116.
70. Derrick Bell, "The Mystique of Affirmative Action," speech at Princeton University, April 1995.
71. Ibid., p. 132.
72. Jennie Farley, *Affirmative Action and the Woman Worker* (New York: Amacon, 1979), p. 14; Carol V. Alstyne et al., "Affirmative Inaction: The Bottom Line Tells the Tale," *Change*, 9, no. 8 (August 1977):39-41, cited in Farley, *Affirmative Action*, p. 15.
73. Judith H. Dobrznski, "Some Action, Little Talk: Companies Embrace Diversity, But Are Reluctant to Discuss It," *New York Times*, April 20, 1995.

74. Kennedy, " Persuasion and Distrust," p. 51.
75. Hacker, *Two Nations*, p. 128.
76. Roger Wilkins, "Racism Has Its Privileges," *The Nation*, March 27, 1995; Kennedy, "Persuasion and Distrust," pp. 51-52; *Thomas Boston, Race, Class, and Conservatism* (Boston: Unwin Hyman, 1988).
77. Terry Eastland and William J. Bennett, *Counting by Race* (New York: Basic Books, 1979).
78. Thomas, cited in the *Wall Street Journal*, July 2, 1991.
79. Russell Nieli, "Ethnic Tribalism and Human Personhood," in Nieli, ed., *Racial Preferences and Racial Justice*, pp. 61-103; Robert Simon, "Preferential Hiring: A Reply to Judith Jarvis Thomson," in Cohen, Nagel, and Scanlon, eds., *Equality and Preferential Treatment*, pp. 40-48.
80. William Julius Wilson, *The Declining Significance of Race*, 2nd ed. (Chicago: University of Chicago Press), p. 182.
81. Robert L. Woodson, Sr., Capitol Hill hearing testimony, Washington, D.C., September 7, 1995.
82. Stephen Carter, *Reflections of an Affirmative Action Baby* (New York: Basic Books, 1991).
83. William Bowen, *Ever the Teacher* (Princeton: Princeton University Press, 1987), p. 432.
84. Thomas Sowell, "Are Quotas Good for Blacks?" *Commentary*, June 1978, pp. 39-43.
85. Thomas Sowell, *Preferential Policies: An International Perspective* (New York: William Morrow, 1990), p. 13.
86. Glenn Loury, *One by One from the Inside Out: Essays and Reviews on Race and Responsibility in America* (New York: Free Press, 1995), p. 118.
87. Ibid., p. 119.
88. Peter Gabel, "Affirmative Action and Racial Harmony," *Tikkun*, May-June 1995, pp. 33-36.; Hacker, *Two Nations*, p. 118.
89. Paul M. Sniderman and Thomas Piazza, *The Scar of Race* (Cambridge, Mass.: Harvard University Press, 1993).
90. Ibid., p. 102.
91. Ibid., p. 103.
92. Ibid.
93. *The New Political Landscape* (Washington, D.C.: Times Mirror Center for the People and the Press), p. 30.
94. Peter Applebome, "Helms Kindled Anger in the Campaign, and May Have Set the Tone for Others," *New York Times*, November 8, 1990.
95. Ibid.
96. Gary Esolen, "David Duke's Use of Television," in Douglas Rose, ed., *The Emergence of David Duke and the Politics of Race* (Chapel Hill: University of North Carolina Press), pp. 137-138.
97. Ibid.

98. "The White Male Vote," CBS/*New York Times* exit polls, *USA Today*, November 11, 1994; Juan Williams, "How Black Liberal Strategy Failed Its Followers," *Washington Post National Weekly Edition*, November 28–December 4, 1994, p. 25.

99. B. Drummond Ayres, Jr., "Conservatives Forge New Strategy to Challenge Affirmative Action," *New York Times*, February 16, 1995.

100. Senator Bob Dole, quoted in Steven A. Holmes, "G.O.P. Lawmakers Offer a Ban on Federal Affirmative Action," *New York Times*, July 25, 1995.

101. Michael Kinsley, "The Spoils of Victimhood," *New Yorker*, March 27, 1995, p. 69.

102. Richard Bernstein, "Racial Discrimination or Righting Past Wrongs?" *New York Times*, July 13, 1994.

103. Antonin Scalia, "The Disease as a Cure," in Nieli, ed., *Racial Preferences and Racial Justice*, p. 221.

104. Richard Herrnstein and Charles Murray, *The Bell Curve: Intelligence and Class Structure in American Life* (New York: Free Press, 1994), chap. 19.

105. William Julius Wilson, *The Truly Disadvantaged* (Chicago: University of Chicago Press, 1987), p. 155.

Chapter 2

Racial Classifications

April Chou

Since the 1960s, American society has adopted many race-conscious remedies to address incidents of past and present discrimination. These antidiscrimination measures and affirmative action policies are based upon a system of racial and ethnic categories. As a result, data on race and ethnicity have been used to enforce and monitor civil rights in areas such as employment, voting rights, housing, health care services, and education.[1] But as Luther Wright, Jr., notes: "Amid all the evidence that racial classification is of great importance in American society, the law has provided no consistent definition of race and no logical way to distinguish members of different races from one another. The reality that race is hopelessly intertwined with significant social opportunities and legal protections raises some very serious concerns about racial classification."[2] This essay focuses on the difficulties in defining race and ethnicity and the problems that classifications present for data collection and the administration of public policies.

Controversial Cases

Two highly publicized examples demonstrate some of the inherent difficulties in classifying people by race and ethnicity. Together they reveal that official definitions, nomenclature, and methods of data collection for racial and ethnic classification are constantly in flux, both within levels of government and between them. The second example illustrates the potential abuse of racial and ethnic categories through questionable membership claims.

In 1978 Susie Guillory Phipps requested her birth certificate from the Louisiana Bureau of Vital Statistics while applying for a passport and was shocked to discover that she and both of her parents were listed as "colored." Because she was afraid of her husband's reaction, Phipps secretly tried to get her birth certificate changed through administrative channels.[3] Eventually she hired a New Orleans attorney, Brian Begue, to challenge the Louisiana statute which provided that "a person having one-thirty-second or less of Negro blood shall not be deemed, described, or designated by any public official in the state of Louisiana as 'colored,' a 'mulatto,' a 'black,' a 'negro,' a 'griffe,' a 'Afro-American,' a 'quadroon,' a 'mestizo,' a 'colored person' or a 'person of color.'"[4] The one-thirty-second standard, passed in 1970, had been originally intended as a reform to replace Louisiana's long-standing "one drop of blood" rule, in which a person with any "black blood" was considered black.[5] Despite such legal definitions, Phipps, who is light-skinned with almond eyes and black hair, insisted that she was white.[6]

Nevertheless, both at trial and on appeal Louisiana courts upheld the constitutionality of the fractional classification statute and Phipps's birth certificate was not changed.[7] At trial, attorneys for the state argued that Phipps's birth certificate should not be altered because the racial information was supplied by the midwife who delivered her.[8] In addition, a genealogist testifying for the state presented evidence that traced Phipps's ancestry to a "free Negress" named Margarita, who married a Guillory in 1760.[9] Taking into account more recent ancestors who also had some "black blood," the genealogist calculated that Phipps was 3/32 black.[10] In an interview following the first trial, Phipps said, "Nothing is bad about being black if you're black, but I'm white. I never was black. I was raised white. . . . My Social Security card says I'm white. . . . My driver's license says I'm white. . . . My birth certificate is the only thing that says I'm black."[11]

In July 1983 Louisiana Governor David C. Treen signed a law repealing the statute that designated as black anyone with more than "one-thirty-second [of] Negro blood."[12] Lee Frazier, the state legislator who wrote the law repealing the formula, attributed its successful passage to the national attention attracted by the Phipps case.[13] As a result, "for the first time in U.S. history, no state [had] any explicit racial calculus written into law."[14] Despite the repeal of the statute, in March 1986 the Louisiana Supreme Court refused to reverse rulings by lower courts which said that Phipps could not force the state to change her or her parents' race on her birth certificate.[15]

The Phipps case illustrates the conflicts created by differences between self-identification and third-party observation as methods of racial classification. A midwife recorded Phipps's race as "colored" on her birth certificate, and the determination became an official record. Simultaneously, Phipps's self-identity and many other administrative documents classified her as white. The legal battle also reveals the arbitrary nature of the state's definition of race and the evolving nomenclature of specific categories, which both changed over time. The following example demonstrates a conflict over the racial classification of two men. In this situation, however, they were accused of "racial fraud," a term used to characterize situations in which individuals misclassify themselves racially in order to obtain some tangible benefit.[16]

In 1975 the twin brothers Philip and Paul Malone applied to be firefighters in the city of Boston, but they were not hired because of their low scores on the civil service test. In 1977 the brothers reapplied, changing their racial classification from "white" to "black."[17] By that time the Boston Fire Department had become subject to a court-mandated affirmative action program.[18] As a result of the Malones' self-identification as black, they were hired in 1978 because they qualified as minority candidates.[19]

Ten years later, when the Boston fire commissioner was reviewing the twins' applications for promotion to lieutenant, he was surprised to find that they had listed their race as black.[20] Following a state hearing which determined that the Malones had falsified their documents, the brothers were fired by the state's administrator for the personnel administration department. The Malones appealed, claiming that between 1975 and 1977 they had learned that their great-grandmother was a light-skinned black woman.[21] Their attorneys argued that the department had required only self-identification in 1977 and that the

Malones' race should be measured by the standards in place at the time.[22]

Justice Herbert Wilkins of the Supreme Judicial Court for Suffolk County, Massachusetts, affirmed the conclusion of the personnel administration official and ruled that the Malones misidentified themselves as black to take advantage of a 1975 consent decree establishing minority preference hiring guidelines.[23] This decision was based upon a three-part test for adjudicating racial identification claims. Under such a scheme, the Malones could have supported their claim to be black through visual observation, documentary evidence, or evidence that they or their families held themselves to be minorities and were considered to be minorities.[24] Wilkins wrote that neither brother met any of these criteria, and that "the Malones did not claim to black status honestly or in good faith. They had a powerful incentive to seize on any means to enhance their chances of appointment as firefighters."[25]

The Malone case caused a furor when it became public, and local black and Hispanic groups criticized the city for allowing the Malones to work for ten years before questioning their racial identity.[26] In response, the mayor ordered an investigation into the fire, police, and school departments to determine whether any other individuals had fraudulently claimed minority status.[27] Eleven Boston firefighters who had self-classified as Hispanic were investigated, and two of them resigned.[28]

This incident illustrates the difficulty in verifying or enforcing claims of racial or ethnic membership in a particular group. The Massachusetts Department of Personnel Administration had developed a specific set of criteria for adjudication, and in court, Assistant Attorney General Lawrence P. Fletcher-Hill argued, "If you accept the Malones' assertion here, anyone can say, 'I believe I am black . . . therefore it is true.' A simple assertion that they have basis to believe they are black is insufficient."[29] In contrast, however, self-identification is the method of classification used for many federal data collection procedures. The Phipps and Malone cases exemplify inconsistencies in methods of collecting data on race and ethnicity as well as differences among administrative definitions of race and ethnicity. These discrepancies are a direct result of variations in the conceptualization of race in American society.

Evolving Concepts of Race

Although the concept of race invokes biologically based human characteristics (so-called "phenotypes"), selection of these particular human features for purposes of racial significance is always and necessarily a social and historical process. In contrast to the other major distinction of this type, that of gender, there is no biological basis for distinguishing among human groups along lines of race. Indeed the categories employed to differentiate among human groups along racial lines reveal themselves, upon serious examination, to be at best imprecise, and at worst completely arbitrary.[30]

With these facts in mind, the authors of *Racial Formation in the United States* propose an alternative definition of race as "a concept which signifies and symbolizes social conflicts and interests by referring to different types of human bodies."[31] This contemporary conception of race is quite different from earlier racial classifications. Carolus Linnaeus, writing in the eighteenth century, described five subspecies or races of *Homo sapiens*:

Four-footed, mute, hairy. *Wild Man.*

Copper-coloured, choleric, erect. *American.*
Hair black, straight, thick; nostrils wide, face harsh; beard scanty; obstinate, content free. Paints himself with fine red lines. Regulated by customs.

Fair, sanguine, brawny. *European.*
Hair yellow, brown, flowing; eyes blue; gentle, acute, inventive. Covered with close vestments. Governed by laws.

Sooty, melancholy, rigid. *Asiatic.*
Hair black; eyes dark; severe, haughty, covetous. Covered with loose garments. Governed by opinions.

Black, phlegmatic, relaxed. *African.*
hair black, frizzled; skin silky; nose flat; lips tumid; crafty, indolent, negligent. Anoints himself with grease. Governed by caprice.[32]

Classifications were often based upon such nonbiological criteria and inherent biases. The eighteenth century also witnessed debates among naturalists over whether human races constituted separate species and how different "colored peoples" had evolved. More recently, in the early twentieth century, anthropologists employed classifications based upon morphological types and established prototypes for a given race. Some anthropologists measured skulls and defined groups on the basis of cephalic index, length-height index of the skull, and nasal index; others observed nonskeletal characteristics such as color, hair texture, and lip thickness.[33]

On July 18, 1950, the United Nations Educational, Scientific, and Cultural Organization (UNESCO) issued a "Statement by Experts on Race Problems" after consulting with international scientists representing the fields of anthropology, genetics, biology, social psychology, sociology, and economics.[34] The document concludes that the term "race"

> designates a group or population characterized by some concentrations, relative as to frequency and distribution, or hereditary particles (genes) or physical characters, which appear, fluctuate, and often disappear in the course of time by reason of geographic and/or cultural isolation. The varying manifestation of these traits in different populations are perceived in different ways by each group. What is perceived is largely preconceived, so that each group arbitrarily tends to misinterpret the variability which occurs as a fundamental difference which separates that group from others.[35]

Despite their recognition that race is often perceived arbitrarily, the experts still identified the anthropological classification of humans into three racial divisions known as Mongoloid, Negroid, and Caucasoid.[36] Thus they differentiated between biological and social conceptions of race and argued that "for all practical purposes 'race' is not so much a biological phenomenon as a social myth."[37] Seventeen years later, in 1967, the "Fourth UNESCO Statement of Race" described the division of the human species into "races" as partly conventional and partly arbitrary and does not imply any hierarchy whatsoever. Many anthropologists stress the importance of human variation, but believe that 'racial' divisions have limited scientific interest and may carry the risk of inviting abusive generalization."[38]

In a study conducted in 1972, the geneticist Richard Lewontin found that the overwhelming majority of human genetic variations

occurs within populations, not between them.[39] By analyzing the data
for gene frequencies of seventeen genes in "Caucasians, black Africans,
Mongoloids, South Asian Aborigines, Amerinds, Oceanians, and
Australian Aborigines," he found that "85.4% of the diversity in gene
frequencies was accounted for within populations of the same race,
while differences between these populations accounted for only 8.3%
of the diversity, and even less—6.3%—was accounted for by racial
classification."[40] Thus "the biological definition of race is statistical.
*Races are simply populations of the same species which differ in the
frequencies of some genes.* . . . racial differences are due to differences
in the frequencies of alleles, not necessarily or generally in the kinds
of alleles."[41] Under a statistical genetic classification of race, boundaries
are arbitrary, the number of races defined is arbitrary, and there is no
average genotype or average phenotype involved in the classification.[42]

More recent scholarship by social scientists has also come to accept
race as a concept with varying definitions that are highly influenced by
social, cultural, and historical contexts. In their analysis of prejudice
and discrimination, George Eaton and J. Milton Yinger write, "The
term race has many levels of meaning, scientific, administrative, and
popular. The meanings are so diverse, even contradictory, that some
authors believe the word ought not be used."[43] Similarly, the sociologist
Howard F. Taylor states that race is a multidimensional concept.
Different definitions of race may be based upon semibiological
distinctions of perceived characteristics, cultural identification,
nationality or geographic origin, socioeconomic distinctions, status or
prestige, and self-definition.[44] Clara Rodriguez and Hector Cordero-
Guzman also confirm that "race is more complex than is generally
assumed."[45] In an article examining the racial self-identity of Puerto
Ricans, they argue that race is a cultural construct, and that the meaning
of the term race as well as how races are determined varies from culture
to culture. Historical context is important in determining race, and in
the United States, "race is generally seen as a fact of biology;" other
countries may emphasize other conceptions of race.[46]

These definitions of race generally converge in the recognition
that racial categories are social constructs that are highly influenced
by historical and cultural contexts. Even if we accept race as a nebulous
and ill-defined concept, however, should we reject racial categorization
in a public policy context? For example, the ACLU advocated the
removal of the race question from the 1960 census, and the state of
New Jersey stopped entering race information on its birth and death

certificates in 1962 and 1963.[47] Many argue that such an approach is naive, as it ignores the role that race continues to play in structuring both state and civil society; today, as in the past, "race continues to shape both identities and institutions in significant ways."[48]

In the context of antidiscrimination measures, the government relies heavily on racial data to support Equal Employment Opportunity (EEO) laws and existing legislation such as the Civil Rights Act of 1964 and the Voting Rights Act of 1965. Without a system of racial categories, affirmative action programs based on race and ethnicity would be defunct. U.S. Representative Thomas C. Sawyer (D-Ohio), chair of the former House Subcommittee on Census, Statistics, and Postal Personnel, states, "Today we measure race in order to preserve rights against discrimination, when in fact those very categories were the vehicles used to discriminate."[49] Echoing the irony in the existing system of racial classification, a medical researcher who studies race and health care says, "We need these categories essentially to get rid of them."[50] Yet the existence of a system of racial categories should not be assumed to be inherently pernicious. There is an important question to consider when discussing the termination of racial categories— to whose best interest would the end of such a system be?

OMB Statistical Policy Directive No. 15

The racial and ethnic categories used by all federal agencies adhere to the guidelines established by the Statistical Policy Directive No. 15, "Race and Ethnic Standards for Federal Statistics and Administrative Reporting," issued by the Office of Management and Budget (OMB) in 1977. Prior to the uniform set of standards created by the directive, each federal agency used its own categorization policy.[51] Although Directive No. 15 states explicitly that its classifications "should not be interpreted as being scientific or anthropological in nature," the OMB specifies that federal agencies must collect and present data on four racial categories—American Indian or Alaska Native, Asian or Pacific Islander, Black, and White—as well as two ethnic categories—Hispanic Origin and Not of Hispanic Origin.[52] The directive also allows for the collection of additional detail in racial and ethnic categories, on the condition that the data can be aggregated into the basic five categories. Directive No. 15 specifies:

When race and ethnicity are collected separately, the number of White and Black persons who are Hispanic must be identifiable, and capable of being reported in that category. If a combined format is used to collect racial and ethnic data, the minimum acceptable categories are: American Indian or Alaskan Native; Asian or Pacific Islander; Black, not of Hispanic Origin; Hispanic; White, not of Hispanic Origin.[53]

Although Directive No. 15 has remained unchanged since 1977, the standards have "come under increasing criticism from those who believe that the minimum categories set forth in Directive No. 15 do not reflect the increasing diversity of our Nation's population."[54] In response, the House Subcommittee on Census, Statistics, and Postal Personnel held four hearings to review federal measures of race and ethnicity in 1993. At the July 1993 hearing, a representative of the OMB testified that the Clinton administration planned to consider revising the directive.[55] The OMB is currently undergoing a comprehensive review and possible revision of Directive No. 15. In 1994 the review process included: (1) a workshop organized by the Committee on National Statistics (CNSTAT) of the National Academy of Sciences; (2) public hearings in Boston, Denver, San Francisco, and Honolulu; (3) comments by federal agencies on their requirements for racial and ethnic data; (4) development of a research agenda; and (5) an open public comment period.[56] In addition, an Interagency Committee for the Review of the Racial and Ethnic Standards has been created to assist the OMB in assessing proposed changes in the system of classifications.[57]

This interagency committee designated a Research Working Group to evaluate proposals for revising categories and the potential effects on data quality that would result from such changes. The first project of the research agenda was a supplement to the May 1995 Current Population Survey (CPS) conducted by the Bureau of Labor Statistics. The supplement, as we shall see below, tested the effects of using a multiracial category, adding "Hispanic" to the list of racial categories, and employing preferences for alternative names for racial and ethnic categories.[58] Any changes to Directive No. 15 must be made by 1997 in preparation for the 2000 census.[59]

Sally Katzen, director of the Office of Information and Regulatory Affairs at the OMB, is responsible for making the final recommendations on revising racial categories. She emphasizes the limited purpose of the OMB distinction: "When OMB got into the business of establishing categories, it was purely statistical, not programmatic—purely for the purpose of data gathering, not for defining or protecting different categories. It was certainly never meant to *define* a race."[60] Yet because Directive No. 15 is effectively functioning in that capacity, the current debates over categories are especially critical. On a separate occasion, however, Katzen said that there is no reason to worry that changes will affect regulatory programs. "Americans may be given more choices in racial and ethnic categories, but statisticians will be given the tools to aggregate the findings so that results can fit the original racial categories."[61]

Classification Methods of the EEOC and OFCCP

Antidiscrimination statutes and federally mandated affirmative action programs are regulated by the Equal Employment Opportunity Commission (EEOC) and the Office of Federal Contract Compliance Programs (OFCCP), agencies that both fall under Directive No. 15 guidelines. The EEOC is an independent commission, mandated by Title VII of the Civil Rights Act of 1964, which focuses on acts of discrimination against identifiable victims. It investigates and conciliates claims in all sectors and administers many equal employment opportunity laws.[62] The EEOC also administers affirmative action within federal agencies and has written guidelines on affirmative action where Title VII and Executive Order 11246 intersect. Although the regulatory and persuasive powers of the EEOC are strong, it cannot enforce corrective measures without court intervention. The OFCCP is a branch of the Labor Department with a specific focus on affirmative action. Unlike the EEOC, the OFCCP can impose strong remedies on employers. It administers Executive Order 11246 for minorities and women in nonfederal entities as well as affirmative action orders for age and disability.[63]

Any changes to Directive No. 15 will have a direct impact on the racial categories used by the EEOC and the OFCCP. Under current EEOC and OFCCP guidelines, there are five specific categories used to designate race and ethnicity. They are based upon Directive No. 15 and defined as follows:

White—an individual, not of Hispanic origin, with origins in any of the original peoples of Europe, North America, or the Middle East.

Black—an individual, not of Hispanic origin, with origins in any of the Black racial groups of Africa.

Hispanic—a person of Mexican, Puerto Rican, Cuban, Central or South American, or other Spanish culture or origin, regardless of race. This does not include persons of Portuguese descent or persons from Central or South America who are not of Spanish origin or culture.

Asian or Pacific Islander—a person with origins in any of the original peoples of the Far East, Southeast Asia, the Indian Subcontinent, or the Pacific Islands. This area includes, for example, China, Japan, Korea, the Philippine Republic and Samoa; and, on the Indian Subcontinent, includes India, Pakistan, Bangladesh, Sri Lanka, Nepal, Sikkim and Bhutan.

American Indian or Alaskan Native—a person with origins in any of the original peoples of North America who maintains cultural identification through tribal affiliation or has community recognition as an American Indian or Alaskan Native.[64]

Problems often stem from the arbitrary nature of these categories. Why are "Black" and "White" defined in terms of color while "Hispanic" is designated in terms of "culture or origin, regardless of race" and "Asian or Pacific Islander" is described as a geographic or national origin group? Are the panethnic categories "Hispanic" and "Asian or Pacific Islander" too broad to have any significant meaning? Does an "American Indian or Alaskan Native" need to demonstrate "tribal affiliation" or "community recognition"? Furthermore, the issue of nomenclature is magnified by the language used in the OFCCP guidelines for utilization analysis. Written in 1978, the terminology used for group designations of "Blacks, Spanish-surnamed Americans, American Indians, and Orientals" is already outdated.[65]

Another example that points to potential problems is the use of third-party identification for determining racial categories. The OMB writes that federal agencies concerned with monitoring and enforcement of civil rights "prefer to collect data on racial and ethnic data by visual observation. Since discrimination is based on the perception of an individual's race or Hispanic Origin, these agencies oppose any changes that would make it more difficult to collect data by observation."[66] An EEOC instruction booklet explains:

> An employer may acquire the race/ethnic information necessary for this section either by visual surveys of the work force, or from post-employment records. For the purpose of this report, an employee may be included in the group to which he or she appears to belong, identifies with, or is regarded in the community as belonging. However, no person should be counted in more than one race/ethnic category.[67]

These guidelines raise a number of important questions. Are visual surveys accurate as a method for racial classification? Is an observer able to differentiate an "American Indian" from a "White"? How should an employer classify an employee with a multiracial background, especially someone whose heritage is partly of a protected group and partly of the unprotected "White" group? For the "Hispanic" group, which by definition encompasses individuals who may be racially "Black" or "White," federal procedures suggest the use of a "Spanish surname" to classify individuals. Yet of all people in the United States who identified themselves as "Hispanic" in the 1970 census, one-quarter did not have Spanish surnames.[68]

One of the policies that depends on these categories and definitions is the mandatory development of affirmative action programs by federal contractors. Under current OFCCP guidelines, an affirmative action program is defined as

> a set of specific and result-oriented procedures to which a contractor commits itself to apply every good faith effort. The objective of those procedures plus such efforts is equal employment opportunity. . . . An acceptable affirmative action program must include an analysis of areas within which the contractor is deficient in the utilization of minority groups and women, and further, goals and timetables must be directed to correct deficiencies and, this to achieve prompt and full utilization of minorities and women, at all levels and in all segments of its work force where deficiencies exist.[69]

In order to gauge underutilization, a contractor must conduct a work force analysis and an availability analysis on an annual basis.[70] How do the difficulties of accurate data collection for racial and ethnic categories affect "work force analyses" and the affirmative action programs based upon them? For instance, "it is not known whether the race/ethnicity designation ascribed by the applicant or employee is the same as that reported by the applicant or employee to the Census Bureau."[71] The Census Bureau uses self-identification as the method for collecting racial and ethnic data, yet census data is often the source of the "availability data" with which the employer compares his/her work force. Despite the recognition by government agencies that "final tabulations give the data an appearance of comparability among data sets when there are actually differences caused by data collection methods," the data "are widely accepted by courts and governments as reliable indicators of change . . . in labor markets."[72]

The U.S. Bureau of the Census

Many of the complexities of collecting data based on race and ethnicity are encountered by the U.S. Bureau of the Census. In addition, differences between the racial and ethnic categories defined by the Census Bureau and those defined by the EEOC, as well as inconsistencies in the methods of reporting of race and ethnicity between these agencies, have implications for affirmative action policies. Racial and ethnic categories from past censuses also reveal how the concepts of race and ethnicity have been viewed in the United States through time.

Items on Race and Ethnicity

Beginning with the first census in 1790, which classified the population into "free persons," "Indians not taxed," and "three-fifths of other persons," the Bureau of the Census has collected information on race.[73] Since then, it has used a variety of different question formats and terminology; categories for tabulating race and ethnicity have changed every ten years.[74] For example, the categories recording race have included various criteria such as national origin, tribal affiliation, and physical characteristics. Prior to 1960, information on race was based primarily upon observation by the census enumerator.

Today information on race is obtained through self-classification. The method of self-identification "means that responses are based on self-perception and therefore are subjective, but at the same time, by definition, whatever response is recorded is an accurate response."[75]

Yet despite the improved system, inconsistencies still exist. An individual may respond differently to the same question on census forms and job applications, and the wording or sequence on a questionnaire can influence responses.[76] A study of the Current Population Survey revealed that one in three individuals reported an ethnicity in 1972 that was different from the one he or she reported in 1971.[77] Robert Tortora, associate director for statistical design, methodology, and standards at the Census Bureau, comments: "Basically, what you're asking is a person's judgment of their race or ethnicity. And since we don't have precise definitions of every possible category, people's perceptions of themselves can change from census to census."[78]

The 1990 question regarding race was asked of all respondents, and each person was asked to select the group with which he or she most closely identified. The question had fourteen specific categories: white; Black or Negro; Indian; Eskimo; Aleut; nine Asian Pacific Islander (API) groups; and two residual categories: "other API" and "other race." Beside the three boxes marked "Indian", "other API," and "other race," respondents are asked to write in their tribal affiliation or race.[79] The only question regarding ethnicity asked by the 1990 census inquired whether or not one was of "Spanish-Hispanic" origin. The section listed a "No" category followed by four "Yes" categories: "Yes, Mexican, Mexican American, Chicano"; "Yes, Puerto Rican"; "Yes, Cuban"; and "Yes, other Spanish-Hispanic." Prior to the current self-identification method of ethnicity, the Spanish-Hispanic origin population was estimated by the Census Bureau through indirect measures based on birthplace, language spoken, and Spanish surnames.[80]

Currently, when individuals refuse to limit their self-definition by checking a designated box, the census computer usually does it for them. If a person does not select an existing category, computers scan the other answers on the form and assign that individual to a category that seems appropriate. Those who check more than one box are assigned the first race that they report.[81]

Thus the information collected on race and ethnicity by the Census Bureau differs from the data required by EEOC guidelines in several ways. First, although each breaks down groups into five basic categories, the census is more specific in its treatment of national origin and tribal identity. Second, the census includes a category for "other race," whereas EEOC and OFCCP forms stipulate that "no person should be counted in more than one race/ethnic category."[82] Third, the Census Bureau employs a system of racial categories based upon self-designation, while the EEOC allows employers to use "visual surveys." An individual may be categorized under one group on the census and under another by an employer. On the aggregate, these differences may affect the construction of and compliance to affirmative action programs.

Issues for the 2000 Census

The Bureau of the Census is currently evaluating the racial and ethnic data collected through the 1990 census in its efforts to develop race and ethnic identifiers that will produce high-quality data for the 2000 census. It plans to conduct two tests in 1996 as part of the Directive No. 15 review process. In March, the National Content Test (NCT), designed to test selected population and housing questions, will include panels that test suggested changes to racial and ethnic categories. The Race and Ethnic Targeted Test (RAETT), scheduled for June, will be administered to a sample of 90,000 diverse racial and ethnic households and will "provide the most extensive opportunity to test several options for collecting racial and ethnic data."[83]

The revision of measures of race and ethnicity is a difficult endeavor, especially because the issues are highly politicized.[84] During the past several years, advocacy groups, social scientists, and other users of data have questioned the conceptual foundations behind the categories designated by OMB Directive No. 15. In addition, a fundamental tension exists between the desire for descriptive accuracy that reflects changing sociopolitical realities and the importance of consistency in reporting that affects longitudinal comparisons of data. Greg Robinson, chief of population and analysis for the Census Bureau, states, "The demand [for detailed data] is going in one direction, and the quality and consistency in counting is going the other way . . . the quality of the race and ethnic data is deteriorating."[85]

The "Multiracial" Box

One of the most controversial issues is the inclusion of a "multiracial" classification. Between the 1960 and 1990 censuses, the number of interracial marriages in the United States increased from 148,000 to 953,000. In 1990 interracial couples accounted for 1.9

percent of the 51.1 million married couples nationwide.[86] During that same year, over 125,000 babies born were classified as biracial.[87] As a result, there is an increasing population of individuals who are asked too choose a single racial category that does not accurately reflect their identity.

Racial mixing has a long history in this country. Much of the early intermixing of blacks and whites occurred as a result of rape and coercion of black slaves by white slaveholders. In contrast, there were also consensual unions between whites, blacks, and Indians in both the North and the South.[88] For brief periods of time, this intermixing was reflected in the census. For example, the 1890 census had a race item that included "mulatto," "quadroon," and "octoroon" as categories.[89] More often, however, the offspring of these unions were subjected to the "one drop of blood" rule, and were defined as black if they had any "black blood." The practice was rooted in a long-discredited belief that each race had its own blood type, correlated with physical appearance and social behavior, and had been implemented in the antebellum South to create as many slaves as possible.[90] In 1920 the government legitimized the one-drop rule by stating that in future censuses, anyone with any African ancestry was to mark his or her race as "Black."[91] It is estimated that 75 to 90 percent of people who now check the "Black" box could check a "Multiracial" box if it were created.[92]

Currently about a third of the one million multiracial people in the United States check "Other" on the census form. According to a study conducted in 1980, the other two-thirds check "Black."[93] Roderick Harrison, head of the Census Bureau's Racial Statistics division, estimated in 1994 that about 10 percent of individuals who check the "Black" box would select the multiracial category if there were one.[94] The creation of a multiracial box, however, would also affect other minority communities. For example, most Native Americans and Latinos also have mixed ancestry as a result of European colonialism in the Americas. In addition, recent interracial marriages more often involve a white and an American Indian or Asian partner than a black and white couple.[95] Preliminary results of the May 1995 "CPS Supplement for Testing Methods of Collecting Racial and Ethnic Information" reveal that when a multiracial category was included, the proportion of American Indians, Eskimos, and Aleuts dropped while the proportions of Blacks and Asian Pacific Islanders were not significantly affected.[96]

Advocates of a multiracial box argue that current categories are inadequate because they force persons to deny the racial heritage of one parent, causing adverse effects on self-esteem, sense of family, pride, and psychological well-being.[97] There are numerous anecdotes about multiracial individuals who do not "fit" any of the designations provided by the census and other federal and local forms. A biracial male explained, "My military records have me as white, my birth certificate has me as black. . . . Now I check 'other' until maybe we can get 'multiracial.'"[98] Kwame Anthony Appiah clarifies an important point:

> What the Multiracial category aims for is not people of mixed ancestry, because a majority of Americans are actually products of mixed ancestry. This category goes after people who have parents who are socially recognized as belonging to different races. That's OK—that's an interesting social category. But then you have to ask what happens to their children. Do we want to have more boxes, depending on whether they marry back into one group or another?[99]

Opponents of the creation of a multiracial box, however, include those who are concerned about the effect of such a category on the enforcement of federal civil rights-related legislation. They note that if a large proportion of people choose to define themselves as multiracial, legislative districts, school desegregation, and regulatory programs addressing housing, employment, and education would all have to be reassessed. One government analyst said, "There's no concern on any of these people's part about the effect on policy—it's just a subjective feeling that their identity needs to be stroked. . . . What they don't understand is that it's going to cost their own groups."[100] Although the arguments in favor of a new box may be easily comprehended by traditional civil rights groups, most activists oppose the creation of the multiracial box on the grounds that it would "dilute" counts of minorities and result in reduced federal funding for targeted programs.[101] At a 1993 House committee hearing Tony Gallegos, chairman of the EEOC, testified that "the addition of a multiracial category may remove significant numbers of employees from current categories . . . this reduction would thus understate the pool of individuals of a given race or ethnicity available for jobs. Compliance monitoring would not be possible."[102]

In addition, it is difficult to predict how individuals who select the multiracial category would be treated in relation to affirmative action programs. It could increase the number of eligible individuals by allowing those with any nonwhite ancestry to be counted as minorities, or it could have the opposite effect by excluding "partial" minorities from all programs.[103] After soliciting public comment from various federal agencies on this issue, OMB concluded that "Federal laws have been written with the assumption that persons identify with one racial group; these laws would either have to be changed or some method would have to be devised to meet legislative requirements."[104]

"Hispanic Origin" and the Overlap with Racial Categories

Another major issue concerning the Census Bureau is the confusion surrounding the ethnic category "Hispanic" and its overlap with racial categories. The Spanish/Hispanic origin item was first included in the 1970 census and has tested and refined for each subsequent census.[105] Prior to the creation of this self-designated category, Hispanic origin was determined through a variety of methods. In 1930, "Mexicans" were included as a category; in 1940, "persons of Spanish mother tongue" were reported; and during 1950 and 1960, "persons of Spanish surname" were reported.[106] Since 1950 a surname list has been used to classify individuals as Hispanic when self-identity is unspecified.[107]

Currently the race and ethnic items are separate questions; a respondent may check one of the racial categories and later indicate his or her ethnicity. For example, this structure enables an individual of Caribbean descent to identify as both "Black" and "Hispanic." Nevertheless, many respondents perceive "Hispanic" as a race and not an ethnic category.[108] Over 97 percent of the 9.8 million "other race" responses in the 1990 census were from individuals who also indicated their Hispanic origin.[109] This figure constitutes 40 percent of all Hispanic respondents and indicates that the 22 million Hispanics in the United States are not willing to identify themselves as belonging to another racial group such as black or white.[110] Instead, a Hispanic person may check "other race," enter a national origin group such as "Mexican," and then not respond to the Hispanic origin item. Likewise, an individual may leave the race item blank and check a Hispanic origin category. During field tests preceding the 1990 census, researchers observed that many individuals gave identical answers to race, ethnicity, and ancestry questions because they did not recognize differences among them. In addition, the 1980 and 1990 censuses experienced a high degree of nonresponse in the Hispanic origin category, either because the question was not understood or because respondents thought that they had already provided their ethnicity in another section.[111]

Many Hispanic activists argue that these discrepancies are the result not of misunderstandings by respondents but, rather, of the Census Bureau's failure to acknowledge the racially mixed character of Hispanics. They state that the majority of Hispanics in the United States have a mixture of Indian, Spanish, and African blood. They believe that respondents who selected the "other" category did so either with an awareness of their indigenous or mixed heritage or because the available racial categories seemed inadequate.[112] As a result, the National Council of La Raza demanded a Hispanic race box at the House committee hearings in 1993.[113] Similarly Jorge del Pinal, the chief of Ethnic and Hispanic Statistics at the Census Bureau, proposes "one unique and mutually exclusive category" for each individual, resulting in no overlap between race and ethnicity. He cites the main deficiency of OMB Directive No. 15 as allowing some individuals to belong to two groups without specifying how to reallocate them when unique and mutually exclusive categories are needed.[114] Early findings from an analysis of the May 1995 CPS supplement provide additional information about this issue. The results show that a higher percentage of people identified themselves as Hispanic when they were asked a separate Hispanic origin question than when "Hispanic" was included as a racial category. At the same time, however, the analysis also revealed that the majority of Hispanic respondents preferred a Hispanic racial category over a separate ethnicity question.[115]

Other Proposed Changes

The data standards on race and ethnicity have been criticized in many other areas as well. Native Hawaiians, for example, oppose their inclusion in the Asian and Pacific Islander category. First, they contend that the current placement implies that the original inhabitants of Hawaii were immigrants to the United States like other Asians or Pacific Islanders. Second, they argue that the aggregate data from the panethnic category do not accurately reflect social and economic conditions faced by Native Hawaiians. Senator Daniel K. Akaka has proposed that Native Hawaiians be placed in the same category as other indigenous peoples, Indians and Alaskan Natives. American

Indian and Alaskan Native organizations, however, do not support this idea. They are worried that such a change would have an adverse impact on both the accuracy of data collection and the administration of federal subsidies to their groups.[116] Nevertheless, there is a precedent for the movement of a group into another category. In 1977 the creation of OMB Directive No. 15 removed Asian Indians from the "White" category and placed them into the "Asian Pacific Islander" category.[117]

In addition, many Middle Easterners charge that their members are grossly undercounted; they have suggested the inclusion of an ethnic category recognizing them.[118] OMB Directive No. 15 classifies people from the Middle East and North Africa as white. Some advocates suggest an "Arab American" category, based on linguistic and cultural ties; others support a geographically based category termed "Middle Easterner."[119] Changes have also been suggested for the revision of nomenclature designating categories. For example, many groups have requested the alteration of the term "Black/Negro" to read "African American." Similarly, advocates have asked for a change from the categories "Indian" and "Eskimo" to "Native American."

It is not a coincidence that the scrutiny over racial and ethnic categories has occurred at a time when policies that were designed to redress social and economic inequalities are also under attack.[120] As political conservatives call for the creation of a race-blind society, various minority groups are fighting for official inclusion and governmental recognition. Simultaneously, advocates of civil rights legislation are attempting to defend a system that enables the enforcement of civil rights-related legislation. Representative Sawyer comments on the debate over racial classification:

> We recognize the importance of racial categories in correcting clear injustices under the law. The dilemma we face is trying to assure the fundamental guarantees of equality of opportunity while at the same time recognizing that the populations themselves are changing as we seek to categorize them. . . . Part of the difficulty is that we are dealing with the illusion of precision. We wind up with precise counts of everybody in the country, and they are precisely wrong. They don't reflect who we are as a people. To be effective, the concepts of individual and group identity need to reflect not only who we are but who we are becoming. The more these categories distort our perception of reality, the less useful they are. We act as if we knew what we're talking about when we talk about race, and we don't.[121]

Conclusion

Although race is largely an arbitrary social construct, it has developed significant meanings in the context of American society. Data on race and ethnicity have been collected by the government throughout the history of the United States, but the definitions, nomenclature, and methods of collection for racial and ethnic categories have evolved with changing political climates and societal attitudes. In 1977 the Office of Management and Budget created standard measures of race and ethnicity through Statistical Policy Directive No. 15 in order to facilitate data analysis and monitor regulatory policies among federal agencies.

The fact that race-conscious remedies are often tied to social opportunities and legal protections for individuals raises significant questions about the nature of racial and ethnic classifications. Racial and ethnic categories are central to the affirmative action programs and antidiscriminatory policies established by Executive Order 11246 and Title VII of the Civil Rights Act of 1964. The Equal Employment Opportunity Commission and the Federal Contract Compliance Programs, regulatory agencies that monitor civil rights-related legislation, use five categories—"White," "Black," "Hispanic," "Asian or Pacific Islander," and "American Indian or Alaskan Native"—to designate race and ethnicity. Federal government employers and contractors that fall under specified criteria are required to use these categories as they develop affirmative action programs based upon measures of "underutilization" and an annual comparison of a "work force analysis" and an "availability analysis." Census Bureau data on the racial and ethnic composition of the United States is often used as the basis for the "availability analysis" conducted by employers. Unlike the federal regulatory agencies, the most recent census asked separate questions on race and ethnicity and used self-designation as opposed to visual surveys as the primary method for classification. As a result, final tabulations give the appearance of comparability among data sets despite differences resulting from collection methods.

In recent years, the classification system created by Directive No. 15 has come under increasing criticism for its failure to represent the nation's growing diversity. As a result, the OMB is currently reviewing its racial and ethnic categories in preparation for the 2000 census. The issues facing the Census Bureau illustrate the different views and concerns regarding racial and ethnic classification. These debates have become very sensitive political issues. Various groups are fighting for official recognition just as others are calling for a color-blind, race-blind society. A system of clearer and more widely accepted racial and ethnic categories will facilitate the debate over race-based policies in the months and years ahead.

Notes

1. Office of Management and Budget (OMB), "Standards for the Classification of Federal Data on Race and Ethnicity," 60 *Federal Register* 166 (1995), p. 44674.
2. Luther Wright, Jr., "Who's Black, Who's White, and Who Cares: Reconceptualizing the United States' Definition of Race and Racial Classifications," *Vanderbilt Law Review* 48 (March 1995): 519.
3. Kent Demaret, "Raised White, a Louisiana Belle Challenges Race Records That Call Her 'Colored,'" *People*, December 6, 1982, p. 155.
4. Louisiana statutes, 1970 LA. ACTS 46 at 1, repealed by LA. REV. STAT. ANN. ACTS 1983 no. 441, at 1 as annotated in Neil Gotanda, "A Critique of 'Our Constitution Is Color-Blind,'" *Stanford Law Review* 44 (November 1991): 35.
5. "Color Bind; Louisiana Reforms—Sort of," *Time*, July 18, 1983, p. 17.
6. Dorothy Gilliam, "Black/White," *Washington Post*, October 2, 1982, final ed., p. B1.
7. Gotanda, "A Critique," p. 350.
8. Mary Schlangenstein, "Appeal Filed on Blood Law," *United Press International*, May 20, 1983.
9. Demaret, "Raised White," p. 155.
10. Art Harris, "Louisiana Court Sees No Shades of Gray in Woman's Request," *Washington Post*, May 21, 1983, A3.
11. Ibid.
12. Frances Frank Marcus, "Louisiana Repeals Black Blood Law," *New York Times*, July 6, 1983, p. A10.
13. "La. Racial Law Repealed," *Facts on File World News Digest*, August 5, 1983, p. 586 G1.
14. Marcus, "Louisianna Repeals."
15. "U.S. Woman Loses Court Battle to Change Race Classification," *Reuters North European Service*, April 1, 1986.
16. Annotated in Wright, "Who's," p. 516.
17. Wright, "Who's," p. 515.
18. Christopher A. Ford, "Administering Identity: The Determination of 'Race' in Race-Conscious Law," *California Law Review* 82 (October 1994): 1232. For a discussion of "ethnic fraud" among individuals claiming to be Native Americans, see Mitchell Zuckoff, "More and More Claiming American Indian Heritage," *Boston Globe*, April 18, 1995, p. 1.
19. Peggy Hernandez, "Many Chances to Dispute Malones Firefighters' Minority Status Unchallenged for 10 Years, *Boston Globe,* November 7, 1988, p. 1.
20. Peggy Hernandez, "SJC Considers Firefighters' Claim of Unfair Hearing in Minority Hiring Case," *The Boston Globe,* May 25, 1989, p. 36.

21. Annotated in Wright, "Who's," p. 516.
22. Ford, "Administering," pp. 1232-1233.
23. Peggy Hernandez, "Firemen Who Claimed to Be Black Lose Appeal," *Boston Globe*, July 26, 1989, p. 13.
24. Ford, "Administration," p. 1233; Hernandez, "SJC Considers," p. 36.
25. Quoted in Hernandez, "Fireman," p. 13.
26. Wright, "Who's," p. 516.
27. Hernandez, "Fireman," p. 13.
28. Peggy Hernandez, "Two Boston Firefighters, Probed for Minority Claim, Resign," *Boston Globe*, May 17, 1989, p. 29; see also Wright, "Who's," p. 516.
29. Quoted in Hernandez, "SJC Considers," p. 36.
30. Michael Omi and Howard Winant, *Racial Formation in the United States: From the 1960s to the 1990s* (New York: Routledge, 1994), p. 55.
31. Ibid.
32. Ayesha E. Gill, "The Misuse of Genetics in the Race-IQ Controversy," *San Jose Studies* 4 (November 1978): 31.
33. Ibid., pp. 32-33.
34. Ashley Montagu, *Statement on Race: An Annotated Elaboration and Exposition of the Four Statements on Race Issues by the United Nations Educational, Scientific, and Cultural Organization*, 3rd ed. (New York: Oxford University Press, 1972), pp. x, 4.
35. Ibid., p. 8.
36. Ibid., p. 9.
37. Ibid., pp. 118-119.
38. Ibid., p. 158.
39. James Shreeve, "Terms of Estrangement: Race and Science," *Discover*, November 1994, pp. 56+.
40. Gill, "Misuse," p. 35.
41. Ibid., p. 27. Emphasis in original.
42. Ibid.
43. George Eaton Simpson and J. Milton Yinger, *Racial and Cultural Minorities: An Analysis of Prejudice and Discrimination* (New York: Plenum Press, 1985), p. 27.
44. Howard F. Taylor, personal interview, December 12, 1995.
45. Clara Rodriguez and Hector Cordero-Guzman, "Placing Race in Context," *Racial and Ethnic Studies* 15 (October 1992): 523.
46. Ibid., pp. 524-526.
47. Lawrence Wright, "One Drop of Blood," *New Yorker*, July 25, 1994, p. 50.
48. Omi and Winant, *Racial Formation*, p. vii.
49. Ted Olson, "What Is Race, Anyway? Dividing People by Race," *Scholastic Update*, November 18, 1994, pp. 6+.
50. Ibid., p. 6.

51. Barry Edmonston and Charles Schultze, eds., *Modernizing the U.S. Census* (Washington, D.C.: National Academy of Sciences, 1995), p. 149.
52. U.S. Office of Federal Statistical Policy and Standards, "Race and Ethnic Standards for Federal Statistics and Administrative Reporting," Directive No. 15 (Washington, D.C., May 1978).
53. Ibid.
54. OMB, "Standards for the Classification of Federal Data on Race and Ethnicity," p. 44674.
55. Edmonston and Schultze, *Modernizing*, p. 149.
56. OMB, "Standards for the Classification of Federal Data on Race and Ethnicity," p. 44674.
57. Suzann Evinger, "How Shall We Measure Our Nation's Diversity?" *Chance* 8 (1995): 10.
58. Bureau of Labor Statistics, U.S. Department of Labor, "A CPS Supplement for Testing Methods of Collecting Racial and Ethnic Information: May 1995" (Washington, D.C., October 1995), p. 1.
59. Kathy Wallman, panel discussion, "Measuring Race and Ethnicity in an Age of Diversity," Population Reference Bureau, Washington, D.C., November 15, 1995.
60. Wright, "One Drop," p. 54.
61. Allan Holmes, "Countdown to 2000," *Government Executive* (March 1995).
62. The EEOC administers Title VII of the Civil Rights Act of 1964, the Equal Pay Act of 1963, the Age Discrimination in Employment Act of 1967, as amended, the Rehabilitation Act of 1973, and the Americans with Disabilities Act of 1990. Arthur Gutman, *EEO Law and Personnel Policies* (Newbury Park, Calif.: SAGE Publications, 1993), p. 7.
63. Gutman, *EEO* Law, p. 7.
64. Order taken from Equal Employment Opportunity Commission, "EEOC Form 221, Higher Education Staff Information (EEO-6)" (Washington, D.C.), pp. 6-7. Definitions from "OFCCP Federal Contract Compliance Manual" (Chicago: Commerce Clearing House, 1993).
65. Sec. 60-2.11, "Required Utilization Analysis," Office of Federal Contract Compliance Programs of the U.S. Department of Labor, *Chapter 60: Equal Employment Opportunity*, Title 41, Part 60 of the Code of Federal Regulations, p. 116.
66. OMB, "Standards for the Classification of Federal Data on Race and Ethnicity," p. 44679.
67. "EEOC Form 221," p. 6.
68. "Summary Notes on the Statistics of Federal Affirmative Action Programs," *American Journal of Economics and Sociology* 41 (October 1982): 324.
69. Sec. 60-2.1, "Purpose of Affirmative Action Programs," *Chapter 60*, p. 115.

70. Gutman, *EEO Law*, p. 245.
71. Ibid.
72. OMB, "Standards for the Classification of Federal Data on Race and Ethnicity," p. 44678.
73. Edmonston and Schultze, *Modernizing*, p. 142.
74. Ibid., p. 140.
75. Ibid., p. 150.
76. Ibid., pp. 150-151.
77. OMB, "Standards for the Classification of Federal Data on Race and Ethnicity," p. 44675.
78. Gabrielle Sandor, "The 'Other' Americans," *American Demographics* (June 1994): 36.
79. Nampeo R. McKenney and Claudette E. Bennett, "Issues Regarding Data on Race and Ethnicity," *Public Health Reports* 109 (January 1994): 16+.
80. Ibid.
81. Sandor, "Other."
82. "EEOC Form 221," p. 6.
83. OMB, "Standards for the Classification of Federal Data on Race and Ethnicity," p. 44691.
84. Martha Farnsworth Riche, "Census 2000 and New Paradigms," lecture at Princeton University, Princeton, N.J., November 15, 1995.
85. Sandor, "Other."
86. Charlotte E. Bennett, Nampeo R. McKenney, and Roderick J. Harrison, "Racial Classification Issues Concerning Children in Mixed-Race Households," paper presented at the annual meeting of the Population Association of America, April 6-8, 1995, San Francisco, p. 1.
87. Jack Sirica, "Question of Race; Census Query Has Many People Asking: Who Am I?" *Newsday*, February 5, 1995, p. A7.
88. Mary C. Waters, "The Role of Lineage in Identity Formation among Black Americans," *Qualitative Sociology* 14 (1991): 60.
89. Edmonston and Schultze, *Modernizing*, p. 142.
90. Wright, "One Drop," p. 48.
91. Sirica, "Question."
92. Wright, "One Drop," p. 47.
93. Hanna Rosin, "Boxed-in: America's Newest Racial Minority; 'Multiracial' Groups Seek Separate Census Status," *New Republic*, January 3, 1994, pp. 12+.
94. Ibid.
95. Bennett, McKenney, and Harrison, "Racial Classification," p. 1.
96. It is important to keep in mind, however, that CPS questions were administered by interviewers via telephone, and self-administered forms may offer different results. "A CPS Supplement for Testing Methods of Collecting Racial and Ethnic Information: May 1995," pp. 2-3.
97. Evinger, "How Small," p. 11.
98. Sirica, "Question."

99. Wright, "One Drop," p. 49.
100. Ibid., p. 47.
101. Sirica, "Question."
102. Holmes, "Countdown."
103. Rosin, "Boxed-in."
104. OMB, Standards for the Classification of Federal Data on Race and Ethnicity," p. 44677.
105. Edmonston and Schultze, *Modernizing*, p. 143.
106. Ethnic and Hispanic Statistics Branch, U.S. Bureau of the Census, "We, the Hispanic Americans" (Washington, D.C.: November 1993), p. 1.
107. Karen C. Swallen, Susan L. Stewart, Sally L. Glaser, Pamela L. Horn-Ross, Dee W. West, "Differential Misclassification of Hispanic Ethnicity: Northern California,"107. March 3, 1995, presented at the annual meeting of the Population Association of America, April 6-8, 1995, San Francisco.
108. Edmonston and Schultze, *Modernizing*, p. 150.
109. Ibid., p. 143.
110. Ibid., p. 150; Sandor, "Other."
111. Jorge del Pinal and Susan J. Lapham, "Impact of Ethnic Data Needs in the United States," United States Bureau of the Census, p. 461.
112. Roberto Rodriguez and Patricia Gonzales, "Black, White, and 'Other,'" *San Francisco Chronicle*, March 14, 1994, pp. A21+.
113. Rosin, "Other."
114. Jorge del Pinal, "Social Science Principles: Forming Race-Ethnic Categories for Policy Analysis," paper presented at "Workshop on Race and Ethnicity Classification: As Assessment of the Federal Standard for Race and Ethnicity Classification," National Research Council, Commission on Behavioral and Social Sciences and Education, Committee on National Statistics, February 18, 1994, pp. 9-10.
115. "A CPS Supplement for Testing Methods of Collecting Racial and Ethnic Information: May 1995," pp. 2-3.
116. Evinger, "How Shall," p. 12.
117. Wright, "One Drop," p. 52.
118. Sirica, "Question."
119. Evinger, "How Shall," p. 12.
120. Wright, "One Drop," p. 55.
121. Ibid.

Chapter 3

Attitudes Toward Affirmative Action: Paradox or Paradigm?

Fredrick E. Vars

"Simply telling a defendant to go forth and sin no more does little or nothing to address the unfair advantage it has already gained." Replace the words "a defendant" with "white males," adjust the pronoun, and you have an argument in favor of affirmative action.[1] Ironically, the statement was made by Judge Stanley Sporkin, a Reagan appointee to the Federal District Court, when he dismissed an out-of-court settlement that was to forestall prosecution of the Microsoft Corporation on antitrust charges (Holmes, 1995). Injustice begs for remediation, so the issue of compensatory justice runs deeper and wider than the high-profile affirmative action debate would lead us to believe. Pollsters have fixated on affirmative action as a unique issue and have reduced complex opinion structures to a single number. Social scientists have formulated intricate explanations for the perceived "paradox" between declining white racism on the one hand and continuing opposition to affirmative action on the other. They have run massive

regression analyses to predict single outcome variables that are taken
to summarize an individual's opinion on affirmative action. Independent
variables in such equations range from racism or self-interest to a belief
in individualism. And while valuable insights can be gleaned from
both sources, pollsters and social scientists have generally ignored the
context of the questions asked and the specific details of the programs
considered.

Paul Sniderman and Thomas Piazza have criticized the assumptions
underlying psychological research on attitudes toward race-specific
policies: "People's reactions to a particular policy are presumed to be
a product of social and economic factors—how they make their living,
when and where they were raised and hence how they were socialized,
how they feel about blacks—indeed, nearly every factor *except* the
policy itself" (Sniderman and Piazza, 1993, p. 8). In the context of
affirmative action, opposition has been equated with racism (Kinder
and Sears, 1981; Jacobson, 1985). The real situation is more complex
than purely racial or self-interested explanations assume: "A swirl of
forces—political ideology, prejudice, ideas of fairness and effort—are
at work to shape the public's reactions to specific racial policies"
(Sniderman and Piazza, 1993, p. 9). Traditional explanations ignore
the possibility that more general principles of compensatory justice
can account for the observed pattern of race-specific policy preferences.

Two findings that take seriously the context and justification for
survey questions on affirmative action suggest the relevance of loss
aversion. Racial preference to correct for local discrimination, where
the injury to minorities is most obvious, garners significantly higher
support than when no context is specified or when racial imbalance is
the justification (Stoker, 1994). Ameliorating a loss, past discrimination,
is more compelling than advancing a positive goal, racial imbalance.
Shifting attention from the justification to the outcome, the argument
that affirmative action hurts whites is much more compelling than the
argument that it gives blacks unearned advantages (Fine, 1992). The
unfair loss to whites is weighed more heavily than an undeserved gain
for blacks. Building on the psychological theory of loss aversion, I
consider attitudes toward affirmative action not as a paradox, but as a
paradigm to understand the considerations that individuals bring to
bear when evaluating compensatory policies: Have the beneficiaries
of the policy suffered losses that deserve remediation? If so, from
whom? What are the costs of the policy for the disfavored? I report
findings from an empirical study which demonstrates that people are
sensitive to these considerations in the affirmative action context and

in less politically charged situations. My results suggest that broader notions of distributive fairness shape attitudes toward affirmative action.

Two Findings

Laura Stoker's (1994) analysis of attitudes toward affirmative action shares Sniderman and Piazza's emphasis on the contexts of racial policies. Stoker maintains that we have reached the wrong conclusion about what public opinion on affirmative action looks like because we have not asked questions that situate affirmative action programs in the context in which they are carried out (p. 211). Stoker argues against the conclusion that the public disapproves of racial preferences across the board. She points out that "virtually all of the questions on affirmative action that pollsters and academic survey researchers have posed have either *generalized* over the kinds of contexts that the Supreme Court has deemed so significant, or [have] *ignored* those contexts altogether" (p. 187). Two examples illustrate her first criticism:

> (Caddell/Cambridge Survey Research): Some large corporations are required to practice what is called affirmative action. This sometimes requires employers to give special preference to minorities or women when hiring. Do you approve or disapprove of affirmative action?

> (Gallup): The U.S. Supreme Court has ruled that employers may sometimes favor women and members of minorities over better qualified men and whites in hiring and promoting, to achieve better balance in their work forces. Do you approve or disapprove of this decision?

Not only do "these questions treat the contexts in which affirmative action programs are implemented as irrelevant to the question of what the public thinks of them," the second cites a goal, racial balance, that the Court has consistently deemed illegitimate (p. 187). And when past discrimination is cited as the justification for preferential policies, it is in the global sense rather than discrimination perpetrated by a specific firm in which an affirmative action policy is to be implemented as a remedy (p. 188). Thus these questions do not assess situations in which the Court has deemed affirmative action to be constitutional.

Stoker examined attitudes toward affirmative action in three contexts, using independent sets of respondents.

Question 1: No Context
Do you think that large companies should be required to give a certain number of jobs to blacks, or should the government stay out of this?

Question 2: Under-representation Context
There are some large companies where blacks are under-represented. . . . Do you think *these* large companies should be required to give a certain number of jobs to blacks, or should the government stay out of this?

Question 3: Discrimination Context
There are some large companies with employment policies that discriminate against blacks. . . . Do you think *these* large companies should be required to give a certain number of jobs to blacks, or should the government stay out of this? (p. 190)

The discrimination context was the only case in which affirmative action would pass constitutional muster, and here the level of support for what was in effect a hiring quota contradicted the conventional view that the public universally condemns racial preference in hiring (see Table 1).

Table 1
Opinions on Affirmative Action by Question (in percent)

	Strongly Favor	Weakly Favor	Weakly Oppose	Strongly Oppose
No Context	16.9	11.3	20.6	51.2
Representation	15.9	8.4	25.3	37.5
Discrimination	30.9	15.0	16.6	37.5

Source: 1992 Race and American Values Survey

The lesson from Stoker's analysis is that context matters. Her predictions were based on the assumption that individuals think about affirmative action in a manner similar to the Supreme Court: racial imbalance is considered by most to be a weak justification for affirmative action, but when racial preference for blacks in hiring at a specific company is a remedy for past discrimination against blacks, public opinion (like the Supreme Court) is divided.[2] Stoker demonstrates that principles of compensatory justice affect attitudes toward affirmative action. My contention is that loss aversion and the endowment effect influence the evaluation of all policies designed to achieve compensatory justice. Rather than estimating the relative strength of traditional explanations for attitudes toward affirmative action through regression analysis, similar policy preferences in scenarios that closely parallel affirmative action will demonstrate that a more general psychological theory can account for the observed preferences.

Terri Susan Fine (1992) conducted another analysis that took seriously the nature of the question being asked. She concluded that "public reactions to equal opportunity programs are affected by how these programs are presented to the public" (p. 324). In the 1986 National Election Survey, all subjects evaluated two programs: "preference in hiring and promotion," and "quotas" for black students at colleges and universities. Fine utilized a split-sample design in which each subject read one of two different arguments against the affirmative action policies, either that they "discriminate against whites" or that they "give blacks advantages they haven't earned." Preferential treatment presented as undeserved benefits received stronger support than did preferential treatment as discrimination, a pattern that held in both cases. The data supported Fine's conclusion that "the public prefers each program more often when the frame elevates than when the frame discriminates" (p. 331). The theory of loss aversion will help to explain this result.

Loss Aversion

The underlying intuition for loss aversion dates back to antiquity. In the *Nicomachean Ethics*, Aristotle argues that threats of punishment are more compelling than offers of reward, because avoiding harm has higher priority than seeking gain (Book III, ch. 1). In modern psychology, Daniel Kahneman and Amos Tversky (1979) first formalized this intuition: a loss of X is more aversive than a gain of X is attractive.[3] Loss aversion leads people to weigh direct losses much more heavily than opportunity costs or foregone gains, in violation of economic norms.

Kahneman, Jack Knetsch, and Richard Thaler (1986) illustrated that individuals were less resistant to the cancellation of a discount or bonus than to an equivalent price increase or wage cut. A $200 increase in the price of a car in response to a shortage was deemed unfair if the dealer had previously been selling at the list price, but the same change was acceptable if the dealer had been selling at a discount of $200. Similarly, a majority of subjects considered a 10 percent pay cut unacceptable, whereas the elimination of an expected 10 percent bonus was seen as fair. George Quattrone and Tversky (1988) showed that the Equal Rights Amendment drew higher levels of support when it was argued that it would "help eliminate discrimination against women" than when improving the rights of women was the stated justification (p. 726).[4] The reduction of a loss is more compelling than the advancement of a positive goal.[5]

Loss aversion means that any one-for-one redistribution of social goods will register negatively in a cost-benefit analysis; hence there is a status quo bias.[6] The potential costs of a change loom larger than equal anticipated benefits. Thus the unpopularity of redistributive affirmative action may be explained without reference to any abstract theory of justice. Taking a job away from a white person to give to a black imposes an equal loss and gain, but the subjective value of the job lost outweighs the value of the job gained.[7] To have positive value an affirmative action program must alter the allocation of goods before a status quo distribution has become firmly entrenched. Intuitively, it is much easier to support a program that does not impose direct losses.

And although the losses are usually less obvious than in the straight redistribution case, every preferential policy has losers. Simple economics dictate that in a world of limited resources, every gain to one group imposes a corresponding loss, or at least an opportunity cost, on the out-group.[8] Take the case of a fixed student population in which blacks are "underrepresented."[9] This necessarily implies that nonblacks are overrepresented. By simple arithmetic, any increase in the percentage of blacks will reduce the percentage of nonblacks; thus every affirmative action program, although it may not have an obvious negative impact on the out-group, imposes at least a foregone gain.[10] How one goes about achieving this change and how one describes the policy are critical to perceptions of fairness. For instance, dismissing current nonblack students would be uniformly condemned, but shifting recruiting resources to predominantly African-American high schools would probably be perceived as just. The crucial difference is that the former policy generates clear losses for an identifiable and "innocent" group of students; the latter, although it may in fact impose opportunity costs for nonblack would-be recruits, has a less obvious negative impact. Another essential distinction is the moment of intervention: current students are entitled to continue their studies in a qualitatively different sense than prospective students deserve recruiting information. If one takes spots in the college class to be the resource domain, one can characterize the recruiting strategy as prior to distribution and the dismissal strategy as postdistribution.[11] The sense of entitlement is more profound after an initial allocation. Specifically, prior to distribution, any shift in the distributive rule will impose indirect opportunity costs on would-have-otherwise-been admits; but after distribution, admitted students will feel any redistribution as a direct loss.[12] A key to determining support for a policy intervention is whether the victim of the policy is coded as a nongainer or as a loser, because opportunity costs are less aversive than direct losses.

Hypothesis

My fundamental thesis is that affirmative action can be understood as a paradigm of redistributive justice. As politically charged as the issue has become, positions on a specific policy are influenced by the same considerations that determine support or opposition to less contentious distributive interventions. More general notions of fairness, especially the unwillingness to impose direct losses, can explain the perceived "incongruity" between support for "special consideration" and opposition to "racial preferences." I propose that people consider three questions when formulating attitudes toward affirmative action and other remedial policies:

1. Have the beneficiaries of the policy suffered losses that justify remediation?
2. If so, is the party considering remediation obligated to the past losers?
3. What collateral losses will the policy inflict on individuals who are disfavored?

My three major hypotheses correspond to these queries and to the three parties involved in any preferential program: the preferred, the preferring agent, and the disfavored. The first and third questions are important because of the high psychological weight placed on losses. People want to compensate clear losers, but do not want to impose losses on innocent third parties. The issue of obligation, addressed by the second query, is closely related to the endowment effect and status quo bias.

First Hypothesis

In the affirmative action context, the first question can be rephrased: Have African Americans been unfairly disadvantaged so that remediation is necessary? If an individual believes that blacks have genuine equality of opportunity, this person will not see a need for affirmative action and will therefore oppose it. Conversely, if an individual believes that past discrimination has unjustly diminished African Americans' opportunities, this person at least recognizes an argument in favor of affirmative action. Belief in inequality does not necessarily translate into support for affirmative action; people may believe that alternative solutions, such as increased education, are superior and sufficient.[13] But it follows that support for affirmative action will be strongest when the beneficiaries can demonstrate that they have suffered from discrimination. Thus policies narrowly tailored to compensate individual victims of identified discrimination will be more acceptable than policies that use race as an imperfect proxy for disadvantage. What is true for racial discrimination will hold for other types of injuries. A policy that helps victims as individuals will receive more support than a policy that is aimed at a group in which victims compose only a subset. By giving preference to members of the group who have not suffered, the compelling rationale of compensating for losses is diluted. Divided in so many other ways on affirmative action, the Supreme Court has consistently found past discrimination to be the strongest argument in favor of compensatory action. Loss aversion can explain why correcting for losses is more compelling than promoting gains in the affirmative action debate.

Second Hypothesis

The question of obligation is more subtle. Obviously, someone who intentionally inflicts losses is obligated to compensate the victims, but a status quo relationship between two parties can also establish an obligation. If an individual or group of individuals has come to depend on a particular distributor for good X, then the distributor is obligated to compensate the recipient when X disappears, even if the loss is not the distributor's fault. Good X is not the only thing the recipient comes to expect; help from the distributive agent also becomes an endowment.

Generalized discrimination in the contracting industry was not considered sufficiently compelling to justify a racial set-aside program in *Richmond v. J. A. Croson Co.* (488 U.S. 469 [1989]). A majority of the Court required a "prima facie case of a constitutional or statutory violation" by someone in the Richmond construction industry. In other words, unless the City of Richmond or an affiliated contractor was directly responsible for the disadvantaged position of minorities, the city was barred from instituting a race-conscious program to ameliorate this disadvantage. This notion of responsibility is not unique to affirmative action. Raising rates for longtime customers violates perceptions of fairness, but it is acceptable for public utilities to increase rates for new customers (Zajac, 1985).[14] Similarly, a wage cut for current employees is perceived to be unfair, but employers can lower their wages for new hires since there is no "reference transaction" (Kahneman, Knetsch, and Thaler, 1986). Tom Tyler and Robyn Dawes (1993) made an important observation about this finding: "Interestingly, these rules are generally linked to existing social relations. For example, companies owe fairness to current employees, not to new hires, and landlords owe fairness to current tenants but not to new tenants" (p. 99).[15] In ongoing relationships, people tend to define rules of acceptable conduct and fair rules of outcome distribution. "Expectations . . . coordinate social interactions, and their violation weakens the general trust that people have in them, forcing people to take precautions against their violation by others" (Baron, 1993, p. 118). Whatever the explanation, procedural norms of justice do seem to become part of an individual's endowment. The result is that parties to an ongoing relationship are more obligated to compensate for losses than are third parties.

Third Hypothesis

Answering the first two questions in the affirmative establish a need for remediation and a sense of obligation. The perceived cost of the policy for disfavored individuals then becomes crucial in the evaluation of specific policy proposals. Every preferential policy excludes as well as includes; groups that are not directly benefited by a policy suffer relative to the preferred class of individuals. The magnitude and nature of the loss imposed on the out-group are crucial for the acceptability of a policy. In general, the high valuation of losses will lead people to prefer policies that have invisible costs, but when the sacrifices of a policy for the disfavored are salient, people will reject the policy. For instance, people will be unwilling to redistribute resources because the losses are obvious. This hypothesis follows from the psychological asymmetry between gains and losses and from Supreme Court precedents that accept preference in hiring but reject preference in layoffs.

Survey Design

As Ricshawn Adkins demonstrates in her contribution to this volume, attitudes toward affirmative action are very sensitive to the language used by researchers. In the questionnaire used in my survey, I avoid politically loaded terms like "racial preference," "quota," and "reverse discrimination" in order to measure attitudes toward specific policies without interference from ideological shibboleths. Likewise, I omit references to the federal government to avoid the contaminating effect of attitudes toward big government (Kuklinski and Parent, 1981). The uniqueness of this wording makes it impossible to compare the levels of support I observe with previous research findings. My intent, however, is not to draw conclusions about *what* the public thinks about affirmative action; rather, I examine *how* people think about issues like affirmative action.[16]

The questionnaire consisted of four hypothetical scenarios in which one group of individuals had been disadvantaged through no fault of its own. The four scenarios were Housing, Meals-on-Wheels (abbreviated Meals), Contractors (Contracts) and Firefighters (Fire). In the Housing scenario, a severe fire displaced needy families from an apartment building. Financial woes forced the termination of a meals-on-wheels program to one geographic region (East Side) of an invented city (Belville) in the Meals scenario. Racial discrimination, either general or specific, was the source of disadvantage in the two affirmative action scenarios, Contract and Fire. Table 2 provides an example of each scenario type.

Table 2
Scenario Descriptions (Low Obligation)

Housing

Separate charitable foundations operate two apartment buildings for needy families in the same city. Each foundation maintains a separate waiting list. Once a unit is promised to an applicant family, it stays vacant for a few weeks while it is renovated, cleaned, and painted. The building operated by one of the foundations has been condemned after being severely damaged in a fire. It will take several years to rebuild. The insurance does not cover the housing needs of the families that were displaced by the fire. Although it does not have direct responsibility in the matter, the board of the foundation that manages the undamaged building is considering what it should do to help the families that were displaced by the fire.

Meals

Belville is a mid-size city. A river divides the city into two areas, West Side and East Side. Separate charitable organizations in the two areas have been operating programs of aid for elderly people in their homes. The programs provide meals-on-wheels, housecleaning and help with laundry. The resources of both organizations have been stretched to the limit, and only cases of great need have been receiving help. Once admitted to the program, elderly recipients have normally received help as long as they lived alone at home, usually for several years. There has been a waiting list for help in both areas of the city. The East Side and West Side organizations have only admitted needy recipients from their respective areas. Due to the death of a wealthy benefactor and the closing of several businesses, the East Side organization has been forced to shut down. Although it has no direct responsibility in the matter, the board of the West Side organization considers several ideas for achieving a more equitable distribution of services to the two areas of the city.

(continued)

Table 2 (continued)
Scenario Descriptions (Low Obligation)

Contract

Faced with bankruptcies in hard economic times, the construction industry has been forced to lay off many workers from its racially diverse work force. Instead of using seniority or ability, managers discriminated by race and fired highly-qualified African-American workers. The manager of one construction company has criticized the industry's racism. This efficient company did not have to lay off anyone and is currently in the process of hiring a few workers. The manager presents the board of directors with several options to help the African-American workers who were unjustly laid off and to correct for past discrimination in the construction industry.

Fire

A city personnel officer has noticed that there is a disparity in the representation of African Americans in the fire department and in the community. Due to recent demographic changes the community is 30% African American, but the department is almost entirely white. Several qualified firefighters, some white and some African American, have applied for work. Some of the African-American applicants recently moved to the community, unable to find work elsewhere due to racial discrimination. The other applicants recently lost their jobs when a fire station in a neighboring community was closed. Although the local fire department has no history of racial discrimination, the city council and fire chief are considering several ideas for increasing the representation of African Americans in the firefighting force to reflect the composition of the community.

In each scenario, subjects were asked to imagine themselves as members of a decision-making body that had the power to compensate victims. In the Housing scenario, a charitable foundation operated an undamaged apartment building. Similarly, the board of a charity operating a West Side meals-on-wheels program considered remediation in the Meals scenario. The board of a construction company evaluated proposals to adjust its future hiring policy to compensate victims of racially discriminatory layoffs. In the Fire scenario, the city council considered various racial preference proposals. A range of policies was presented and subjects were asked to indicate whether they would vote for or against each proposal. As a model, Table 3 lists each remedy in the Housing scenario.

Table 3
Housing Scenario Remedies

Priority
The waiting list for future vacancies will be rearranged to give displaced families some priority.

Quota
For the next few months, only displaced families will be considered for units that become vacant.

Broken Promise
Displaced families will be assigned to several units currently under renovation. The families to whom these units were promised will be returned to the waiting list.

Redistribution
Displaced families will be assigned to several units that are currently occupied. To make this possible, some families who moved in recently will be required to leave, and will be returned to the waiting list.

The most benign proposal was to give some *priority* to past victims when making future allocation decisions. A somewhat more radical proposal, *quota*, was to distribute positions exclusively to victims for the next few months. The next step up the ladder of loss salience, *broken promise*, entailed reneging on an agreement in order to provide the resource immediately to the victims. The most intrusive remedies were to evict families, to terminate services, or to lay off workers, in order to provide for victims immediately. This policy level is referred to as *redistribution*. Consistent with the third hypothesis, I predicted support to follow this pattern:

priority > *quota* > *broken promise* > *redistribution*

Independent consideration of each policy was encouraged by a statement equivalent to this sentence from the Housing scenario: "All of the proposals that are supported by a majority of the board will be adopted." The response scale offered four alternatives: "Certainly Against," "Probably Against," "Probably For," and "Certainly For." No intermediate or "undecided" level was included in order to force individuals to choose one of the four options.[17]

The scenarios were also constructed to test the sensitivity of subjects to the inclusion of beneficiaries who were not direct victims. Remedies in the Housing and Contract scenarios were narrowly designed to confer advantages to displaced families and to individual African-American workers who had been victims of racially discriminatory layoffs. In contrast, proposals in the Meals scenario favored not only clients who had lost services but also other residents of East Side, the area in which services had been terminated. The *priority* remedy reads: "The waiting list for admission of new clients will be rearranged to give some priority to former clients of the East Side program *and other East Side residents.*" Similarly, the Firefighters' affirmative action programs used race as an explicitly imperfect proxy for discrimination. From the first hypothesis, I anticipated that subjects would be more likely to vote for remedies narrowly tailored to benefit individual victims than for policies that utilized overbroad proxies for disadvantage, such as geography and race.

I used a split-sample design to test the second hypothesis.[18] Each scenario was phrased in "high obligation" and "low obligation" versions. In the high obligation versions of the Housing and Meals scenarios, a relationship of support had been established between the charitable organization that was considering compensatory action and the victims. In the low obligation versions there was no relationship, because the victims had been under the charge of a second charity. In the Housing scenario, a charity seems more responsible to the victims when the fire is in its own apartment building than when the fire is in someone else's building.[19] Racial discrimination was the "fire" in the affirmative action scenarios. In the high obligation version of the Contract scenario, a company that had discriminated in the past was considering various remedies. In the low obligation case, industrywide discrimination by other companies was the impetus for action. Likewise, in the Fire scenario, qualified African-American firefighters were unemployed owing either to local discrimination or to discrimination elsewhere. The intuition is that a perpetrator of discrimination is more obligated to the victims than is a third party. In all four scenarios, I anticipated more favorable votes in the high obligation condition than in the low obligation condition.

Proviso

My major hypotheses focus on the material losses of parties in distribution situations, but because the allocative principle becomes part of an individual's endowment, the moral calculus is more complex than a simple weighing of two parties' interests. A preferential policy not only imposes material costs on the disfavored, it modifies the existing system of allocation, which people may expect and revere. To support remediation in the Housing and Meals scenarios was to suspend queuing as the allocative principle. In the affirmative action scenarios, the *priority* and *quota* remedies contravened the principle of hiring the most qualified applicant. There is no reason to assume that the strength of attachment to these two allocative principles is equal, so the parallel between the two kinds of scenarios was compromised in this sense. If people subscribe to the individualist ethic of advancement by merit, one might reasonably suspect that the attachment to ability-based hiring is stronger (Lipset, 1992). But all four scenarios ignored relevant differences among applicants, thereby minimizing the extent to which the compensatory policies would be recognized to violate entrenched principles of allocation. In the Housing scenario, all families were described as "needy," so they were implicitly equal. The Meals programs similarly admitted "only needy recipients." It is perhaps less believable that all applicants for a job are equally qualified, but the affirmative action scenarios likewise obscured the differences among "qualified" applicants. By effectively removing this variable from the moral equation, the scenarios were maximally favorable to redistribution and affirmative action. This had the advantage of focusing attention on the variables of interest to the present study, but makes it difficult to draw solid conclusions about the relevance of the findings to other contexts in which this consideration is central. Previous poll data indicate opposition to racial preference is most resounding when it is pitted against ability as the "main consideration" (Bunzel, 1986). In political discourse, belief in "color-blind equal opportunity" weighs against affirmative action, which violates purely merit-based allocation systems.[20] And although this consideration is surely important, I would argue that people object more strongly to the loss of an individual than to the loss of an ideal. It is the individual loser, the Alan Bakke, the Sharon Taxman, who captivates public attention and ignites passion.

Results

The questionnaire was administered to 152 Princeton University students on March 2, 1995. Students filled out a battery of unrelated questionnaires at the same time and received $6 for their participation. In order to simplify subsequent analyses, "Certainly Against" and "Probably Against" responses were considered negative votes, and the two favorable responses were lumped together as positive votes.[21] As expected, support for the *priority* remedy was highest and support for *redistribution* was lowest, with support for the two intermediate policies falling in between (see Table 4).

Table 4
Percentage of Votes in Favor of Each Policy

Policy	Scenario			
	Housing	*Meals*	*Contract*	*Fire*
Priority	90.8	82.9	88.8	73.0
Quota	69.1	49.3	61.2	37.5
Broken Promise	31.6	28.3	25.7	11.8
Redistribution	2.0	7.9	16.4	7.2

In every scenario, the percentage of votes in favor of each policy was consistent with the expected pattern: *priority > quota > broken promise > redistribution*. Support diminishes as the losses to the disfavored become more salient.

A more demanding formulation of the third hypothesis is that the four items form a scale. If the items form a perfect scale, a vote in favor of a more radical policy would always imply a favorable vote for a less radical proposal, and this would hold true for all two-item comparisons. Thus from a single score, the number of yes votes, one could fully reproduce an individual's response pattern. For instance, if I knew that John voted for two policies and that the items formed a scale consistent with my expectations, I could conclude that John voted for the *priority* and *quota* proposals (the two least radical remedies).

In every scenario, a near perfect scale emerged.[22] For this reason, subsequent analyses utilize individual scores, the number of favorable votes for remedies in a given scenario. Scores take on values from zero to four, and fully describe a subject's response pattern. Using a single value to describe a response pattern greatly simplifies analysis.

The first analysis using mean scores tests sensitivity to the overinclusiveness of remedies. From my first hypothesis I predicted that subjects would be more likely to support remedies in the Housing and Contract scenarios because these policies were narrowly tailored to benefit past victims, whereas remedies in the other two scenarios used geography and race as rough proxies for victimhood. Table 4 provides rough evidence to support this hypothesis: majorities endorsed the *quota* remedy in the Housing and Contract scenarios, but rejected *quotas* in the Meals and Fire cases. I conducted a more formal comparison: scores in the Meals and Fire cases were subtracted from the sum of scores in the Housing and Contract scenarios. A single sample t-test revealed that the mean of the individual differences was significantly greater than zero, so I rejected the null hypothesis of equal support in the narrowly tailored and overinclusive cases ($t = 7.94$, df $= 151, p < 0.0005$). In other words, the level of support for remedies was significantly higher in the narrowly tailored scenarios, Housing and Contract. This finding supports my hypothesis that people object to the inclusion of beneficiaries who are not direct victims.[23]

The obligation manipulation had very significant effects in all four scenarios. Table 5 shows significantly lower mean scores in the low obligation condition than in the obligation case for all four scenarios.

Table 5
Mean Scores By Obligation Level
(t-statistics in parentheses, df > 140)

Manipulation	Condition	Scenario			
		Housing	Meals	Contract	Fire
Obligation	High	2.16	1.95	2.24	1.46
	Low	1.71	1.42	1.61	1.13
		(-3.53)	*(-3.38)*	*(-3.79)*	*(-2.07)*

A one-tailed *t*-test is appropriate since I predicted the direction of this effect. I rejected the null hypothesis of equal means in favor of the hypothesis that $X_{High} > X_{Low}$ in all four scenarios ($p < 0.0005$ in the Housing, Meals, and Contract scenarios, and $p < 0.025$ in the Fire scenario). The data supported my prediction that the high obligation scenario versions would elicit higher support for remedies than would the low obligation versions.

My fundamental thesis is that attitudes toward affirmative action can be understood as a paradigmatic application of redistributive fairness norms. The striking similarity in favorable votes for remedies in all four scenarios supports this assertion (see Table 4). If people think about various issues of redistributive justice in the same way, their responses will be highly correlated. Table 6 presents average correlations for all six two-scenario pairings.[24]

Table 6
Average Correlations

	Housing	Meals	Contract	Fire
Housing	-			
Meals	0.48	-		
Contract	0.26	0.32	-	
Fire	0.30	0.39	0.47	-

The positive correlations suggest that there exist underlying principles of redistributive fairness that were tapped by each of the scenarios.

Summary and Discussion

The data supported my hypothesis that people consider the closeness of the fit between past losers and would-be beneficiaries when evaluating remedial policies. When a group-regarding policy favors individuals who have not suffered personal losses, it is less acceptable than an individual-based policy in which the compelling rationale of compensating for losses is undiluted.   The mean scores were significantly higher in the Housing and Contract scenarios than in the Meals and Fire scenarios.   Thus remedies narrowly tailored to compensate individual victims were more acceptable than policies that used geography or race as an imperfect proxy for disadvantage.

Disdain for overinclusive remedies is consistent with the premise that individuals' reasoning about the issue of affirmative action is sensitive to the same considerations that guide legal reasoning. People agree with the Court that discrimination is the strongest argument in favor of affirmative action, and they would therefore prefer to limit compensation to direct victims. Much of the social science literature presumes an incongruity between the decline in overt, public racism and opposition to affirmative action, but there may be a causal relationship. People who believe that racial discrimination is disappearing along with overt racism will perceive little need for preferential treatment (Devroy, 1995). In preferring to limit remedies to direct victims, people seem to apply the logic that "if there isn't a problem, you don't need a solution" (Kluegel, 1985). This principle transcends the issue of racial discrimination, so that compensating for unfair losses in other contexts, such as meals-on-wheels service, is perceived to be more important than geographic equity. It follows that framing a redistributive intervention as "restorative" instead of "preferential" will probably heighten its perceived fairness.[25]

People not only consider the fit between the solution and the problem, they want the party responsible for the problem to solve it. Subjects considered the perpetrators of discrimination to be more obligated to the victims than they did third parties who were in a position to provide similar compensation. One might argue that identifying the perpetrator was important to prove discrimination. I think it unlikely, however, that subjects doubted the existence of racial discrimination, since it was explicit in the descriptions of the Contract and Fire scenarios. Furthermore, the losses were undeniable in both versions of the Housing and Meals scenarios, where the obligation manipulation was similarly effective. Housing providers were considered more obligated to their current tenants than to new applicants, and meals-on-wheels programs were more obligated to maintain service than to expand it.   The endowment effect and the development of fairness expectations in social relations heightens the sense of obligation in a variety of contexts.

Jon Elster (1993) has proposed that a sense of responsibility may account for the "norm of thoroughness" in medical treatment. Because of diminishing marginal returns, doctors could better contribute to total health by spreading themselves over a larger number of patients (p. 264). A Norwegian parliamentary commission finding that eye specialists tend to admit too few patients and treat each of them very thoroughly illustrates the norm of thoroughness (p. 265). Elster speculated that "the most important factor may be that doctors get to know their patients and feel responsible for them. The non-patients, by definition, have no face" (p. 265). My findings suggest that direct personal contact is not necessary to establish a sense of responsibility. Board members of a charitable foundation have probably never met the families living in the apartment building they oversee, but the impersonal status quo relationship nonetheless heightened their obligation to provide for these families.

In both the affirmative action scenarios and in the less political cases, subjects preferred remedies narrowly tailored to help individual victims. Similarly, subjects considered perpetrators of discrimination and parties in established relationships to be more responsible than third parties. But perhaps the most striking pattern to emerge in all four scenarios was the diminished support for policies in which the collateral losses were obvious. Table 4 shows what the scale analysis concluded more formally: people were willing to give the victims some priority in future decisions, but withheld support for policies that broke promises or imposed direct losses through redistribution. The same pattern is evident in Supreme Court decisions, which have generally struck down racial preferences in layoffs but have upheld them in hiring and promotions.[26] I contend that loss aversion and the endowment effect can account for this pattern.

There are other explanations for this result. First, high transaction costs may reduce the attractiveness of redistributive proposals. Second, job-specific skills and interactions with colleagues may increase the subjective value of a position so that losing a current job is more painful than missing an opportunity at a new job (Elster, 1992). The same argument can apply to the housing case, in which relationships with neighbors may carry value above the market price of a given location. Neither of these arguments, however, applies to the meals-on-wheels case: subjects probably did not believe that the cost of delivery varied substantially among houses in a given city, or that clients developed important relationships with their servers. Nonetheless, exactly the same pattern of differential support emerged in this scenario, which suggests that explanations based on transaction costs and substantive differences are insufficient to account for this phenomenon. Loss aversion, which has been demonstrated in numerous other contexts, provides a more complete and intuitively compelling explanation.

Conclusion

Traditional explanations for attitudes toward affirmative action ignore the specific policy and the context in which it is implemented. Public opinion polls likewise obscure these essential details. For this reason, researchers miss the impact of loss aversion and the regularities evident in political debate and legal reasoning: (1) programs implemented to compensate individual losers, victims of past discrimination, are more popular than policies that promote gains (such as racial diversity) or that benefit nonvictims; (2) actual perpetrators of past discrimination are more obligated to provide remediation than are third parties; (3) policies that impose obvious losses on the out-group are unacceptable. These principles extend beyond the affirmative action debate to other compensatory situations.

The experimental findings confirm the role of loss aversion in other contexts by demonstrating the significance of these considerations. The remarkably similar pattern of overall support for remedies and the high correlations among scores in the four scenarios suggest that basic attitudes toward affirmative action are in conformity with broader moral principles. Explanations for opinions on affirmative action that treat the issue in isolation are incomplete at best and blatantly political at worst, as when opposition is equated with racism. Race is certainly important, but broad notions of fairness are not suspended when race is involved. Sympathy for individual losers extends beyond African-American victims of racial discrimination, and a sense of obligation to past victims heightens support for compensation in a variety of contexts. And yet people simultaneously reject remedial policies that impose clear losses on anyone, not just "angry white males." In short, attitudes toward affirmative action are no more paradoxical than attitudes toward other policies designed to restore distributive fairness. Affirmative action can even serve as a useful paradigm to understand general principles of justice. Political leaders on both sides of the affirmative action debate would be well advised to consider the power of loss aversion on public opinion.

Notes

1. In this essay, "affirmative action" will describe any remedial policy that confers benefits to individuals on the basis of their gender or minority status. I also use the terms "preferential treatment" and "racial preference," generally in reference to policy interventions after the redistribution stage. The bulk of the discussion applies equally to preference for ethnic minorities and for women, but sometimes I limit myself to racial preference for two reasons: (1) the black-white paradigm dominates the popular discourse on affirmative action; (2) the arguments concerning preference for blacks have generally received the most articulate expression. My thanks to Daniel Kahneman, professor of psychology and public affairs at Princeton University, without whose guidance and grant this project would not have been possible.

2. This pattern of support is consistent with the theory of loss aversion, which will be explained in depth below; the elimination of a loss, discrimination, is a more compelling justification for affirmative action than the achievement of a gain, racial balance. And while the latter justification could be framed negatively, it is intuitively awkward to consider racial imbalance a loss in the absence of discrimination.

3. On the basis of experimental evidence, Tversky and Kahneman (1992) estimated the coefficient of loss aversion to be 2.25. In other words, a given loss is 2.25 times as aversive as an equal gain is attractive.

4. This experimental design recalls Fine (1992).

5. In the affirmative action context, this finding suggests that the name of the policy may be a political liability. "Antidiscrimination" would perhaps evoke higher levels of public support. Nonetheless, people consider affirmative action *for* blacks to be more acceptable than preference *against* nonblacks.

6. In several domains, researchers have demonstrated that a given alternative becomes more appealing when it is designated as the status quo (Samuelson and Zeckhauser, 1988). From his analysis of public utility regulation, Edward E. Zajac (1985) concluded that "the beneficial retention of a status quo is considered a right whose removal is considered unjust" (p. 141).

7. An exactly inverted formulation and positive valuation of affirmative action can be structured in the case of intervention prior to an otherwise unjust distribution. Assume that the black applicant deserves the spot more than her white counterpart, although the white would win without affirmative action. The program can thus be coded as avoiding a loss for the black while forcing the white to forgo a gain. The foregone loss to the black denied the position may subjectively outweigh the foregone gain to the white. This may explain why correcting for past discrimination by the relevant actor has been the most compelling constitutional argument in favor of affirmative action policies.

8. This is not strictly true if the resource domain expands with more efficient allocation, but it is true in the case of fixed resources, like jobs or openings for students in college. In personal correspondence, William G. Bowen, former president of Princeton University, raised this objection to a zero-sum perspective on racial preference in higher education: "Promoting diversity will both: (a) enrich the educational experience for all students (or at least for most of them); and (b) make a positive long-term contribution to the welfare of the country by sending out into it individuals from diverse backgrounds who can help to guide a pluralistic society." By focusing narrowly on the individuals involved, I understate the importance of such "spillover" effects. But even Bowen admits that "societal" arguments are nebulous and also hard to sell, suggesting that perceptions of unfairness play a larger role in determining public opinion on affirmative action. And it is attitude formation, not policy evaluation, that is the subject here.

9. "Underrepresented" will be taken to mean that the group constitutes a lower percentage of the population than advocates of affirmative action desire. Some comparison to the qualified applicant pool is a likely way to evaluate representation.

10. "To be effective, affirmative action policies must engage in 'reverse discrimination.' In other words, increasing the probability that an individual from a minority group will gain access to a limited resource necessarily implies that the chances of majority group members will be decreased" (Dawes, 1994, p. 223).

11. Of course, if one takes recruiting information to be the resource domain, this distinction breaks down. But I would argue that information in this case has only instrumental value; increasing the number of blacks in college is the goal.

12. This division of affirmative action policies relative to the moment of distribution differs from traditional program definitions. Often, "compensatory action," denoting predistributive interventions like better education and recruiting, is contrasted with "preferential treatment," which occurs around the moment of distribution. This misleading distinction mirrors the unequal subjective weighting of opportunity costs and losses. Compensatory action for blacks denies nonblacks equal benefits, so it imposes costs on the out-group just as preferential treatment does.

13. See Lipset (1992) for evidence that this alternative is very popular.

14. My brother receives preferential treatment at the barber shop where he has been a steady customer for many years. The barber has raised rates during this time, but still charges his longtime customers at the old price. My brother and most other customers would not leave if asked to pay the new price, so the barber's pricing policy cannot be explained by the standard profit-maximizing model of economic behavior.

15. I would add that landlords also do not owe fairness to someone else's tenants. The obligation manipulation in the Housing scenario follows from this assertion (see below).

16. This project is at once narrower and broader than the "comprehensive survey" proposed by Adkins, more limited in its selection of policies to be evaluated, but more expansive in its attempt to elucidate compensatory norms with implications beyond affirmative action.

17. This omission was also justified by the finding that "people who consider an attitude unimportant or whose attitudes are not intense flock to a middle alternative disproportionately often when it is offered" (Krosnick and Schuman 1988, p. 949). Because I hypothesized that attitudes toward affirmative action are more intense, I would have expected fewer subjects to select a middle alternative in the affirmative action scenarios than in the Housing or Meals scenarios.

18. The survey was split in a 2 x 2 x 2 factorial design along three dimensions: obligation, scenario order, and remedy order. The observed order effects are omitted from the present discussion.

19. The low obligation version explicitly noted: "Although it does not have direct responsibility in the matter . . ." the board of the surviving charity is considering several proposals to help displaced families.

20. Pure meritocracy is perhaps an illusion, but it is nonetheless a compelling ideal (Kinsley, 1995).

21. By and large, the omission of a middle response was successful, but one subject (out of 152) inserted an intermediate space for the broken promise remedies in the Housing and Meals scenarios. This response was coded as a no vote.

22. The Coefficient of Reproducibility, CR, is a measure of how accurately one can reconstruct response patterns on the basis of scores, and is obtained by the formula: $CR = 1 - (Errors / Total Responses)$. For each of the four scenarios, the CR was well above the 0.90 cut-off that Guttman suggested (Menzel, 1953, p. 279).

23. Unintended differences between the two types of scenarios may have confounded this result. The scenarios were designed to be as parallel as possible in other respects to minimize the likelihood of confounding variables. Splitting each scenario across this dimension would have been a more rigorous test of the hypothesis, but this would have required twice the number of treatments and a larger sample size.

24. Correlations were calculated separately for each of the eight survey versions. I converted these correlations to z-values using the Fisher transformation. The mean of the z-values was then reconverted to obtain the correlation values shown in Table 6.

25. See note 5 for a parallel line of reasoning.

26. The Court explicitly condemns policies that violate "legitimate, firmly rooted expectations" (*Johnson v. Transportation Agency, Santa Clara County*, 480 U.S. 616 [1986]).

References

Baron, Jonathon. 1993. "Heuristics and Biases in Equity Judgments: A Utilitarian Approach." In Mellers and Baron, eds., *Psychological Perspectives on Justice: Theory and Applications*. New York: Cambridge University Press.

Bunzel, John H. 1986. "Affirmative Re-Actions." *Public Opinion* (February/March): 45-49.

Dawes, Robyn M. 1994. "Affirmative Action Programs: Discontinuities between Thoughts about Individuals and Thoughts about Groups." In Health et al., eds. *Applications of Heuristics and Biases to Social Issues*. New York: Plenum Press, pp. 223-239.

Devroy, Ann. 1995. "Clinton Orders Affirmative Action Review." *Washington Post*, February 23.

Elster, Jon. 1992. *Local Justice*. New York: Russell Sage Foundation.

———. 1993. "Justice and the allocation of scarce resources." In Mellers and Baron, eds., *Psychological Perspectives on Justice: Theory and Applications*. New York: Cambridge University Press, pp. 259-278.

Fine, Terri Susan. 1992. "The Impact of Issue Framing on Public Opinion toward Affirmative Action Programs." *Social Science Journal* 29, no. 3: 323-334.

Holmes, Steven A. 1995. "Affirmative Action, by Another Name." *New York Times*, March 9.

Jacobson, Cardell K. 1985. "Resistance to Affirmative Action: Self-Interest or Racism?" *Journal of Conflict Resolution* 29, no. 2 (June): 306-329.

Kahneman, Daniel, Jack L. Knetsch, and Richard Thaler. 1986. "Fairness as a Constraint on Profit Seeking: Entitlements in the Market." *American Economic Review* 76, no. 4 (September): 728-741.

Kahneman, Daniel, and Amos Tversky. 1979. "Prospect Theory: An Analysis of Decision under Risk." *Econometrica* 47, no. 2 (March): 263-291.

Kinder, Donald, and David Sears. 1981. "Prejudice and Politics: Symbolic Racism versus Racial Threats to 'the Good Life,'" *Journal of Personality and Social Psychology* 40: 414-431.

Kinsley, Michael. 1995. "The Spoils of Victimhood." *New Yorker* March 27, pp. 62-69.

Kluegel, James R. 1985. "'If There Isn't a Problem, You Don't Need a Solution': The Bases of Contemporary Affirmative Action Attitudes." *American Behavioral Scientist* 28, no. 6 (July/August): 761-784.

Krosnick, Jon A., and Howard Schuman. 1988. "Attitude Intensity, Importance, and Certainty and Susceptibility to Response Effects." *Journal of Personality and Social Psychology* 54, no. 6: 940-952.

Kuklinski, James H., and Wayne Parent. 1981. "Race and Big Government: Contamination in Measuring Racial Attitudes." *Political Methodology* 7: 131-159.

Lipset, Seymour Martin. 1992. "Affirmative Action and the American Creed. *Wilson Quarterly* 16, no. 1 (Winter): 52-62.

Menzel, Herbert. 1953. "A New Coefficient for Scalogram Analysis." *Public Opinion Quarterly* (Summer): 268-280.

Quattrone, George A., and Amos Tversky. 1988. "Contrasting Rational and Psychological Analyses of Political Choice." *American Political Science Review* 82, no. 3 (September): 719-736.

Samuelson, William, and Richard Zeckhauser. 1988. "Status Quo Bias in Decision Making." *Journal of Risk and Uncertainty* 1: 7-59.

Sniderman, Paul, and Thomas Piazza. 1993. *The Scar of Race.* Cambridge, Mass.: Harvard University Press.

Stoker, Laura. 1994. "The Moral Basis of Political Choice." Manuscript pp. 179-217.

Tversky, Amos, and Daniel Kahneman. 1992. "Advances in Prospect Theory: Cumulative Representation of Uncertainty." *Journal of Risk and Uncertainty* 5: 297-323.

Tyler, Tom, and Robyn M. Dawes. 1993. "Fairness in Groups: Comparing the Self-interest and Social Identity Perspectives." in Mellers and Baron, eds., *Psychological Perspectives on Justice: Theory and Applications.* New York: Cambridge University Press, pp. 87-108.

Zajac, Edward E. 1985. "Perceived Economic Justice: The Example of Public Utility Regulation." In Young, ed. *Cost Allocation: Methods, Principles, Applications.* New York: North-Holland, pp. 119-153.

Chapter 4

Affirmative Action and Public Opinion Polls

Ricshawn Adkins

In the effort to "open the entire, rusted arsenal of federal 'affirmative action' programs to real, meaningful debate at last, and remove from American law ugly manifestations of race-consciousness," the Republican anti-affirmative action coalition has spared no expense.[1] The artillery of the coalition includes testimonies from 'self-propelled' high-achieving minorities and slighted white male casualties, from the legacies of fallen civil rights heroes, and from a battery of superficially convincing statistics. All of these components have played a crucial role in the fight against affirmative action, yet, arguably, none has had as much influence as the surveys and polls that have been cited in support of the assault. The use of polling data to substantiate and thereby validate political views is not unique to the struggle over affirmative action and the problems associated with this approach are not new. Conclusions drawn from polls and surveys have assumed such a large role in this national debate, however, that the considerable inadequacies of the underlying data merit attention.

In *The Scar of Race*, Paul Sniderman and Thomas Piazza cite the "pliability of policy positions of substantial numbers of whites on specific issues of race" as their most important finding concerning contemporary American racial attitudes.[2] They go on to say that "majorities are not the inevitable facts of life permanently dictated by deep-lying social and economic forces."[3] These observations call into question the anti-affirmative action movement's portrait of itself as a response to what the majority of Americans unequivocally and unambiguously want.[4] Laura Stoker comments:

> We reach a different conclusion about where the public stands when we ask about affirmative action programs that are situated in circumstances that the Supreme Court has deemed legitimate. One no longer gets the impression that while opposition to affirmative action is so deep and unyielding that the issue need no longer be debated and, if peaceful race relations are to ensue, that the programs had best be abandoned. One sees an issue that is controversial among whites, not settled, where opinion is polarized, not lopsided—where there is still plenty of room in which to carry out debate.[5]

What is so often referred to as the "dominant public opinion on affirmative action" is more often the dominant public perception of some aspect of a larger issue, indiscriminately labeled affirmative action. In polls Americans, particularly white Americans, often reject the whole affirmative action pie, but not because all of the vast array of programs that fall under this rubric are unpalatable. They reject it because they find one or several pieces of the pie fundamentally unjust and are given no knife with which to separate these pieces from the rest. Currently, polls ostensibly conducted in order to gauge public opinion on affirmative action do not ask the specific kinds of questions that would allow a complete picture of support and opposition to various policies to emerge.

These methodological flaws are not limited solely to polls on affirmative action but can be found in polls surveying public opinion on a variety of issues—they are inherent flaws about which a substantial body of literature exists.[6] In spite of these flaws, however, numbers from public opinion polls are consistently used as ammunition on both sides of major policy issues.

Here I explore not whether public opinion poll respondents really know what they want when they respond to survey questions, but whether politicians and interest groups may be incorrectly interpreting respondents' answers. In contrast to Sniderman and Piazza's negation of "the conventional wisdom [which holds that] opposition to affirmative action is driven by racism, with the vehemence of whites' opposition to racial quotas and preferential treatment taken as proof of the tenacity of their prejudice against blacks," I examine the possibility that opposition to affirmative action is driven by a number of factors, including methodological deficiencies, the fact that the concept has become so value laden, and racism.[7]

What are the causes of the confusion that prompt the inaccurate and incomplete interpretation of survey results? They include definitional and contextual ambiguities and issue-framing and question-wording concerns.[8] An analysis of the work of two scholars, Terri Susan Fine and Laura Stoker, will provide the foundation for discussion of these areas. Fine focuses on how public opinion can be altered by the way in which affirmative action is framed in polling questions. Stoker has explored whether polling questions have even aptly described the policy of affirmative action in the first place.[9]

Methods

To substantiate the findings of Stoker and Fine, I initially searched all possible sources for polling data. I ultimately decided to use survey question data from three major polls, Harris, Gallup, and Roper, collected between 1990-1995. I anticipated comparing responses to questions which varied according to the word used to denote the policy (affirmative action, preferential treatment, quota, equal opportunity program, special training, and so on), the circumstance in which the program was implemented, and the definition of affirmative action given.

Issues of noncomparability, however, are involved in analyzing such data. By and large the national polls cited are not designed to identify trends more sophisticated than those general ones found in asking "Do you oppose or favor affirmative action"—just the type of questions I was trying to avoid. That being the case, consistent variations in question content, question wording, and question context are not always evident in the sample of questions gathered. Nevertheless these questions remain useful. Despite the noncomparability issues, there are certain similarities in the questions gathered, and comparisons can be made.

Definition

Randall Kennedy, in discussing the fact that affirmative action means different things to different people, suggests four possible definitions of the term: (1) an incentive to encourage women and minorities to "enter the race" with regard to jobs and college attendance; (2) a racial "tie-breaker" when choosing between two *equal* candidates; (3) a tool for giving substantial preference to a candidate based on race, ethnicity, or gender; and (4) an outright quota system.[10] The lack of a sole, generally agreed-upon formulation means that when polling questions do not provide specific definitions of the policies they ask about, respondents have had to construct their own in coming up with their answers. This process has involved not only choosing among reasonable definitions but negotiating the minefield of misconceptions, false allegations, and overgeneralizations that have come to define affirmative action over time.

Michael Frisby alluded to the original intent and definition of affirmative action in a *Wall Street Journal* article entitled "Clinton's Choice to Review Affirmative Action Underscores Delicate Nature of Undertaking": "It was not originally devised as a quota system or a ceiling system or much more than a set of goals and aspirations for employers . . . to bring capable and competent and qualified workers who had traditionally been excluded for reasons of race into the workplace."[11] Lincoln Caplan, in *Newsweek*, explained the change in perception from the original definition to its current one:

> Now laden with derogatory meaning, "affirmative action"— like the word "quota"—covers a broad spectrum of government and privately sponsored activity. In employment alone, it ranges from trying to attract an inclusive group of applicants (by placing job ads in papers read by minorities or recruiting at schools attended by minorities) to seeking a diverse pool of candidates (by using race as a factor for selecting who is interviewed) to favoring minorities in hiring and promotion if other things are equal (by treating race as a positive factor).[12]

Affirmative action has not only become like the word "quota," it has also become synonymous with it, as well as with other derogatory terms such as reverse discrimination and preferential treatment.

The following questions and the responses shown in Figure 1 illustrate the range and support of the programs and policies that have at one time or another fallen under the rubric of affirmative action.[13]

Question 1: Minorities and women are not entitled to any special consideration. (Harris, 1991)

Question 2: After years of discrimination, it is only fair to set up special programs to make sure that women and minorities are given every chance to have equal opportunities in employment and education. (Harris, 1991)

Question 3: As long as there are no rigid quotas, it makes sense to give special training and advice to women and minorities so that they can perform better on the job. (Harris, 1991)

Figure 1
Special Consideration vs. Special Programs vs. Special Training

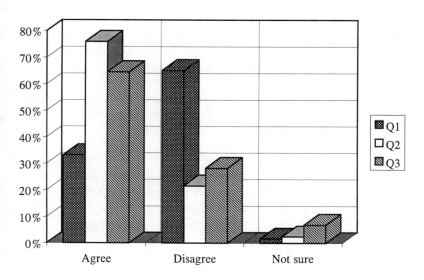

The support for "affirmative action" indicated by the responses to these three questions derives from a combination of factors. One reason for the support is the ambiguity of the programs mentioned: it is not clear what "special consideration" and "special programs" really entail. In addition, Question 2 is worded to appeal to the respondent's sense of fairness, expressing the egalitarian ideal of equal opportunity that the majority of Americans claim to support. Question 3 promotes measures that garner the most support of any affirmative action program included in this sample for at least two reasons: it eliminates the fear of institutionalized quotas and, more important, the proposed measures are to be enacted after the women and minorities have already been hired (presumably in a strictly meritocratic fashion).

Four additional questions also concern affirmative action, with differing emphases. Responses are given in Figure 2.

Question 1: Generally speaking, are you in favor of affirmative action programs designed to help minorities get better jobs and education, or are you opposed to them—or haven't you heard enough to say? (If favor or oppose, then ask whether that opinion is strong or partial.) (*Los Angeles Times*, 1991)

Question 2: All in all, do you favor or oppose affirmative action programs in business for blacks and other minority groups? (NBC News/*Wall Street Journal*, 1991)

Question 3: Do you favor or oppose federal laws requiring affirmative action programs for women and minorities in employment and in education, provided there are no rigid quotas? (Harris, 1991)

Question 4: Do you favor or oppose federal laws requiring racial preference for minorities in employment and education, provided there are no rigid quotas? (Roper, 1991)

Figure 2
Affirmative Action[1]

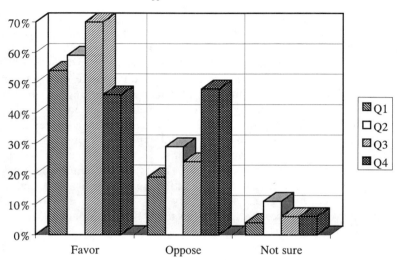

1   Q1: Haven't heard enough to say = 22%, Favor strongly = 30%, favor
          somewhat = 24%, Oppose somewhat = 10%, Oppose strongly = 9%, Not
          sure = 4%, Refused = 1%;
     Q2: Favor = 59%, Oppose = 29%, Not sure = 11%;
     Q3: Favor = 70%, Oppose = 24%, Not sure = 6%;
     Q4: Favor = 46%, Oppose = 48%, Not sure = 6%.

The first three questions all ask specifically about affirmative action
but with significant variations in wording. Question 1 supplies the
intent of the affirmative action program ("to help minorities to get
better jobs and education") as well as providing an attractive alternative
to either favoring or opposing such programs ("haven't heard enough
to say"). Question 2 specifies blacks and other minority groups and
pertains only to business; Question 3 attempts to gauge support for
legislatively mandated affirmative action programs.

Questions 3 and 4 differ in target group and program type. Laws
requiring affirmative action programs for women and minorities clearly
receive more support than those requiring preference only for minorities
such as those programs advocated in Questions 1 and 2. The disparity
could be due to two factors: the inclusion of women may make such
policies seem more favorable, and/or racial preference has more
negative connotations than does affirmative action. These two factors
have important consequences both for the interpretation of survey
results and for the design of future survey questions.

Context

"The term 'affirmative action' is a potent stimulus. It is all the same an empty phrase to many in the public whose meaning depends on context."[14]   Laura Stoker argues that "previous research has led us to misunderstand the nature of public opinion on affirmative action."[15] She seeks to demonstrate the role compensatory justice plays in our explanation of public opinion on affirmative action and to force a rethinking of what public opinion on affirmative action looks like.[16]

Stoker advances the thesis that "if people care about considerations of compensatory justice, then we would expect their opinions about affirmative action programs to be sensitive to the context in which those programs are implemented."[17]   That is, public opinion pollsters should expect different assessments of the merits of affirmative action programs depending on whether they were intended, as should be indicated by the question, to "compensate blacks for historical and society-wide practices of discrimination to which they have been subject" or were introduced "where discriminatory hiring has been taking place in an effort to dismantle those practices and to compensate those subject to discrimination."[18]

In her analysis of the questions previous researchers have asked, Stoker concludes that most have "generalized over the kinds of contexts that the Court has deemed so significant, or have ignored these contexts altogether."[19]   Stoker states that these types of questions treat the contexts in which affirmative action programs are imposed as irrelevant to the question of what the public thinks of them.   These types of questions ultimately lead to a misrepresentation of the level of public support for the programs involved.[20]

To investigate the effect of considerations of compensatory justice on public opinion on affirmative action, Stoker analyzed the results of three different questions from the 1992 Race and American Values Survey, a national survey administered to randomly selected individuals. These questions did not specifically use the term "affirmative action" but rather indicated a policy similar to the notion of quotas.   The first of these questions was context free, the second inquired about public support for a policy undertaken in a company where blacks were underrepresented, and the third, where companies had been engaging in discriminatory practices.   The second question represents a "polling middle ground," the first is the abstractly framed question most frequently asked, and the last is situated in the context that is most representative of what the Supreme Court has deemed legitimate. The responses are given in Figure 3.

Question 1—No Context[21]: Do you think that large companies should be required to give a certain number of jobs to blacks, or should the government stay out of this?

Question 2—Underrepresentation Context: *There are some large companies where blacks are underrepresented....* Do you think that *these* large companies should be required to give a certain number of jobs to blacks, or should the government stay out of this?

Question 3—Discrimination Context: *There are some large companies with employment policies that discriminate against blacks....* Do you think *these* large companies should be required to give a certain number of jobs to blacks, or should the government stay out of this?

Figure 3
Context: None vs. Under-representation vs. Discrimination

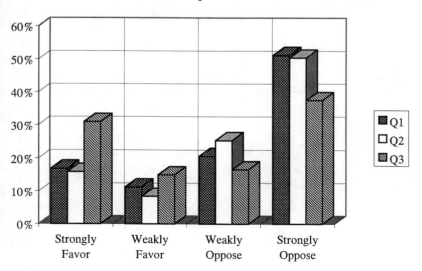

Analysis of the responses to these three questions leads to three conclusions. First, it is not true that "mass opinion remains invariably opposed to preferential treatment" or that "there is no ambiguity about where the majority stand." Rather, affirmative action is an issue upon which the public is sharply divided. Second, response similarities in Question 1 and 2 suggest that people ordinarily think of affirmative action as being implemented in circumstances where there is manifest racial imbalance in the work force. And third, dissimilar responses in Questions 2 and 3 suggest that people generally do not consider racial imbalances in the work force to be indicative of discriminatory hiring practices.[22]

These findings have significant implications both for analysts and for future pollsters. According to Stoker, when a question supplies no context, respondents will tend to think that affirmative action programs were implemented where racial imbalance but not racial discrimination existed. In addition, the responses from Question 3 indicate that affirmative action programs may still be supported even though it is recognized that the actual victims of the discriminatory behavior may not gain and that innocent people, not necessarily the wrongdoers, will experience a loss.

The following five questions represent tiers of support for preferential policy.

Question 1: We should make every possible effort to improve the position of blacks and other minorities, even if it means giving them preferential treatment? (Times Mirror, 1991)

Question 2: Do you favor or oppose federal laws requiring racial preference for minorities in employment and education, provided there are no rigid quotas? (Roper, 1991)

Question 3: Do you think blacks and other minorities should or should not receive hiring preference to make up for past discrimination against them? (NBC News/*Wall Street Journal*, 1991)

Question 4: Some people say that to make up for past discrimination, women and members of minority groups should be given preferential treatment in getting jobs and places in colleges. Others say that their ability, as determined by test scores, should be the main consideration. Which point of view comes closer to how you feel on the subject? (Gallup, 1991)

Question 5: As you may know, a measure has been proposed in Congress that would make it unlawful for any employer to grant preferential treatment in hiring to any person or group on the basis of race, color, religion, sex, or national origin. Do you favor or oppose this proposal? (*Los Angeles Times*, 1995)

Preferential policy is a term that is often used interchangeably with affirmative action, to the latter's detriment, in education and employment. The first question includes virtually every possible policy that exists under the affirmative action rubric and will speak favorably primarily to respondents who do not attribute the position of minorities to such dispositional factors as lack of ability. The second question introduces the looming specter of legislation and intrusive big government to the debate while including a more narrowly defined range of policies (it excludes quotas). The third and fourth questions offer a general explanation for why preferential treatment needs to exist (past discrimination), but the latter includes women and also provides an alternative to preferential policies—the strict meritocracy. Question 5 was asked in a 1995 *Los Angeles Times* survey. The responses are given in Figure 4.

Figure 4
Preferential Treatment[2]

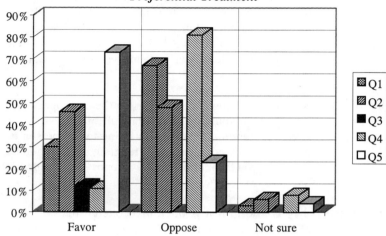

2   Q1: Completely agree = 10%, Mostly agree = 20%, Mostly disagree = 33%,
        Completely Disagree = 34%, Don't know = 3%;
     Q2: Favor = 46%, Oppose = 48%, Not sure = 6%;
     Q3: White Favor = 12%, Black Favor = 51%;
     Q4: Preferential Treatment = 11%, Test Scores = 81%, Don't Know = 8%;
     Q5: Favor = 73%, Oppose = 23%, Don't Know = 4%.

The policy advocated in Question 2 receives the most support in this set of questions and serves as a slight indication that the public favors legislative mandates.[23] Results from Question 4 indicate that the mention of past discrimination does not outweigh the considerable sway of the meritocracy. The difference between Questions 2 and 5 could represent a change in public opinion over time or the effect of excluding quotas from preferential policies.[24]

Issue Framing

In "The Impact of Issue Framing on Public Opinion toward Affirmative Action Programs," Terri Susan Fine addresses issues associated with reactions to equal opportunity programs as they relate to the framing of survey questions designed to measure attitudes. She argues that whether or not questions are phrased with a positive or negative bias, the specific concepts and terms used to present choices and the way and extent to which counterarguments and alternative policies are presented all affect public reactions to equal opportunity programs.

Fine used data from the 1986 American National Election Survey conducted by the Center for Political Studies at the University of Michigan's Survey Research Center to test the effects of issue framing on public opinion. Respondents were asked about preferential treatment in higher education and employment, with opposition to such treatment framed in one of two ways: either as giving blacks advantages they haven't earned or as discriminating against whites. I have included only Fine's preferential treatment questions and results that pertain to employment; the education-based questions, however, yield similar trends. The following question was asked of both blacks and whites, in two different formulations. Responses are given in Figures 5 and 6.

"Some people say that because of past discrimination, blacks should be given preference in hiring and promotion. Others say that such preference in the hiring and promotion of blacks is wrong because it (either 'discriminates against whites' or 'gives blacks advantages they haven't earned'). What about your opinion—are you for or against preferential hiring and promotion of blacks?"

Figure 5
White Opinion

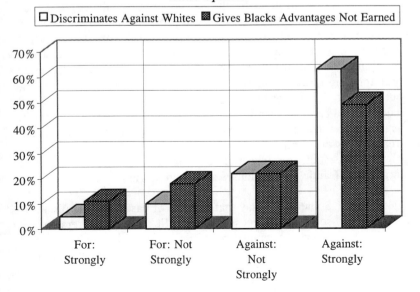

Figure 6
Black Opinion

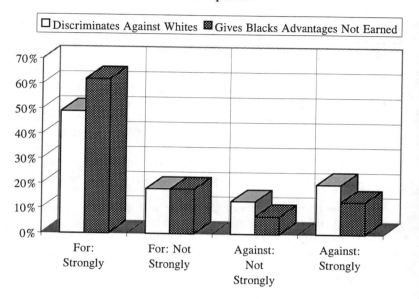

□ Discriminates Against Whites ▓ Gives Blacks Advantages Not Earned

Fine's results illustrate that the way preferential policies are framed does indeed influence support of these programs and that "question effects are not caused by substantive changes in policy or target population. Rather, the cues that are used for issue presentation affect reactions."[25] Fine's finding that whites, more than blacks, opposed preference in hiring promotion was consistent with previous studies, but she also found that framing the program in terms of losses and gains caused respondents to react differently. "Preferential treatment as undeserved benefits garners stronger support than does preferential treatment as discrimination."[26]

Two questions on education facilitate a comparison of different targets and framings. Responses are given in Figure 7.

Question 1: Some people say that because of past discrimination it is sometimes necessary for colleges and universities to reserve openings for black students. Others oppose quotas because they say quotas give black advantages they haven't earned. What about your opinion—are you for or against quotas to admit black students? (If favor, ask:) Do you favor quotas strongly or not strongly? (If oppose, ask:) Do you oppose quotas strongly or not strongly? (American National Election Study 1988-Post election, 1989)

Question 2: There is a controversy over special admissions procedures and quotas for blacks and other minority students in colleges and graduate school programs. Some say quotas and programs are necessary to increase the number of minorities in these schools and make up for past discriminations. Others say this practice discriminates against whites who cannot be considered for the places in the quota. What is your feeling—that the quotas should be kept to insure a certain number of minority students or that they should be illegal? (Roper Report, 1985)

Figure 7
Advantage Not Earned vs. Discrimination Against Whites[3]

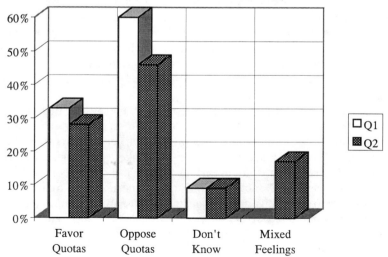

---

3   Q1: Favor strongly = 18%, Favor not strongly = 15%, Oppose not strongly = 18%, Oppose Strongly = 42%, Don't Know/Refused = 9%;
    Q2: Quotas Kept = 28%, Quotas illegal = 46%, Mixed feelings = 17%, Don't Know = 9%.

Both of these questions deal with quotas in higher education (an area in which public opinion on affirmative action policies is almost always more favorable than in employment) and mention past discrimination. However, the former specifically targets blacks and frames opposition to affirmative action as a positive gain to someone who does not deserve it. The latter encompasses blacks and other minorities and frames opposition as a negative loss to someone who doesn't deserve it. According to Fine, to the extent that public opinion varies according to the question's emphasis on loss or gain, educational quotas as presented in the first question should engender greater support.

At first glance, Question 1 seems to garner both more favor and more opposition than Question 2. Such seemingly ambiguous results could and are being used to the detriment of affirmative action programs. Those interpretations, however, conveniently ignore the nearly one-fifth of respondents to Question 2 that have mixed feelings and are therefore not counted in opposition to or in favor of such policies.

Conclusion

There are more than enough reasons to oppose affirmative action, including its purported negative effects on black initiative and self-confidence; the message of black inferiority and white superiority and the ensuing stigma that it may engender; and the alleged paltry benefits of such policy at considerable personal and group expense. There is no need to provide more reasons by misinterpreting public opinion polls.

The conclusions of Stoker and Fine on the effects of question context, wording, and issue framing on public support for and against affirmative action substantiate the work of earlier scholars interested in a variety of social and political issues. Stoker finds that opposition to affirmative action is not as unequivocal as has been advertised and that "old-fashioned racism looms larger as a source of political opposition to affirmative action than the typical analysis would reveal."[27] Both scholars emphasize the importance of notions of compensatory justice to survey respondents in their responses to questions about affirmative action. Fine further concludes that the question of compensation can often outweigh an initial negative reaction to the proposed method of policy implementation.[28]

The survey questions considered here highlight and confirm the contributions made by Stoker, Fine, and other scholars. For example, the wide disparities in public opinion on affirmative action found in polls taken in Los Angeles in 1991 versus 1995 and in other areas where the affirmative action debate has been less politically salient in both time periods is evidence of Donald Kinder and Lynn Sanders's thesis that "by examining the alterations in opinion induced by alterations in question wording that mimic the ongoing debate among elites, it becomes possible to learn how changes in public opinion can be induced by changes taking place *outside* the survey, in the ordinary, everyday, process of democratic discussion."[29]

Toward a More Comprehensive Survey

There is an urgent need for a comprehensive survey of public opinion on the range of policies and programs collectively referred to as affirmative action. Such a survey would require careful design, with attention to as many factors that affect survey responses as possible.

Defining the language used in such a survey is important. Definitions help ensure that respondents are responding to the same concept. In addition, survey administrators must remain aware of their questions' ideological import. Definitions of affirmative action may minimize a hostile reaction, for example, by excluding any mention of quotas or preferential treatment. Programs mentioned in questions can be conceptualized to an extent that makes them appear to the respondent as benign. As demonstrated by Stoker and Fine, incorporating considerations about question wording and issue framing are critical to developing a valuable survey.

The location of questions assessing public opinion on affirmative action in relation to one another and to other questions in a larger questionnaire is also important.[30] There are a number of as yet unasked questions, moreover, that would be helpful to include in the effort to better understand public opinion on affirmative action. They include questions similar to ones asked previously but with a clear distinction between federally mandated programs and voluntary ones; questions on support for means-tested preferential treatment policies, which are steadily gaining support from politicians, policymakers, and academics; questions on support for the enforcement of tougher antidiscrimination laws; questions on the motivation of attitudes and opinions; and questions on both the real extent of affirmative action programs and the perception of that extent. This last category includes asking women and minorities how often they have been told, or think, that they have gotten a job or promotion or entrance into an academic institution because of affirmative action; asking white male respondents how often they have been told, or think, that they failed to get a job or a promotion or lost a job because of affirmative action; and candidly asking the federal government, businesses, and admissions committees how affirmative action policies play a role in their deliberations, if at all.

As a nation, we are standing at an important crossroads in the history of the affirmative action debate. Public opinion polls need not always be foe to those who advocate measures, affirmative action included, that are considered more liberal. According to Howard Schuman and his colleagues, "Social 'reporting,' as originally conceived, was integral to the underlying political purpose of social science: the accommodation of a plurality of interests in the context of expanding popular expectations."[31] Now is the time to make good on this original intent and so utilize the survey method. Those who support affirmative action have at least two options: they can launch a rhetorical retooling campaign and/or a massive truth campaign.[32] (Either strategy would benefit from conducting the comprehensive survey which I have suggested.) Each of these options, though not mutually exclusive, will appeal to different constituencies on the ideological spectrum.

Rhetorical Retooling

If the public does not support affirmative action as it is now described in polls, in the media, and by politicians, how can it be repackaged to make it more appealing? Neither Fine nor Stoker explicitly focused on devising a method of publicly redefining affirmative action programs in order to make them more socially and politically acceptable, but their results could be used toward that end.

The repackaging of affirmative action includes redefining the language used to describe affirmative action-type programs and tailoring the concept to include those aspects of affirmative action that do garner positive response and exclude those that do not. This may simply mean changing the general name of such programs from affirmative action to something that has not become so politicized and value laden, for example, antidiscriminatory policy or diversity enhancement programs. Changing the name might also, however, mean being more specific and diligent about identifying and qualifying these programs. A comprehensive survey would be invaluable as a tool to help assess the strengths and weaknesses of the current affirmative action program as derived from public opinion.

Truth Campaign

> Despite all feasible precautions, however, it is evident that not every variation, nor even every statistically significant variation, necessarily reproduces real change over time in the attitudes of the population.[33]

One need not concede the battle over affirmative action to those who oppose it using public opinion polls; instead, one can expose the shortcomings of such data. For example, Stoker's finding that racism is a significant contributor to people's opinions on affirmative action contradicts many who have argued to the contrary. This finding could have a major impact on the affirmative action debate, making it difficult for opponents of affirmative action to maintain their cloak of propriety while advocating their policies. Any finding that undermines their claims of racial neutrality will shed new light on such policies.

Policy Recommendations

Beyond specific recommendations for the pro-affirmative action party — i.e., a rhetorical retooling campaign or massive truth campaign — are there more general implications of this analysis for the future of affirmative action policy? The answer is yes. A future devoid of any type of affirmative action is inconceivable precisely because affirmative action has so many different connotations. In the words of Randall Kennedy, "the very ambiguity of the term shall serve to preserve, to an extent, its practice."[34]

1) The debate over affirmative action has become even more complicated because of the ambiguities now involved in defining exactly what it is. A national definition of affirmative action is needed to aid those programs that are federally mandated and to frame further political debate.
2) There is currently a lack of empirical evidence on the subject of affirmative action: its impact and its perception.

Race Versus Class

Furthermore, these types of issues must be critically examined before making policy. A comprehensive survey of public opinion on affirmative action is part of the further research needed.

Notes

1. William Kristol, "Affirmative Action: Democratic Confusion and Republican Principle," Project for the Republican Future Memorandum to Republican Leaders, March 14, 1995, pp. 1-2.
2. Paul M. Sniderman and Thomas Piazza, *The Scar of Race* (Cambridge, Mass.: Harvard University Press, 1993), p. 178.
3. Ibid. Affirmative Action and Public Opinion Polls.
4. It may seem ironic that the very issue on which Sniderman and Piazza conclude that "preferences are so one-sided as to seem irreversible" is the one about which I suggest there is a great deal of pliability. Sniderman and Piazza's definition of affirmative action (ensuring that a predetermined proportion of jobs or college admissions go to blacks whether or not they are qualified) is a narrow one, however, that closely resembles the type of quota system that respondents to public opinion polls consistently oppose.
5. Laura Stoker, "The Moral Basis of Political Choice," September 1994, p. 210.
6. Donald R. Kinder and Lynn M. Sanders, "Mimicking Political Debate with Survey Questions: The Case of White Opinion on Affirmative Action for Blacks," *Social Cognition*, 8, no. 4 (1990): 73-74. Citing the current abortion debate, Kinder and Sanders discuss how the same issue may be discussed in very different ways and argue that how a policy is described affects its reception and success among the general public: "Surveys not only measure public opinion but also shape, provoke, and occasionally create it. We recognize that what may appear to be real shifts in opinion can be produced by ostensibly innocuous alterations in question wording, format, and placement." See also Howard Schuman, Charlotte Steeh, and Lawrence Bobo, *Racial Attitudes in America: Trends and Interpretations* (Cambridge, Mass.: Harvard University Press, 1986).
7. Sniderman and Piazza, *The Scar of Race*, p. 176.
8. Schuman, Steeh, and Bobo, include the larger questionnaire in which the questions are embedded, sampling considerations, consistency of question wording, organizational differences, the race of the interviewer, the mode of administration, the effects of context, and missing data as features of surveys that must be taken into account if one is to avoid serious misinterpretation (*Racial Attitudes in America*, pp. 58-68).
9. See W. A. Gamson and K. F. Lasch, "The Political Culture of Social Welfare Policy," in S. E. Spiro and E. Yuchiman-Year, eds., *Evaluating the Welfare State* (New York: Academic Press, 1983), and W. A. Gamson and A. Modigliani, "The Changing Culture of Affirmative Action," in R. D. Braungart, ed., *Research in Political Sociology*, vol. 3 (Greenwich, Conn: JAI Press, 1987) for a more detailed analysis of issue framing.

10. Randall Kennedy, Harvard Law School, presentation to WWS 402g, March 30, 1995. See also Lee Sigelman and Susan Welch. *Black Americans' Views of Racial Inequality: The Dream Deferred* (Cambridge: Cambridge University Press, 1991). Sigelman and Welch have found that "in addition to assessing the effects of affirmative action differently, many blacks and whites actually define affirmative action differently" (p. 134).

11. Michael K. Frisby, "Clinton's Choice to Review Affirmative Action Underscores Delicate Nature of Undertaking," *Wall Street Journal*, March 14, 1995.

12. Lincoln Caplan, "Why Affirmative Action Is Divisive, Difficult—and Necessary" *Washington Post*, February 12, 1995.

13. Unless otherwise noted, questions are from telephone surveys of the national population of adults. Schuman and colleagues find that the data obtained from telephone surveys is not equivalent to data obtained in face-to-face interviews because (to the extent that question response is influenced by the race of the interviewer) the use of telephone surveys introduces an ambiguity in regard to racial identification that is not present in face-to-face interviews. (Schuman, Steeh, and Bobo, *Racial Attitudes in America*.)

14. Sniderman and Piazza, *The Scar of Race*, p. 130.

15. Stoker, "The Moral Basis of Political Choice," (p. 180).

16. Ibid., pp. 178-179.

17. Ibid., pp. 179, 182, 185. The Supreme Court has based its rulings on the legitimacy of affirmative action programs on a notion of compensatory justice which supports the use of race-conscious hiring programs if they are narrowly tailored to remedy specific practices of discrimination. Compensatory justice requires that when it has been established that a given company or governmental unit has wrongfully discriminated against blacks, then their discriminatory hiring practices must be dismantled and compensatory or remedial actions undertaken. The alternative theory of consequential justice demands race-conscious measures to eliminate workplace castes, to promote diversity in the educational process, to ensure a balanced police force in the interest of community service, or to accomplish a range of other goals. Different conceptions of affirmative action policies emerge as a function of which theory is endorsed: the former conceives affirmative action as a response to identifiable breaches of past and present duty while the latter conceives it as an effort to overcome social subordination of the relevant groups. The former sanctions affirmative action responses that take the form of discrete remedies for discrete harms while the latter sanctions a much broader set of affirmative action policies.

18. Ibid., p. 186.

19. Ibid., p. 187.

20. According to Schuman, Steeh, and Bobo, the "main implication of the possibility of context effects is to emphasize the importance of looking for evidence of systematic change, or lack of change, over as many points as possible. Single outliers don't deserve too much effort at substantive interpretation in terms of change because they may result from questionnaire context rather than from events in the external social or political environment" (*Racial Attitudes in America*, p. 68).

21. This set of questions is representative of the consistency of question wording needed for a comprehensive analysis of public opinion on affirmative action from which substantive conclusions can be drawn.

22. Stoker, "The Moral Basis of Political Choice," p. 193.

23. As demonstrated earlier this question gets more favorable response when affirmative action, women, and minorities are substituted for racial preference, black, and minorities.

24. Questions might also serve as an interesting example of how ongoing political debate can frame public opinion poll responses and the corresponding responses. See Kinder and Sanders, "Mimicking Public Debate."

25. Terri Susan Fine, "The Impact of Issue Framing on Public Opinion Toward Affirmative Action Programs," *Social Science Journal*, 29, no. 3 (1992): 324.

26. Ibid., p. 327.

27. Stoker, "The Moral Basis of Political Choice," p. 210.

28. Fine, "The Impact of Issue Framing," p. 325. The public prefers compensatory to preferential treatment. Lipset and Schneider find that compensatory action is supported because it elevates discriminated against groups to society's established standards. Preferential treatment is viewed as suspending those social standards so that minorities can be integrated into society.

29. Kinder and Sanders, "Mimicking Political Debate," p. 73.

30. Kinder and Sanders, "Mimicking Political Debate."

31. Schuman, Steeh, and Bobo, *Racial Attitudes in America*, p. v.

32. Randall Kennedy provided the original endorsement for the former option.

33. Schuman, Steeh, and Bobo, *Racial Attitudes in America*, p. 70.

34. Kennedy, March 30, 1995.

Chapter 5

Philosophical Perspectives

Justin McCrary

More so than most policy debates, the furor over affirmative action is driven by philosophical disagreement. Rigorous, clear philosophical discussion is a prerequisite of democratic consensus. Yet lack of such discussion plagues the affirmative action issue. As Nicolaus Mills succinctly states, "Three decades after the first affirmative action programs, we lack basic agreement on the justification for them."[1] This chapter examines the utilitarian, egalitarian, libertarian, and contractarian conceptions of justice and their implications for affirmative action.

Most policy analysts are utilitarians, either explicitly or implicitly. Utilitarians compare the costs and benefits of a policy and advocate those policies with positive sums. Such calculations are not the focus here, however, as I address utilitarian justice only briefly.

Egalitarians are prevalent among New Deal-style Democrats and civil rights advocates. Egalitarians receive sparse press in the mid-1990s, and their arguments are less relevant to policymakers concerned with making policy changes in the current conservative political climate.

The egalitarian perspective, like the utilitarian perspective, receives only cursory treatment below.

Libertarians are the vanguard of the shift to the right in America, and their philosophy pervades Americans' political views in subtle yet important ways. Although few mainstream politicians present themselves as libertarians, the meteoric rise of ultra-conservative figures such as Rush Limbaugh and Bob Grant underscores the extent to which libertarian ideals resonate with the American public. Any attempt to tailor affirmative action policies to the 1990s electorate must carefully consider the support libertarian ideals enjoy.

Finally, the contractarian conception of justice, with its Rawlsian emphasis on justice as fairness, resides closer to the political mainstream than egalitarianism and deserves an in-depth discussion. Those looking to anchor neo-affirmative action policies around a consistent conception of justice should consider the implications of the contractarian perspective.

Utilitarian Justice

Utilitarians desire to maximize welfare. Such a straightforward concern makes for easy policy choices; calculating costs and benefits in a zero-sum world may be a logistical nightmare, but addition is no moral Catch-22. The beauty of utilitarianism lies in its simplicity.

Above all, pure utilitarians are opposed to any form of government action that reduces the efficiency of markets. Affirmative action requires no small amount of overhead, and would seem to be a prime target for a utilitarian budget axe. The way in which affirmative action affects markets, however, depends on two factors: (1) the efficiency of the market absent affirmative action; and (2) the scope, character, and manner of the affirmative action program's impact.

In a perfect world, employers would always hire workers solely on the basis of their merit, universities would always admit students solely on the basis of their potential contribution to the educational community, and real estate agents would always sell to the first qualified buyer. In this perfect world, affirmative action programs would give women and minorities a competitive advantage. Critics charge that affirmative action robs Peter to pay Paul, with gains and losses simply shifting hands. Utilitarians, concerned with efficiency, are indifferent to such zero-sum changes in allocations. But if affirmative action discourages hard work, then utilitarians quickly become concerned that affirmative action shrinks all the pieces of the pie—minority as well as white, female as well as male. These fears do not seem ill founded. Affirmative action could have a negative impact on the self-esteem of beneficiaries, reduce incentives for hard work by lowering standards, and stigmatize beneficiaries.

Other utilitarians have pointed out, however, that markets are virtually never efficient. If employers, universities, and landlords all discriminate against women and minorities, especially unconsciously, then affirmative action may militate against inefficiencies. If a white hiring officer is suspicious of young black males generally, she may form a negative impression of a potential employee who happens to be young, black, and male. Affirmative action would try to counter that negative impression, giving the hiring officer added incentive to consider the young man for the job.

Robert Fullinwider prefers the straightforward utilitarian argument that affirmative action has positive income effects for the black community. One African-American family's improved employment status will have positive effects on the black community surrounding that family. Fullinwider asserts that the employment loss to a white family should affect only that family. But do black Americans tend to affect the economic well-being of their communities more than white Americans affect theirs? I have no reason to believe that this is true. Moreover, the logical conclusion of Fullinwider's argument would seem to be that African Americans living in white neighborhoods would not be eligible for affirmative action. If there is something inherent in black communities that entails the sharing of income, then should whites living in black communities be eligible for affirmative action?

Michael Rosenfeld asserts that Fullinwider may be able to find alternative justification for affirmative action within the framework of utilitarianism. Perhaps there are good psychological reasons why improvements in black income provide more benefit than decreases in white income amount to loss. Espousing the traditional "role model" argument, Rosenfeld comments:

> In the midst of poverty and a general lack of opportunities, visible success could quite possibly enhance hope and pave the way toward the improvement of prevailing material conditions. In contrast, a relatively small number of additional individual failures to secure scarce positions by whites are unlikely to have a great negative impact on the white community.[2]

If Rosenfeld is correct, the overall benefit of affirmative action is positive. Rosenfeld however, despite his good intentions, does not necessarily come to Fullinwider's rescue. Rosenfeld fails to recognize that the African-American community is diverse—in fact, increasingly so. The number of black doctors, lawyers, and professors has grown in the 1980s and 1990s, as has the number of black children growing up in poverty. Affirmative action will help middle- and upper-class blacks get into good colleges and obtain good jobs, but middle- and upper-class blacks often live in the suburbs, far away from those most in need of help. Unless we are sure that inner-city minority youth are inspired by the Cosby family, we should not base our support of affirmative action on a presumed class-breaching identification with role models.

Further, Rosenfeld's role model argument seems to apply only to those communities beset with concentrated "poverty and a general lack of opportunities." He fails to address whether affirmative action for women is then unjustified within a utilitarian framework. Women are not disproportionately residents of communities plagued by poverty and lacking opportunity.[3]

In sum, utilitarianism fails to provide us with clear philosophical grounds for either opposition to or advocacy of affirmative action. The utilitarian would base her support of affirmative action on the result of empirical investigations demonstrating the cost or benefit of the policy. Within the foreseeable future, however, we are unlikely to be able to accurately measure the impact of affirmative action on self-esteem, incentives to work, or negative stereotypes of beneficiaries.

The Egalitarian Perspective

Best articulated in recent years by Jesse Jackson's "rainbow coalition" vision, egalitarians are in favor of equality or equity, depending upon their perspective.[4] Some egalitarians are in favor of total equality and feel that the United States should strive to emulate the social welfare policies of Western European democracies. Other egalitarians simply argue for equality of opportunity, but expand the definition of equality of opportunity to include the provision of equal life chances—an inclusive definition encompassing parity of health care and education.

William Julius Wilson is probably best categorized as an egalitarian. In his work *The Truly Disadvantaged*, he criticizes affirmative action's class bias. Wilson's argument is that affirmative action benefits wealthy members of beneficiary groups who have the resources, say, to send their children to prep school before Ivy League college. Simultaneously, per Wilson, affirmative action recipients are most likely to take jobs away from whites with low socioeconomic status—whites with high incomes and educational attainment are less likely to be in competition with minorities for jobs.

The egalitarian does not oppose affirmative action for its attempt to level the playing field; rather, she opposes affirmative action because it does not go far enough. Wilson also makes the important argument that affirmative action steals precious political capital from "race neutral policies" that might benefit the poor.

Although egalitarian tendencies are strong in the United States, support for egalitarian policies is lower than in Europe. For historical and other reasons, Americans have tended to be more individualistic in their political views. In Europe welfare is perceived as necessary to stave off hunger; in the United States we fear that recipients are not pulling their fair share.

Given the recent shift to the right in American politics, it seems that egalitarian arguments in favor of affirmative action will fall on deaf ears. Americans are not now compelled by the compassion of Lyndon Johnson's Great Society programs. Any attempt to retool affirmative action for the 1990s must look beyond old-guard egalitarian arguments and toward the rise of the New Right of Rush Limbaugh.

The Libertarian Perspective

Libertarians, true to their name, are dedicated to the principle of "overall maximization of freedom."[5] This position entails unwavering support of individual freedoms, private property rights, and the freedom of contract. The libertarian further values the integrity of individual liberties above every other concern. Libertarians are well known in today's political arena for being the most vocal group opposed to virtually all government programs.

The popular talk-radio host Rush Limbaugh is probably best categorized as a libertarian, and his rabid opposition to anything remotely akin to New Deal policies is apparently not falling on deaf ears. Jonathan Freedland comments: "Across the country, right-wing talk radio is entrenched. The king of the medium, Rush Limbaugh, is estimated to reach 20 million people a week on 660 stations, all tuning in to a daily monologue of Clinton-bashing and welfare-trashing, punctuated by Limbaugh's much-imitated riff, the angry cry of the put-upon white male."[6]

Pierre Blondeau, a longtime member of the Libertarian Party in Texas, was a candidate for the U.S. Senate in November 1994. His platform mirrored that of the prototypical libertarian. He called for an end to the income tax, elimination of public schools, and replacing Medicare with cash awards to the elderly. Consistent with the libertarian desire to maximize individual freedoms, he opposes government intervention into social issues and victimless crimes. He is staunchly pro-choice and collects guns. He objects to any restriction on sexually explicit materials. He advocates drug legalization, especially for marijuana. His potential constituency represents an intriguing political cross-section. In Blondeau's words: "I'm in the enviable position of being pro-business, pro-labor, pro-minority, any group you want to pick, except large government and pressure groups."[7]

A libertarian like Blondeau would defend the individual's right to engage in irrational behavior, and deny the proposition that an individual has any right to a potential benefit that could be distributed by a fellow citizen. All distribution of private benefits must take place in a manner consistent with the property owner's preferences.

A firm in the libertarian universe, then, is equally justified in hiring no African Americans or only African Americans. The libertarian would thus argue against antidiscrimination legislation. But libertarians like Blondeau want to maximize individual freedoms; to the extent that discrimination limits the freedom of women and minorities, antidiscrimination legislation would seem to increase liberty. Few would assert that southerners enjoyed more freedom two generations ago than they do today. Most would agree that the extent of one's freedom depended upon one's color. The federal government became an enemy to many white southerners in the 1960s because of the intrusiveness of civil rights legislation, but that legislation undoubtedly increased the liberties of black southerners and northerners alike. A laissez-faire federal government like the one libertarians espouse would have left the system of Jim Crow in place.

Rush Limbaugh and other libertarians who join him on the radio spend much of their air time denouncing the lack of "personal responsibility." Yet, importantly, libertarian justice means that those engaging in discrimination do not bear responsibility for the consequences of their discrimination.

A coal-mine owner in West Virginia who refuses to hire women may induce a good deal of hunger in single mothers and their children. Indeed, that hunger may even be the direct outgrowth of his malevolence. The libertarian is forced to reach one of two somewhat uncomfortable conclusions: (1) no one is responsible for the harms that stem from discrimination, or (2) there are those who are responsible for discrimination, but their responsibility entails no obligation. Yet the libertarian would remain opposed to any restriction of his hiring preferences, falling back on the premise that liberty must precede social welfare considerations and that no one has a right to any job. To the extent that libertarians oppose antidiscrimination legislation, they diverge from the predominant American political sentiment.

Given the libertarian position on antidiscrimination legislation, government-imposed affirmative action seems unlikely to tickle libertarian fancy. Policies of preference require increased representation of minorities and women in the workplace, the housing market, and institutions of higher learning—necessarily infringing upon the absolute, unassailable freedom of employers, property owners, and universities to hire, house, and admit whomever they want to. Even if it were effectively demonstrated that affirmative action would improve the lot of African Americans, who are disproportionately represented among the ranks of the poor and the jobless, the libertarian would remain unconvinced. Individual freedoms, for the libertarian, trump welfare considerations. Moreover, enforcement of affirmative action would require that government overstep the bounds of the minimal state. The libertarian's stance on affirmative action, however, depends fundamentally on his interpretation of history.

Few Americans would deny that racism, sexism, xenophobia, and heterocentrism remain part of American society. Yet libertarian principles are at odds with this reality. If employers are willing to pay the economic price of discrimination, as they were in the South a generation ago, then the laissez-faire principles of the libertarian may imply oppression.

It is important to note, however, that the libertarian is not opposed to affirmative action per se. Rather, the libertarian is opposed only to government imposition of affirmative action. If Rush Limbaugh assumed complete control of the American polity tomorrow, affirmative action would not disappear altogether. To the extent that firms and universities support affirmative action, policies of preference could continue.[8]

Given the respect libertarians have for private property rights, America's history of slavery is troubling. American government has historically violated libertarian principles and deprived African Americans, Latinos, and Asian Americans of the right to hold property. Rush Limbaugh and his partners in talk-radio would deny that they have a responsibility to pay for historical wrongdoings. Stuttering John, Howard Stern's sidekick, grumbles: "I didn't keep any slaves."[9]

But the libertarian philosopher Robert Nozick disagrees asserting that society has a responsibility to compensate those illegally deprived of property. Nozick's "principle of rectification" establishes that if you steal something, you have no right to it. The stolen good should be returned to the individual from whom it was stolen. Nozick's principle of rectification is not unfamiliar to Americans. Every first grader knows that when Bobby steals Jane's pencil, Bobby should return Jane her pencil, say he's sorry, and be reprimanded. Any course of action falling short of this would unjustly deprive Jane of a pencil which is rightfully hers, would unjustly improve Bobby's wealth, and would lead to a rash of pencil thefts on the part of Bobby and others encouraged by his example.

Many would seek to justify affirmative action on similar grounds. Policies of preference stem from a period when racial unrest was sending city after city up in flames. Affirmative action may have been an attempt to provide some sort of compensation to African Americans in order to increase the legitimacy of the social order. Many who advocate affirmative action today, especially those in the black leadership such as Jesse Jackson and Donald Payne, remain committed to it because of its compensatory component.

Compensatory justice is an important concept particularly in the United States where economic wealth was, and to a lesser extent probably still is, accumulated with the sweat of oppressed labor. The institution of slavery meant the evisceration of labor costs over multiple centuries for propertied white males choosing to engage in labor-intensive agriculture; the construction of American urban centers was largely the product of ill-paid immigrant labor both from abroad and from the former slave South; and women have only rarely and inadequately been compensated for centuries of what has traditionally been known as "women's work." One could argue that there has never been a just distribution of the spoils of economic competition in the United States. In this context, the familiar concept of "property rights" loses its prima facie validity.

The Supreme Court agrees in principle with the black leadership that minorities and women may benefit from affirmative action if they have been discriminated against in the past. Exactly how one keeps track of past discrimination is, however, a contentious issue. The black leadership, which sees discrimination as historically and currently pervasive, insidious, and immeasurably significant, presumes that in the absence of information to the contrary, affirmative action or some other means of compensation is justified.

The Supreme Court, in contrast, views affirmative action with libertarian suspicion. The Court has held that federally funded institutions may only implement a program of affirmative action if it can be demonstrated that the institution had intentionally discriminated in the past against beneficiary groups. However, like advocates of libertarian justice, the Court—as the protector of individual rights—has been loath to hold constitutional those affirmative action programs that attempt to redistribute admissions slots or jobs solely on the basis of distributive justice.

The executive branch of government, in contradistinction to the judiciary, seems to base its justification of affirmative action not on compensatory but on distributive grounds. As Hugh Graham notes in his book *The Civil Rights Era*, the inclusion of Cuban Americans in the mosaic of beneficiaries casts doubt upon compensatory justification for affirmative action: "If the chief rationale for affirmative action was to compensate for historic discrimination against a disadvantaged minority, then the Cubans had little credible claim—except perhaps against Fidel Castro's government—and it is not clear that the proud and upwardly mobile Cubans ever pressed such a claim."[10] The apparent intentions of the executive branch would imply a more egalitarian or perhaps contractarian perspective on affirmative action. The interpretation of the judiciary implies a more libertarian perspective. There is tension between these views.

Nozick's principle of rectification implies that a libertarian's support of or opposition to affirmative action depends fundamentally on the libertarian's interpretation of history. If the current distribution of resources has little to do with coercion and theft, then affirmative action is profoundly unjustified. But if current beneficiaries of affirmative action have historically been deprived of property rightly theirs, then some form of compensation is necessary. Thus the libertarian historian would seem compelled to support either affirmative action or another program that benefits historical victims.

Contractarian Justice

Contractarian justice is intuitively familiar to all of us. From the Judeo-Christian credo, "Do unto others as you would have done unto you" to the American folk wisdom "Never judge a man until you walk a mile in his shoes," justice is implicitly understood to be that which you would like to have happen to you. In *A Theory of Justice*, John Rawls formalizes this theory of justice as fairness.[11]

He begins his discussion with a hypothetical situation that is not unlike a group of children deciding upon the rules of a new game. The actors are called social contractors, and they do not know their stratum in society, their innate abilities and talents, their level of intelligence, their value system, their lifeplan, the extent of their risk aversion, or their tendency toward optimism or pessimism. In short, the social contractors know nothing that would bias them toward any distribution of goods that is not entirely equitable. The social contractors know only the ways in which society functions, not the place within that functioning they might possess. In Rawlsian terminology, the social contractors are placed behind a "veil of ignorance."

The social contractors are placed in this unbiased position so they may establish the rules governing society with an even hand. The contractors so situated come to espouse two principles of justice. The first principle of justice bears remarkable resemblance to the libertarian principle of liberty. As Rawls expresses it, "Each person is to have an equal right to the most extensive basic liberty compatible with a similar liberty for others."[12]

Rawls's second principle of justice, commonly termed the difference principle, is based on his conviction that privilege in a capitalist economy accumulates inertia—that is, the disadvantaged will be further disadvantaged with the passage of time. According to the difference principle, "social and economic inequalities are to be arranged so that they are both: (a) to the greatest benefit of the least advantaged . . . and (b) attached to offices and positions open to all under conditions of fair equality of opportunity."[13]

The difference principle, like contractarian justice more generally, is also quite intuitive. In professional football, the object of every coach is to produce the best team possible, and the object of the football league is to produce high-quality competition between teams.[14] It is in the best interests of every coach to obtain the highest-quality players possible, which means that a strict meritocracy is the basis of selection for the team. Yet the football league, like the American government, has a vested interest in providing healthy competition. The football league knows that the stronger teams, if left to their own devices, will earn more money and perpetually be in a better position to pick the best players available. This would lead to a few very powerful teams and many weak teams. In order to counter this tendency toward inequality, the National Football League provides that the team finishing last in the championships has the first-round draft pick. In essence, the football league ruled that since somebody had to receive it, the first pick for players should go to the least-advantaged team— in this case, the last-place finishers. It is difficult to conceive of a more perfect embodiment of Rawls's difference principle.

Rawls's conception of justice as fairness seems at least theoretically compatible with a program of affirmative action, advocating as he does providing greater opportunities to those with lesser opportunity.[15] A conclusive determination of the choices of the social contractors, however, would depend in large part on their perception of the functioning of society. If the football league decided that the last-place team was at a horrible disadvantage when it came to picking good players, it might advocate granting the first two draft picks to that team. But if the league decided that the disadvantage of the last-place team was only slight, they would probably propound the current system, whereby the last-place team gets only the first draft pick. Finally, if the league determined that the disadvantage of the last-place finisher was at best minimal, it might advocate abolishing the system of preferences altogether.

Unfortunately, we will never be able to place ourselves fully behind Rawls's veil of ignorance. Self-interested rich white males have an incentive to believe that society functions quite fairly. They also have far less contact with discrimination and disadvantage and may feel that the world is a fair place. Self-interested Latinas, however, would charge that discrimination is still pervasive and that minorities are disproportionately represented among the ranks of the disadvantaged. Social science research must attempt to improve on the understanding of how society works. Only better science will enable us to discount those arguments that distort the extent to which American society is a meritocracy or an aristocracy.

Affirmative action, even in the ideal case, does not by itself reconcile the reality of American economic competition with a Rawlsian universe of distributive justice. The prototypical social contractor, knowing neither race nor gender nor social status, would know that if she were black and highly skilled, affirmative action would improve her chances of securing a job. If she were white and highly skilled, affirmative action would be unlikely to affect her. If she possessed only low skills, she would be less likely to get a job regardless of her race. Affirmative action will never be able to implement the redistribution of life chances that Rawls feels is called for by distributive justice. Yet it is also true that in a society without affirmative action inequalities would be distributed even less in favor of the disadvantaged. Although not a panacea, affirmative action represents a marginal policy shift toward Rawlsian justice—if discrimination and disadvantage are important factors in labor market outcomes, university admissions, and housing decisions.

Conclusion

Even if we feel that affirmative action can be justified under a contractarian framework, we need to consider whether alternative policies might better reach our goals. Proponents of affirmative action argue primarily that the policy compensates for past wrongs and creates a more equitable distribution of wealth. Yet if these are noble goals, society would be better served by separate, complementing policies specifically tailored to separate and to redistribute. Affirmative action is hard pressed to achieve both of these goals efficiently.

Conservatives are clear in their stance on affirmative action. Philosophically, they have shifted toward an ahistorical libertarian conception of justice. Grass-roots organizing is being carried out by mass media icons like Rush Limbaugh and Howard Stern, and their popularity implies that the American public is impressed with the apparently principled stance of affirmative action conservatives. The ahistoricism of this stance may appeal to a nation that enjoys happy illusions about its past.

Progressives have yet to articulate a clear moral vision of equal force. The rigor and intuitive appeal of contractarian justice establishes it as a philosophical perspective around which progressives could anchor policy recommendations. By appealing to Americans' sense of justice as fairness, calling for a set of complementing policies with broadly tailored benefits that would *replace* affirmative action, and standing staunchly behind those policies and their philosophical perspective, progressives could steal current conservative momentum.

Notes

1. Nicolaus Mills, ed., *Debating Affirmative Action* (n.p., n.d.) p. 27.
2. Rosenfeld, *Affirmative Action and Justice: A Philosophical and Constitutional Inquiry* (New Haven: Yale University Press), p. 97.
3. Throughout his book, Rosenfeld fails to address the place of women, Latinos, Asians, or homosexuals within affirmative action.
4. Egalitarians may also differ in their definition of equality or equity.
5. Alan Goldman, *Justice and Reverse Discrimination* (Princeton University Press, 1979), p. 39.
6. Jonathan Freedland, "The Right Stuff," *Guardian*, January 31, 1995, p. T2.
7. Alan Bernstein, "Libertarian Candidate Seeks End to Income Tax," *Houston Chronicle*, August 8, 1994, p. A13.
8. There is good reason to believe that both firms and universities would continue affirmative action programs in the absence of government regulation, at least for the foreseeable future. "Affirmative Action: Why Bosses Like It," *Economist*, March 11-17, 1995, p. 29, and Joann Mitchell, affirmative action officer of Princeton University, interviewed Spring 1995.
9. Freedland, "The Right Stuff," p. T2.
10. Hugh Davis Graham, *The Civil Rights Era: Origins and Development of National Policy, 1960-1972* (New York: Oxford University Press, 1990), p. 327.
11. John Rawls, *A Theory of Justice* (Cambridge, Mass.: Harvard University Press, 1971), p. 4.
12. Ibid., p. 60.
13. Ibid., p. 302.
14. Jack Greenberg is, to my knowledge, the first to have made this observation in the context of the affirmative action debate.
15. This assertion depends in large degree, of course, on the efficacy of affirmative action. One might well argue that ineffective affirmative action programs would *not* satisfy Rawlsian criteria of fairness, because they would not, in effect, increase opportunities for the least advantaged.

References

"Affirmative Action: Why Bosses Like It," *Economist*, March 11, 1995, p. 29.

Alter, Jonathan. "Affirmative Ambivalence: Why the Mushy Middle Is Where the Action Should Be," *Newsweek*, March 27, 1995, p. 26.

Bernstein, Alan. "Libertarian Candidate Seeks End to Income Tax," *Houston Chronicle*, August 8, 1994, p. A13.

Bittker, Boris I. *The Case for Black Reparations.* New York: Random House, 1973.

Cahn, Steven M., ed. *Affirmative Action and the University: A Philosophical Inquiry.* Philadelphia: Temple University Press, 1993.

Citizens' Commission on Civil Rights. *Affirmative Action to Open the Doors of Job Opportunity.* June 1984.

Clayton, Susan, and Faye Crosby. *Justice, Gender, and Affirmative Action.* Ann Arbor: University of Michigan Press, 1992.

Cohn, Bob, Bill Turque, and Martha Brant. "What about Women?" *Newsweek*, March 27, 1995, pp. 22-25.

Combs, Michael, and John Gruhl, eds., *Affirmative Action: Theory, Analysis, and Prospects.* Jefferson, N.C.: McFarland and Company, 1986.

Conyers, John, U.S. Congressman. Interview via telephone. April 26, 1995.

Cose, Ellis. "The Myth of Meritocracy" *Newsweek*, April 3, 1995, p. 34.

Dworkin, Ronald. "DeFunis v. Sweatt." In Marshall Cohen, Thomas Nagel, and Thomas Scanlon, eds., *Equality and Preferential Treatment.* Princeton: Princeton University Press, 1977, pp. 63-83.

Elledge, Paul, Bob Cohn, Tom Morganthau, Vern E. Smith, and Peter Annin. "Battleground Chicago." *Newsweek*, April 3, 1995, pp. 26-33.

Fineman, Howard. "Bob Dole's Surprising Kingmaker." *Newsweek*, March 27, 1995, p. 29.

———. "Race and Rage." *Newsweek*, April 3, 1995, p. 23-25.

Freedland, Jonathan. "The Right Stuff." *Guardian*, January 31, 1995, p. T2.

Fullilove v. Klutznick, 448 U.S. 448 (1980).

Galanter, Marc. *Law and the Backward Classes in India.* Delhi: Oxford University Press, 1984.

Goldman, Alan. "Affirmative Action." In Marshall Cohen, Thomas Nagel, and Thomas Scanlon, eds., *Equality and Preferential Treatment.* Princeton: Princeton University Press, 1977, pp. 192-209.

———. *Justice and Reverse Discrimination.* Princeton: Princeton University Press, 1979.

Graham, Hugh Davis. *The Civil Rights Era: Origins and Development of National Policy, 1960-1972.* New York: Oxford University Press, 1990.

Greenberg, Jack. "Affirmative Action in Other Lands: A Summary." In *International Perspectives on Affirmative Action*, Rockefeller Foundation Conference Report, 1990.

Greene, Kathanne W. *Affirmative Action and Principles of Justice*. New York: Greenwood Press, 1989.

Gutmann, Amy. Interview. Spring 1995.

Hacker, Andrew. *Two Nations: Black and White, Separate, Hostile, Unequal*. New York: Ballantine Books, 1995.

Hazelwood School District v. United States, 433 U.S. 299 (1977).

Horne, Gerald. *Reversing Discrimination: The Case for Affirmative Action*. New York: International Publishers, 1992.

Kaufman-Rosen, Leslie with Claudia Kalb. "Holes in the Glass Ceiling Theory." *Newsweek*, March 27, 1995, pp. 24-25.

Kramer, Michael. "The Political Interest." *Time*, April 24, 1995, p. 52.

McCormick, John. "How to Help the 'Truly Disadvantaged,'" *Newsweek*, April 3, 1995, p. 33.

Mills, Nicolaus, ed., *Debating Affirmative Action*.

Mitchell, Joann. Interview. Spring 1995.

Nagel, Thomas. "Equal Treatment and Compensatory Discrimination." In Marshall Cohen, Thomas Nagel, and Thomas Scanlon, eds., *Equality and Preferential Treatment*. Princeton: Princeton University Press, 1977, pp. 3-18.

Podberesky v. Kirwan, Nos. 93-2527, 03-2585, 1994 WL 587092 (4th Cir. October 27, 1994).

Rawls, John. *A Theory of Justice*. Cambridge, Mass.: Harvard University Press, 1971.

Rosenfeld, Michel. *Affirmative Action and Justice: A Philosophical and Constitutional Inquiry*. New Haven: Yale University Press, 1991.

Rosenstiel, Thomas. "Politics, Oprah Style: Gingrich Struggles to Repair GOP Ruptures over Abortion, Term Limits and Taxes," *Newsweek*, March 27, 1995, p. 27.

Skelton, George. "An Issue Drawn in Black and White," *Los Angeles Times*, April 24, 1995, p. A3.

Sniderman, Paul, and Thomas Piazza. *The Scar of Race*. Cambridge, Mass.: Harvard University Press, 1993.

Stotts v. Memphis Fire Department, 858 F. 2d 289 (6th Cir. 1988).

Thomson, Judith Jarvis. "Preferential Hiring." In Marshall Cohen, Thomas Nagel, and Thomas Scanlon, eds., *Equality and Preferential Treatment*. Princeton: Princeton University Press, 1977, pp. 19-39.

United States v. Starrett City Association, 840 F. 2d 1096 (2d Cir. 1988).

United Steelworkers of America, AFL-CIO-CLC, v. Weber, 443 U.S. 193 (1979).

University of California Regents v. Bakke, 438 U.S. 265 (1978).

Wards Cove Packing Co. v. Atonio, 490 U.S. 642 (1989).

Washington, James, ed., *A Testament of Hope: The Essential Writings and Speeches of Martin Luther King, Jr.* San Francisco: Harper Collins, 1986.

"Washington Watch," *The San Francisco Examiner*, April 17, 1995, p. A2.

Wilson, William Julius. *The Truly Disadvantaged: The Inner City, the Underclass, and Public Policy.* Chicago: University of Chicago Press, 1987.

Wyzan, Michael L., ed., *The Political Economy of Ethnic Discrimination and Affirmative Action: A Comparative Perspective.* New York: Praeger, 1990.

Yoachum, Susan. *San Francisco Chronicle.* March 10, 1995, p. A1.

Chapter 6

Race-Exclusive Scholarships for Undergraduate Education

Jessica Malman

Struggling with a history of segregation and the present effects of racial discrimination, the United States is forced to address a glaring discrepancy between the ideal of a color-blind society and the reality of continued racial inequalities. This predicament may be most pressing in the system of higher education. More than forty years after the Supreme Court ordered states to offer equal educational opportunities to all students, postsecondary institutions remain relatively homogeneous and a college degree is out of reach for many African-American students. In an effort to address these problems, educators are employing race-exclusive scholarships, grant money reserved for students from particular racial groups. Some scholarships, such as those reserved for poor, African-American students or those for African-American students willing to attend predominantly white, historically segregated institutions, appear reasonable and potentially justifiable.[1] Such scholarships could help to increase enrollment and retention rates of disadvantaged African-American students. Other race-exclusive scholarships, however, benefit economically advantaged African-American students or essentially pay African-American students to maintain good grades.[2] As a result, race-exclusive scholarships have become the focus of legal and political controversy, involving educators, government entities, civil rights advocates, and students themselves.

Legal Framework

Title VI of the Civil Rights Act of 1964 provides that "no person in the United States shall, on the ground of race, color, or national origin, be excluded from participation in, be denied the benefits of, or be subjected to discrimination under any program or activity receiving Federal financial assistance."[3] Title VI applies to all private colleges and universities that receive federal funds and to all public postsecondary institutions.[4] On their face, Title VI regulations allow for "affirmative action:"

> In administering a program regarding which the recipient has previously discriminated against persons on the grounds of race, color, or national origin, the recipient must take affirmative action to overcome the effects of past discrimination. Even in the absences of such prior discrimination, a recipient in administering a program may take affirmative action to overcome the effects of conditions which resulted in limiting participation by persons of a particular race, color, or national origin.[5]

The term "affirmative action," however, is ambiguous. In 1964 the phrase was used "as a critique of merely passive nondiscrimination," which has the effect of maintaining the status quo.[6] But it remains unclear whether such an affirmative action mandate requires more severe penalties for discrimination, more aggressive recruiting of minorities, or preferences for minorities.

The Supreme Court has held that affirmative action measures that utilize racial classifications include "suspect" classifications and are therefore subject to "strict scrutiny" by the courts.[7] Programs that use such classifications can only be justified if they pass a two-pronged test: (1) they must further a "compelling governmental interest," and (2) they must be "narrowly tailored" to serve that interest.[8] In the context of education, the Court has acknowledged the government's compelling interest in remedying past and present discrimination on the basis of race.[9] Furthermore, the Supreme Court recently ruled that a state with a history of *de jure* segregation in its system of higher education has an affirmative obligation to ensure that no vestiges of that *de jure* system have a discriminatory effect on the present system.[10] Although it is not necessary for an institution to wait for a formal finding of discrimination by a court, administrative agency, or legislature, an institution must provide a "strong basis in evidence for its conclusion that remedial action [is] necessary."[11] This evidence must be specific to the particular domain in which race-conscious measures are being taken.[12]

The Supreme Court has also held that the advancement of student body diversity is a compelling government interest.[13] In *Regents of the University of California v. Bakke*, the Court held that a college has a First Amendment right to seek a "robust exchange of ideas" by diversifying its student body.[14] Speaking for the majority, Justice Powell explained:

> Academic freedom, though not a specifically enumerated constitutional right, long has been viewed as a special concern of the First Amendment. The freedom of a university to make its own judgments as to education includes the selection of its student body. . . . [I]t is not too much to say that the "nation's future depends upon leaders trained through wide exposure" to the ideas and mores of students as diverse as this Nation of many peoples.[15]

In several subsequent decisions involving race-conscious programs, the Court has cited this portion of the opinion with approval.[16]

If an institution proves that a race-conscious measure aims to further a compelling government interest, then the institution must prove that the program is "specifically and narrowly framed to accomplish that purpose."[17] In several instances the Supreme Court has upheld race-exclusive programs as narrowly tailored to remedial goals. In the context of higher education, the Court has not "required remedial plans to be limited to the least restrictive means of implementation," but has likened the choice of remedial programs to a "balancing process."[18] The Court has explained that the appropriateness of race-conscious remedies is determined by looking at several factors, including "the necessity for relief and the efficacy of alternative remedies; the flexibility and duration of the relief, including the availability of waiver provisions; the relationship of the numerical goals to the relevant . . . market; and the impact of the relief on the rights of third parties."[19]   In terms of this last consideration, the Court has upheld "limited and properly tailored" programs which "impose a diffuse burden, often foreclosing only one of several opportunities" as long as they do "not impose an *undue* burden on nonminorities."[20]

The authoritative reasoning in cases concerning diversity comes from the *Bakke* opinion, in which Justice Powell held that a set-aside of a fixed number of places for minority students was not a necessary means of attaining a truly diverse student body.[21]   Powell explained that the use of an admissions quota to attain a diverse student body misconceived the nature of the government's interest in diversity: "It is not an interest in simple ethnic diversity. . . . The diversity that furthers a compelling state interest encompasses a far broader array of qualifications and characteristics of which racial or ethnic origin is but a single though important interest."[22]   Powell did, however, find that race and ethnic background could be one of many factors considered in the admissions decision. Powell explained that a program which considers minority status as a "plus" is "flexible enough to consider all pertinent elements of diversity in light of the particular qualifications of each applicant."[23]   Although the *Bakke* decision indicates that diversity may be furthered with race-conscious policies, the Supreme Court has never upheld a race-conscious measure solely on the basis of diversity enhancement.

Since the Supreme Court has not addressed the constitutionality of race-exclusive scholarships, it has been left to the U.S. Department of Education's Office for Civil Rights (OCR) to devise guidelines for colleges and universities that comply with the Supreme Court's decisions.[24]   Until December 1990 OCR approved student financial aid programs based on race or ethnicity when used to overcome minority underrepresentation at a postsecondary institution.[25]   After the *Bakke* decision, OCR concluded that it was improper to extend the decision on admissions to all racial set-asides at universities, saying: "Admissions quotas, the policy at issue in Bakke, unlike many other policies, may result in the exclusion of an individual from a university on the basis of race or national origin. The availability of a particular financial aid program does not have such a far-reaching effect."[26]   Accordingly, OCR required only that an institution show that past discrimination at the school produced underrepresention of the group in question or that the school's current practices or conditions result in limited participation by the targeted group.[27]

The Political Arena

In 1990, the use of race-exclusive scholarships became a highly controversial issue. In an unprecedented statement, Michael L. Williams, assistant secretary of the U.S. Department of Education's Office for Civil Rights, claimed that Title VI regulations prohibited recipients of federal funds from "denying, restricting, or providing different or segregated financial aid or other program benefits on the basis of race, color or national origin [unless] mandated to do so by a court or administrative order, corrective action plan or settlement agreement."[28] Williams, a conservative African American, had served as a policy analyst in the 1988 Bush campaign. A former Justice Department official, he is known for his aggressive prosecution of racial discrimination cases and for his firm opposition, on philosophical grounds, to many programs that grant preferential treatment to minorities.[29]

Williams insisted that he had not formally consulted with White House officials, and claimed that his statement was merely an application of neutral legal principles.[30] His decision, however, had far-reaching political implications. The announcement came at a time when civil rights groups were particularly critical of President Bush, whose recent veto of the Civil Rights Bill of 1990 was taken as a symbol of his opposition to affirmative action.[31] The same week that Williams's scholarship statement was announced, Senator Phil Gramm (R-Tex.) and Representative Newt Gingrich (R-Ga.), two influential conservatives, urged the GOP to press the anti-affirmative action theme embodied in Bush's veto. In addition, William J. Bennett, Bush's then candidate to head the Republican National Committee, announced that he was prepared to challenge the Democrats on the issue of affirmative action.[32]

The OCR's announcement drew sharp criticism from numerous civil rights groups, academic institutions, and business interests, setting off what was described as a "political bomb."[33] Civil rights organizations accused the Bush administration of race baiting, "stirring up a race war" because "there [was] political capital to be gained."[34] Academics were angered by the federal government's contradictory messages, telling them to increase minority participation but denying them the means to do so.[35] Students joined the protest, warning that the policy would have a "chilling effect" on all minority education programs.[36] The U.S. Chamber of Commerce and the Council on

Competitiveness also urged the department to reconsider its guidelines in light of population trends that made it necessary to educate more minority professionals.[37]

Although the administration claimed to be neutral, presidential aides confirmed that the explosive issue had sent the White House into a "madhouse" of debate.[38] Prodded by the administration, Williams modified his statement of policy two weeks later, but the heart of the original prohibition remained.[39] In the turbulent political climate, civil rights advocates accused the federal government of abandoning its commitment to the higher education of minority students.[40] Furthermore, because Williams ignored the proper policymaking procedure, there was little discussion of his suggestion that race-exclusive scholarships be replaced with programs employing race-neutral criteria to target disadvantaged students or with programs using race as a "positive factor amongst similarly qualified individuals."[41]

When the new secretary of education, Lamar Alexander, came into office in February 1991, he called the whole controversy a "mud puddle" which sent the wrong "signal" to minorities.[42] He immediately put a hold on any changes to OCR's original scholarship policy and promised to clear up the issue.

The Pursuit of Information

Although Williams's statement was denounced, his proposals stimulated discussion and generated new data on minority scholarships.[43] It appears that scholarships for specific minority groups come from a variety of sources, including the federal government, several state governments, public and private colleges and universities, and various private organizations. Congress has authorized the use of federal funds for several minority-exclusive programs such as Minority Access to Research Careers (MARC), which provides research awards to minority students at colleges with a substantial level of minority enrollments, and Minority Honors Training and Industrial Assistance (MHTIA), which provides scholarships to needy minority honors students.[44] According to a 1989-90 survey by the National Association of State Scholarship and Grant Programs (NASSGP), nine states have established scholarships, grants, or loan-forgiveness programs for minority students regardless of need, and six states have minority scholarships and grants that take need into account.[45] The Internal Revenue Service also acknowledges the legitimate use of minority-exclusive aid by allowing tax-exempt organizations to maintain funds for scholarships and fellowships that are restricted to minorities as long as their financial aid programs, as a whole, are nondiscriminatory.[46]

A variety of private organizations offer scholarships to minority students. For example, the Jackie Robinson Foundation provides educational scholarships of up to $5,000 for African-American students with "strong capabilities but limited financial resources."[47] African-American students of any income level may receive $1,400 renewable awards from the Herbert Lehman Foundation and the NAACP Legal Defense Fund. To qualify, an individual must be an "outstanding student" planning to attend an institution with less than 8 percent African-American enrollment; preference is given to schools in the South that were once segregated.[48] There is also a "compensatory program" run by the National Achievement Scholarship Program for Outstanding Negro Students, offering up to eight hundred awards between $250 and $2,000 to African-American students based on their PSAT/NMSQT scores.[49] In addition, the National Merit Scholarship Corporation (NMSC) has, since 1964, conducted the National Achievement Scholarship Program for Outstanding Negro Students. This program also provides grants to African-American students based on their PSAT/NMSQT scores.[50]

Results from the College Board's Annual Survey of Colleges indicate that there are a number of minority-exclusive scholarships offered by colleges and universities. In 1990-91, about 24 percent of responding institutions offered minority scholarships without regard to financial need.[51] The percentage of respondents offering need-based minority scholarships was 27 percent.[52] It is estimated that there are about 5,150 minority scholarship programs in the United States, serving approximately 35,000 students.[53] Of these programs, an estimated 740 use minority status as the sole criteria for eligibility.[54] Although minority-targeted scholarships are prevalent, they account for a small percentage of all student aid. It appears that less than 5 percent of minority students receive grants exclusive to race.[55] National surveys also indicate that the estimated $138 million awarded on the basis of race or ethnicity adds up to only 3.3 percent of all scholarship money, and race-exclusive awards constitute just 0.3 percent of all allocations.[56]

Minority scholarships at different institutions have various qualification criteria and funding sources. The College Board found that 46 percent of race-exclusive awards come from the institution's own funds (endowment and tuition), as opposed to federal and state aid or donations from outside sources.[57] For private schools, institutional resources support about 78 percent of the scholarships designated for minority students.[58] Even if funding comes from outside sources, the funds are usually designated exclusively for minority scholarships by the institutions themselves.[59]

Some race-exclusive scholarships are provided regardless of need. For example, since 1990, Florida Atlantic University has offered free tuition to every African-American student admitted.[60] At Penn State and the Miami-Dade Community College, race-exclusive programs are designed to motivate African-American students. Penn State's Black Incentive Grant pays $550 to each African-American student who maintains a grade-point average between 2.5 and 2.74 and the Black Achievement Award pays $1,000 to those who maintain a grade-point average above 2.75.[61] Miami-Dade seeks to encourage minority students with its offer to refund minority students' tuition if, upon graduation, they are unable to find a job in their field of study.[62]

In addition to minority status, most programs establish other criteria for awarding funds. Some scholarships are dependent on need. For example, the University of Nebraska designates some of its need-based state aid for minority-exclusive scholarships.[63] Similarly, Earlham College in Indiana tries to recruit needy African-American, Hispanic, and Native American residents of the state by offering to replace their federal loans with grant aid.[64] Colleges and universities may also provide merit scholarships to recruit high-achieving minority students. Transylvania University, in Kentucky, provides renewable scholarships ranging from $500 to $4,000 to minority students demonstrating high academic ability and financial need.[65] At Rutgers University, New Jersey's state university, over two hundred minority students receive the James Dickenson Carr Scholarship. Named after the university's first African-American graduate, the program provides about two-thirds of the annual cost of tuition, room, and board to minority high school graduates who finish in the top 10 percent of their high school class and score at least 1,100 on their SATs.[66] Other prestigious universities, including the University of Virginia, Duke University, Washington University in St. Louis, and Rice University, also use minority-exclusive merit scholarships to entice high-achieving African-American students.[67]

Recent Controversies over Race-Exclusive Scholarships

After a review of the issue, Secretary of Education Richard Riley issued revised policy guidelines for race-exclusive financial aid in 1994.[68] The revised principles permit race-exclusive financial aid when the funds have been authorized by Congress, when private funds are distributed directly from a private funding source, or when an institution uses private or public funds to remedy past discrimination.[69] An institution may also use private or public money for race-exclusive aid when the programs are "narrowly tailored to the goal of diversity."[70] To determine if such diversity efforts are "narrowly tailored," the department considers whether there is a race-neutral means or a "less extensive or intrusive use of race" to achieve that goal.[71] The department also looks at the extent, flexibility, and regular review of the race-exclusive scholarships, and it questions whether the awards have a "sufficiently small or diffuse" effect on students who do not qualify.[72]

OCR's new guidelines appear quite permissive in comparison with Williams's 1990 proposal, which would have eliminated all race-exclusive scholarships. The department not only condones but encourages race-exclusive scholarships. In a letter to 7,500 colleges and universities participating in federal student loan programs, Riley endorsed race-exclusive scholarships as a "valuable tool for providing equal opportunity and for enhancing a diverse educational environment for the benefit of all students."[73]

Civil rights groups have applauded the Clinton administration for what they perceive to be a restoration of minority education to its rightful status as a legal and moral imperative. An editorial in the *Sacramento Observer* proclaimed, "Racial justice is served through the provision of educational assistance and scholarships for students who come from communities that have been marginalized, exploited and oppressed."[74] Meanwhile, critics view the new scholarship policy as an "unconscionable" statement which is "in violation of the spirit of the Constitution."[75]

Disagreement Among the Courts

Those who oppose the department's position see a possibility for change in light of the Supreme Court's recent behavior with respect to affirmative action. In June 1995, in the case of *Adarand Constructors, Inc. v. Pena,* the Court ruled on the constitutionality of a federal program that gave federal highway construction contractors a 1.5 percent bonus for using minority-owned subcontractors. In its decision, the Court rejected precedent that would subject federal affirmative action programs to more relaxed judicial review than those of the states. Instead the Court declared that any federal programs which use racial classifications will be subject to the same "strict scrutiny" test applicable to state and local programs.[76] Although the Court stopped short of declaring racial preferences unconstitutional, critics of affirmative action are looking to *Pena* as a virtual repudiation of such practices.

The Court maintains that "strict scrutiny" is not "fatal in fact," but its recent action in the case of *Poberesky v. Kirwin* has opened the door for lower courts to use exceptionally rigid strict scrutiny tests for race-exclusive programs.[77] In May 1995, the Court refused to review the *Poberesky* case, in which the Appeals Court for the Fourth Circuit used a particularly rigorous strict scrutiny test to declare a race-exclusive scholarship program at the University of Maryland unconstitutional.[78] The suit was brought by Daniel Poberesky when he was denied one of the university's race-exclusive merit scholarships. Poberesky, a Hispanic student with a high school GPA of 4.0 and a score of 1,340 on his SATs, did not qualify for the Banneker program, scholarships reserved for African-American students with at least a 3.0 GPA and a score of 900 on the SATs.[79] Poberesky contended that the state's refusal to consider him for this scholarship violated Title VI and the fourteenth amendment.[80]

The appeals court found that the university did not have sufficient evidence of present effects of past discrimination to justify the use of race-exclusive remedial measures and that the program was not narrowly tailored to achieve its stated objectives.[81] The court was not persuaded by the university's vast collection of evidence purportedly showing that the present underrepresentation of African-American students resulted from past discrimination at the university. The university provided survey data demonstrating the poor reputation of the university within the African-American community, but the court dismissed this evidence, explaining that if poor reputation is tied solely to knowledge of past discrimination, then "as long as there are people who have access to history books, there will be programs such as this one."[82] The court also dismissed evidence of racial hostility on campus, claiming that the stream of racial incidents there did not necessarily stem from historic discrimination at the university. The court explained that evidence of "present societal discrimination . . . cannot be the basis for supporting a race-conscious remedy" at the University of Maryland.[83]   When the university offered statistical data revealing the underrepresentation and the low retention rates of African-American students, the court failed to see a causal connection between these statistical disparities and past discrimination at the school.[84]

Even if it were to accept this evidence, the court found that the Banneker program was "not narrowly tailored to remedy the underrepresentation and attrition problems" of African-American students at the University of Maryland.[85]   The court questioned the appropriateness of a program which aimed to attract only high-achieving African-Americans saying, "High achievers, whether African-American or not, are not the group against which the University discriminated in the past."[86]   The court also questioned the narrowness of a program that included non-Maryland residents.[87]   Finally, the court criticized the university for its failure to show "that it has tried, without success, any race-neutral solutions" to its problems.[88]

Technically, the Supreme Court's denial of review means that the *Poberesky* decision will only apply to the circuit court's jurisdiction. Many supporters and opponents of race-exclusive scholarships, however, view the Court's action as an example of its conservative shift and an indication of the fate that will befall similar affirmative action cases.   On the other hand, some supporters of race-exclusive scholarships are encouraged by the action of other federal courts that seem to deem such scholarships both legal and effective. Only four months after the *Poberesky* decision, another federal district court endorsed the use of race-based scholarships to diversify Mississippi's system of public higher education. After many years of desegregation suits, this court ordered the state to finance scholarships for white students to induce them to attend the state's historically black colleges.[89] Judge Neal B. Biggers, Jr., found that the use of separate admissions standards for Mississippi's historically white colleges and its historically black colleges was perpetuating the vestiges of past *de jure* segregation and viewed the white-only scholarships as an effective integration mechanism. Janell Byrd, attorney for the NAACP Legal Defense and Educational Fund and an attorney for the state in *Poberesky,* points out that Judge Biggers's demand for race-exclusive scholarships is "bizarre and ironic" in light of the recent Maryland ruling.[90]

Given the discrepancies between federal courts, the Supreme Court may be forced to make a definitive ruling on the legality of race-exclusive scholarships. To do so, the Court will have to consider whether race-exclusive scholarships further a compelling government interest and whether these programs are a justifiable means of achieving the purported goals. Unfortunately, discussions up to this point have been dominated by anxious liberals alarmed by recent civil rights struggles and fervent conservatives determined to abolish affirmative action.

Evaluation

To date, there has been no comprehensive study that systematically analyzes the efficacy of race-exclusive scholarships. There is a great deal of literature, however, examining the connection between financial aid and student outcomes. These studies can be supplemented with anecdotal evidence to predict some of the effects of race-exclusive scholarships. I will focus on race-exclusive scholarships reserved for African-American students, rather than all minority-targeted aid, for two reasons. First, the Supreme Court has specifically identified African Americans as a group which, because of our nation's history of segregation, may be the legitimate recipient of targeted programs. Second, African Americans are the group for which there are the most extensive and reliable data on educational decisions and educational attainment.

Justifications for Race-Exclusive Scholarships

There are two government interests that race-exclusive scholarships may further: improving the educational attainment of African Americans and enhancing the diversity of undergraduate education.   The undereducation of the African-American community is no longer merely a problem of social justice; it is an alarming deficit that threatens the economic future of our nation.[91] Population trends and changes in the U.S. economy indicate that African-American youths represent a "pipeline for the future of higher education and for the workforce."[92] African Americans are becoming an increasing proportion of the U.S. population. Between 1980 and 1990, the African-American population increased by 6.8 percent while the white population decreased by 4.8 percent.[93] By the year 2000, the African-American population is expected to increase another 7.8 percent while the white population should fall another 3.9 percent. As a result, 13.4 percent of the population will be African American and 12 percent of the U.S. labor force between the ages of twenty-four and fifty-six will be African American.[94] Since the job market is demanding workers with greater educational preparation, the educational attainment of African Americans will be essential to the nation's productivity.[95]

Given the current level of African-American education, the supply of educated African Americans is not likely to meet the demands of the labor market. Although the absolute number of African Americans in undergraduate education has increased in the last decade, the college-going rate of African Americans (the percentage of high school graduates who enroll in college) has fallen increasingly behind that of whites.[96] Between 1982 and 1994, the absolute enrollment numbers for African Americans increased 27 percent.[97] The white-black gap in college-going rates increased significantly, however, from a difference of 18.2 percent in 1982 to a difference of 24.9 percent in 1992.[98] As a consequence, African Americans have come to represent a declining proportion of all enrolled students.[99] The increase in enrollment numbers reflects the growth of the African-American population rather than an increase in the percentage of African Americans who avail themselves of expanded educational opportunities or have greater access to higher education.[100] Perhaps even more alarming is the continually low graduation rates of African-American students. From 1980 to 1993, the six-year graduation rate of African-American students remained at about 32 percent, compared with 56 percent for whites.[101]

The government should also have a legitimate interest in the pursuit of a diverse educational community. Postsecondary institutions are expected to prepare students for participation in the economic, political and social life of the nation. Two trends are noteworthy. The first is the diversification of the U.S population and labor force. The nonwhite share of the labor force increased 18.4 percent between 1970 and 1985, and is expected to increase another 29 percent by the year 2000.[102] The second trend is the globalization of the economy. Developments in telecommunications and transportation have enhanced worldwide economic and political relations to such an extent that, as the Brookings Institution explains, "the market for U.S. goods and services has grown to include not only 50 states, but also the 178 countries of the world."[103] Given these major changes, it is imperative that students learn to relate to and work with a diverse array of people; community diversity has therefore become an important measure of school quality.[104]

Research suggests that monetary aid has a significant impact on African-American educational attainment and recruitment. Studies indicate that a grant or scholarship will increase the probability that an African-American student will enroll in and graduate from an undergraduate institution. According to the Citizen's Commission on Civil Rights, 45 percent of African-American students and 40 percent of low-income students cite cost as the factor most affecting their decision not to go to college.[105] In an analysis by Alexander Astin and Carolyn Inouve, increases in the level of grant aid per student were associated with increased enrollments of low- and middle-income students.[106] Another study by the Council for the Advancement and Support of Education (CASE) found that misinformation about college costs is often the reason why students decide not to go to college.[107] The availability of financial aid also offers students the opportunity to attend higher-cost institutions that they would otherwise not consider. Eric Hanushek concluded that "the largest impact of aid is probably in insuring choice among different institutions. [It] allows students without substantial resources to consider attending four-year colleges . . . instead of . . . two-year colleges and the lowest cost alternatives."[108]

Researchers also report that grants and scholarships can improve undergraduate retention rates. After academic difficulties, financial difficulties are the most often cited reason for dropping out of college.[109] As an example of the significance of student aid, it has been found that, other things being equal, the availability of an additional $1,000 in grant aid per semester will increase the likelihood of graduation from a two-year college by 58 percent and from a four-year college by 53.6 percent.[110] At private institutions, monetary grants have an even stronger effect on persistence.[111] Surveying the data on student aid and college persistence, Murdock concluded that aid enables "the low-income student to persist at a level almost equal to that of middle- and upper-income students."[112]

As a recruitment tool, race-exclusive scholarships seem to be quite effective.[113] For low-income students of any race, financial aid has a profound affect on school choice. According to a 1991 survey conducted by UCLA and the American Council on Education, "Low-income freshmen are more than twice as likely to cite the offer of financial aid as a very important reason for selecting the institution where they were enrolled than [are] affluent freshmen."[114] For African-American students, college costs and monetary incentives are two of the factors most likely to convince them to attend a predominantly white institution over a predominantly black institution.[115]

Institutions also use race-exclusive aid to recruit academically talented African Americans. The scarcity of high-achieving African-American students has caused fierce competition among the colleges and universities that want to attract them.[116] Both survey research and anecdotal evidence indicate the effectiveness of monetary incentives on the college choice of high-achieving African-American students. A 1991 study by Stammats Communications surveyed college-bound African-American high school juniors with a GPA of 2.65 or more.[117] Since most of the respondents had GPAs between 3.0 and 3.79 and came from stable, two-parent families, these students would appear to be those that colleges and universities would vie for.[118] The survey found that, after college reputation and range of majors, the availability of financial aid and total cost of attendance were the most often cited reasons for choosing a particular undergraduate institution.[119] Interviews with African-American high school students also reveal the critical impact of money. One student chose to attend the University of South Carolina over Stanford or Harvard because South Carolina offered him a race-exclusive, full scholarship.[120] Similarly, a high-achieving African-American student-body president in Houston declared, "I'll go to the school that gives me the most money."[121]

The evidence suggests that race-exclusive scholarships advance the goals of African-American educational advancement and campus diversity in specific ways. They increase the number of African-American students opting to go to college, graduating from college, and choosing to attend colleges where African Americans are underrepresented. Numerical accomplishments, however, may be deceiving, for they do not necessarily correspond to meaningful, qualitative improvements.

Limits

Despite their apparent utility, race-exclusive scholarships have relatively limited advantages. Moreover, the implementation of such programs may have some unintended, yet deleterious, consequences for disadvantaged African-American students.

Race-Exclusive Scholarships Perpetuate a Low-Income Disadvantage

Evidence suggests that race-exclusive scholarships perpetuate the disadvantage faced by low-income students in need of financial aid. Given that African-American students are much more likely than whites to come from low-income families, they have been disproportionately harmed by recent changes in federal financial aid programs that have reduced available grants.[122] The Pell Grant, the major federal need-based program long relied on by needy students, plummeted in real value throughout the 1980s.[123] The average Pell Grant, which made up 76 percent of the average college cost in 1979, formed only 21 percent of the average college cost in 1994.[124] Meanwhile, virtually all of the increases in federal student aid went to student loans, rather than grants, which tend to benefit middle- and upper-income students.[125] Student loans do little to help low-income students whose families are less likely to take on large, long-term debts to finance higher education.[126] The Citizens' Commission on Civil Rights explained:

> It is hardly surprising that an 18-year-old black high school graduate would be reluctant to borrow ten thousand dollars for college when that is the amount his family has to meet his expenses for an entire year. Thus, the increasing emphasis on loans rather than grants during the past years has been seen as adversely affecting low-income students and thus many minorities in higher education.[127]

The recent focus on student loans rather than grants also threatens persistence levels of African-American students. Although grant aid improves the likelihood of graduation, student loans have been found to have no effect or a negative effect on student retention.[128] Unlike loan programs, work-study has been found to improve one's likelihood of graduating because jobs provide students more opportunities to interact with the campus community.[129] Low-income and African-American students, however, those students who most need help integrating into the community, are underrepresented as recipients of work-study jobs.[130]

Race-exclusive scholarships will not compensate for the disadvantages that low-income students face in the federal financial aid system. When a low-income student receives a special scholarship, her calculated need (the number used to determine the amount of a federal grant) is reduced by the amount of the grant. Thus the true beneficiaries of race-exclusive grants are the relatively well-off African-American students who do not qualify for need-based grants.

Middle-class students also tend to have an advantage over low-income or undereducated students who face a significant information barrier. Information barriers especially hinder African-American youths, who disproportionately come from low-income and/or underinformed families.[131] Several studies indicate that low-income and undereducated families lack access to information about the variety institutional and government assistance programs or how to apply for them.[132] A New Jersey study conducted in 1989 found that over 25 percent of students from families with incomes below $6,000 did not apply for aid, primarily because they lacked information or assistance with the applications.[133] An important study conducted by the Council for the Advancement and Support of Education found that misinformation about financial aid often affects students' enrollment decisions.[134] The study found that 22 percent of junior and senior high school students thought that aid was only available from the federal government, 49 percent thought students could not use aid to go to a more expensive private school, and 29 percent thought that students with average grades could not apply for financial assistance.[135] Even if students are aware of financial aid opportunities, they may not understand the application process. A study conducted by the College Entrance Examination Board found that low-income African Americans were often impeded by complicated forms, complex eligibility requirements, and the need for multiple records.[136] The result of this information barrier is that many needy students, who are disproportionately African American, are not informed of financial aid opportunities early enough in the college search process to raise their college degree aspirations and therefore increase enrollments.[137] Observing these shortcomings of student aid programs, Gary Orfield concludes, "Obviously it is a serious mistake to assume that, simply because a series of programs can work together to help a student, that low-income families and their schools will actually be able to make them work."[138]

Race-Exclusive Scholarships Achieve Only Limited Diversity

Race-exclusive scholarships are an effective means of attracting African-American students; they therefore help to increase the number of African-American students on a campus. Increased attendance, however, may not necessarily result in increased campus diversity. As suggested above, race-exclusive scholarships tend to benefit students from middle-class backgrounds, a group that is already well represented on college campuses.[139]   There is even anecdotal evidence indicating that much scholarship money is spent on students who are already economically or socially advantaged. For example, five recipients of the Jerome Holland Scholarship, a $10,000 merit award for African-American students at the University of Virginia, came from families with annual incomes greater than $100,000.[140]   Several minority-targeted scholarships are also obtained by African-American students at prestigious private schools like Phillips Academy, a prep school in Massachusetts.[141]

William Bowen, the former president of Princeton University, and Neil Rudenstine, former provost of Princeton and now president of Harvard University, argue that race-exclusive scholarships are the most efficient use of diversity-enhancement funds even if they go to middle-class students.[142]   They claim that minority-exclusive scholarships send a positive "signal" to other minority students, indicating that an institution welcomes minorities and is committed to retaining them. Anthony Catanese, the president of Florida Atlantic University, agrees that designated funds serve as proof that an institution is "serious about recruiting minority students."[143]   The claim that race-exclusive scholarships help to create "a positive, caring atmosphere" for minority students seems a bit dubious, however, since these awards are offered by precisely those institutions that continue to be perceived as unsupportive or unwelcoming.[144]

The "signal" argument is also weak because race-exclusive scholarships tend to be offered as part of a much larger, ambitious recruitment effort. A school may encourage minority students to apply with targeted mailings, advertisements in minority newspapers, and/or visits to high schools with high minority populations. To attract lower-income students, schools often provide simplified, encouraging information about the variety of financial aid opportunities available in addition to race-exclusive scholarships.[145]   Furthermore, those schools reporting great strides in African-American student retention have coupled their race-exclusive scholarships with other programs that encourage cultural expression and cultural appreciation. For example, several institutions have made a visible effort to invest in multicultural centers, seek out minority faculty members, and diversify their curricula.[146]   Acknowledging the limited contribution of race-exclusive scholarships, one university administrator insisted that she would give up all 197 race-exclusive scholarships at her institution in return for greater efforts in these other areas.[147] The reality is that race-exclusive scholarships are but one of many options open to a college or university that wants to send out the right "signal."

Scholarships for middle-class African-American students are also justified by the argument explaining that institutions are "bidding up the price" of African-American students, thereby increasing the value of students whose social contribution has been historically undervalued.[148] The problem with this "value argument" is that it assumes that a student's contribution to campus diversity can be measured by the color of her skin when, in fact, diversity enhancement means much more than that. The goal is a diverse community; this sort of diversity is important because it improves the academic, social, and interpersonal experiences of the entire campus community, including both minority and majority students. To effectuate diversity, minority students must not only attend a school; they must remain there and participate in the community. Minority student retention depends on a student's perception of an institution's ability to serve his or her personal, academic, and social needs, in addition to financial needs.[149] Thus when students are convinced by monetary incentives to attend a school that would not otherwise appeal to them, they tend to be unhappy with their decision. They are therefore less likely to contribute to the campus community or to reap the benefits of the undergraduate experience.[150] As a result, the monetary value of a race-exclusive scholarship may have little relationship to true diversity enhancement.

Race-Exclusive Scholarships Exacerbate
Racial Tensions on Campus

Race-exclusive scholarships may, in fact, be undermining African-American students' ability to become part of or promote a diverse community, for race-exclusive policies tend to exacerbate racial tensions on campus. Michael L. Davis, director of the Minority Information Center at the University of Texas, is concerned that monetary set-asides for minority students have stirred up an "undercurrent of antagonism."[151] He explains that white students often resent the "special treatment" given to African-American students, who appear less needy than many white students.[152] On some campuses, anger over race-exclusive policies has prompted students to form White Student Unions (WSUs) to protest these practices.[153] For example, when the University of Nebraska at Lincoln established a $1 million endowment to be used solely for minority scholarships, a group called the White Organization of Concerned Students posted fliers in protest and tried to organize a demonstration.[154]   At the University of Florida in Gainsville, a WSU was founded by Mark Wright, an electrical engineering major who opposed the fact that almost half of the engineering scholarships at Gainsville were reserved for African Americans or Native Americans. Having served in the air force to put himself through college, Wright explained his resentment: "I have a 3.6 average, and I didn't get a scholarship. I have black engineering friends with less who get $2,000 Westinghouse scholarships."[155]   White students are trying to organize WSUs on dozens of other campuses where they perceive race-exclusive programs as "racist and discriminating against whites."[156] Although WSUs represent a minority of students' opinions, their presence is indicative of fermenting tensions. The National Association of Scholars (NAS) regrets that educational practices have so contributed to this regression of racial attitudes. In a special advertisement taken out in the *Chronicle of Higher Education*, the NAS severely criticized educators for fostering racial tensions: "Educators have failed to reassess policies and practices that, far from promoting tolerance and fairness, are undermining them."[157]

Race-exclusive scholarships appear to have several disadvantages. They provide limited opportunities for students from low-income or undereducated families and serve to lure predominantly middle-class African-American students to otherwise unattractive campuses. Furthermore, the mere existence of racial preferences can threaten the academic achievement and campus diversity these scholarships are intended to promote.

Conclusions and Recommendations

Analytical and anecdotal evidence suggests that race-exclusive scholarships can help both to increase African-American enrollment and retention rates and to lure African-American students to predominantly white colleges and universities. A reexamination of their efficacy, however, indicates that such scholarships appear to serve short-run, narrow interests and tend to obfuscate the deeper or broader problems hindering African-American students and campus diversity. The federal government continues to encourage or provide special-interest scholarships instead of addressing the deficiencies of the federal student aid program, and an information barrier continues to hinder low-income and undereducated students' access to financial aid. Meanwhile colleges and universities use monetary incentives to lure African-American students to institutions that are not suited to address their social and educational needs. Above all, race-exclusive scholarships may, in the long run, undermine the very goals they are intended to achieve. They aggravate racial tensions on campus, and these hostilities in turn pervert the educational experience of African-American students and retard any efforts toward campus diversity.

If colleges and universities want to further their educational and diversity interests without fostering racial hostility, scholarships should be targeted toward disadvantaged students of any race or ethnicity. For example, colleges and universities could establish scholarships or programs based on students' economic status, education status (for example, students from poor school districts), or social status (for example, students from families with few college-educated members).[158] At the same time, policymakers cannot ignore the fact that race continues to be a form of disadvantage in public education, and that such racial impediments undermine our nation's political economy.[159] As an effort to rectify the deleterious effects of present and past discrimination, when all other factors are equal, racial disadvantage should be an overriding consideration in awarding scholarships.

This scholarship policy would necessarily target a large number of African-American students who are more likely to be poor than are whites. Furthermore, while this policy acknowledges the racial inequities of our society, it also ensures that an African-American student from an advantaged background and an already promising future will not enjoy additional economic advantages, by reason of her skin color, over a white student who is struggling financially. Moreover, it ensures that a wealthy African-American student will not deprive a truly needy African-American student of necessary funds.[160]

An additional means of targeting disadvantaged students is through the federal student aid program. Recent changes in federal financial aid policies have disproportionately impaired African-American students, who are much more likely to be poor than are white students. The growth of the student loan program has expanded the choices available to middle- and upper-income students at the expense of grant programs that are the most effective source of aid for low-income students. Although choice is an admirable goal, the federal government should focus on low-income students' access to and matriculation from institutions of higher education before expanding choices for the middle class. This effort would require an increase in the level of Pell Grant awards.[161] To achieve greater vertical equity, the federal government could increase the maximum Pell Grant while simultaneously raising the rate at which Pell Grants are reduced for higher-income families.[162] Meanwhile, educational institutions should minimize the loan burden for low-income students and give preference to low-income students when distributing work-study opportunities.

In addition to scholarship and student aid reform, there must be a coordinated, concerted effort by the federal government and institutions of higher education to disseminate information to low-income and less-informed students, many of whom are minorities. If student funding is expected to raise college degree aspirations, thereby increasing enrollments, funding opportunities must be clarified long before students show interest in a particular college.[163] One way in which colleges and universities can inform families about potential aid is by working together to establish information centers in urban areas or specific low-income communities.[164]

Financial aid will help to enroll and retain disadvantaged minority students, but true diversity in undergraduate education will not be attained unless institutions commit themselves to adaptation and improvement. Schools cannot expect to diversify their campus communities merely by attracting a certain number of students of color. To be effective and meaningful, recruitment of minority students should be part of a "holistic and systemic approach" that takes into consideration not only the financial need but also the social, educational, and psychological needs of minority students.[165]

The factors affecting minority enrollment, choice, and retention are unique to the particular institution.[166] Institutions must conduct comprehensive audits to identify the reasons why few minorities are attracted to a particular campus and the factors, in addition to financial considerations, that affect African-American retention rates. Studies find that, for minority students, academic and social integration are central factors in student persistence.[167] Depending on the institution, colleges and universities may wish to encourage student/faculty interaction and peer tutoring, institute ethnic studies programs, enhance efforts to diversify the faculty, and/or increase support for multicultural social activities.[168] Such an approach to diversity would have multiple benefits for both students and educators. Having chosen an institution perceived as meeting their needs, minority students may have a better undergraduate experience, thus increasing the likelihood of graduation. At the same time, this approach to diversity should enrich the social, artistic, and intellectual environment of the entire campus.

The condition of African-American students in higher education is not a simple, quantifiable problem. Nevertheless, African-American educational attainment and campus diversity are goals that the government and educational institutions must pursue. The use of narrow, short-term solutions like race-exclusive scholarships will not adequately or effectively address the issues. To achieve genuine success, we must make a long-term commitment to systemic change—in scholarship programs, in financial aid policies, and within undergraduate institutions themselves.

Notes

1. Infra., at notes 48-51, 64-68.
2. Infra., at notes 62-64.
3. 42 U.S.C. §2000d (1988).
4. 42 U.S.C. §2000d (1988). Section 606 of Title VI provides: "For the purpose of this title, the term 'program or activity' and the term 'program' mean all of the operations of . . . (2)(a) a college, university, or other postsecondary institution . . . any part of which is extended Federal financial assistance."
5. 34 C.F.R. §§100.3 (b)(6)(i)(ii) (1964).
6. Hugh Davis Graham, *The Civil Rights Era* (Oxford: Oxford University Press, 1990), p. 34.
7. *Adarand Constructors, Inc. v. Pena*, U.S. S. Ct. No. 93-1841, dec. June 12, 1995.
8. Id., at 5.
9. See, for example, *U.S. v. Fordice*, 112 S. Ct. 2727(1992); *U.S. v. Paradise*, 480 U.S. 149, 167 (1987).
10. *Fordice*, at 2736.
11. 59 Fed. Reg. 36, 8759 (1994).
12. In *Wygant v. Jackson Board of Education*, 476 U.S. 267, 276 (1986), the Court held that "societal discrimination, without more, is too amorphous a basis for imposing a racially classified remedy". In *City of Richmond v. J. A. Crosan Co.*, 488 U.S. 469, 497 (1989), the Court found that proof of general discrimination in the construction industry did not justify race-conscious remedial action in the awarding of public contracts in the city of Richmond.
13. The Court has rejected the use of race-conscious measures to provide African-American role models. *Wygant*, at 276.
14. *Regents of the University of California v. Bakke*, 438 U.S. 265, 311-313 (1978).
15. Id., at 311-313 (citations omitted).
16. John A. Ward, "Race-Exclusive Scholarships: Do They Violate the Constitution and Title VI of the Civil Rights Act of 1964?" 18 *Journal of College and University Law* 73 (1991), at 100.
17. Wygant, at 280.
18. Id., at 184 (citations omitted).
19. Id., at 171.
20. *Metro Broadcasting v. FCC*, 110 S. Ct. 2997, n. 15 (1990), at 3026 (emphasis in original).
21. *Bakke*, at 314-315. The university set aside sixteen out of a hundred spots for minority students.
22. Id., at 315.
23. Id., at 317.

24. OCR is responsible for enforcing federal laws that prohibit discrimination on the basis of race, national origin, sex, handicap or age in all educational programs and activities receiving federal funds.

    Minority scholarships were challenged in the case of *Flanagan v. President and Directors of Georgetown College*, 417 F. Supp. 377 (D.D.C. 1976). However, the opinion was based on an interpretation of Title VI that has since been rejected by the Court.

25. As the Supreme Court announces relevant decisions, OCR continually revises and amends its guidelines on minority-targeted financial aid. In 1972, in a memorandum to the presidents of postsecondary institutions regarding their compliance with Title VI, OCR explained that "student financial aid programs based on race or national origin may be consistent with Title VI if the purpose of such aid is to overcome the effects of past discrimination." Office of the Secretary, Department of Health, Education and Human Services, "Memorandum to Presidents of Institutions of Higher Education Participating in Federal Assistance Programs, Summary of Requirements of Title VI of the Civil Rights Act of 1964 for Institutions of Higher Education," Washington, D.C., June 1972. In 1973, OCR indicated that, even in the absence of prior discrimination, an entity which administers a program with federal funds "may take affirmative action to overcome the effects of conditions which resulted in limiting participation by persons of a particular race, color, or national origin." 45 C.F.R. Part 80, § 80.3(b)(ii), 38 Fed. Reg. 17978 (July 5, 1973).

26. Quotation from OCR's 1982 decision to approve MIT's Minority Tuition Fellowship Program. Letter of the Department of Health and Human Services to Unnamed Complainant, Complaint #01802046, March 24, 1982. This approval was based on a 1978 interpretation of Title VI in light of the *Bakke* decision. "OCR Affirmative Action Policy Interpretation," 44 Fed. Reg. 58509 (Oct. 3, 1979).

27. For example, in 1989, OCR held that the University of Colorado could constitutionally limit a financial aid program to African Americans, Hispanics, and Native Americans because the limits were based on historical enrollment data showing underrepresentation of these groups. "Memorandum from Joan Standlee, Deputy Assistant Secretary for Civil Rights, to Gilbert D. Roman, Regional Director, Region VIII," OCR Case #08826001, March 22, 1983. Meanwhile, in 1986, OCR held that a scholarship restricted to Dutch Americans was impermissible because there was neither evidence that Dutch Americans had been discriminated against in the past nor conditions at the universities that resulted in limited participation by Dutch Americans. Letter from Alicia Coro, Acting Assistant Secretary for Civil Rights, to Unnamed Recipient, May 2, 1986.

28. In a letter to the directors of the Fiesta Bowl football game, Williams warned that the universities of Alabama and Louisville would violate Title VI if they assisted the Fiesta Bowl in awarding scholarships designated for African-American students only. The directors were intending to

contribute $100,000 to each participant of the tournament to establish a Martin Luther King, Jr., scholarship fund for African-American students. Letter from Michael L. Williams, Assistant Secretary of the U.S. Department of Ed. Office for Civil Rights to Mr. John Junker, Executive Director, Fiesta Bowl, December 4, 1990. Williams claimed that, although the Fiesta Bowl, a private entity, had complete discretion over the distribution of its funds, Title VI prohibits universities receiving federal funds from using their own funds or distributing private funds for race-exclusive scholarships. *Id.*, citing 34 C.F.R. §§ 10.3(b)(1)-(6) (1989).

29. Barbara Vobejda, "In the Eye of Racial Controversy, Education Official's Action Shocks Some," *Washington Post*, December 14, 1990, p. A22.
30. Neil A. Lewis, "Race and College Aid," *New York Times*, December 13, 1990, p. A12.
31. Id., p. A12. The future of affirmative action and quotas were a major factor in the President's decision to veto the legislation.
32. Maureen Dowd, "Cavazos Quits as Education Chief amid Pressure from White House," *New York Times*, December 13, 1990, p. A1.
33. Maureen Dowd, "President Orders Aide to Review New Minority Scholarship Policy," *New York Times*, December 14, 1990, p. A1.
34. Ibid., quoting Janell Byrd, assistant council, NAACP Legal Defense and Educational Fund.
35. Ibid., p. A23.
36. Amy Goldstein and Mary Jordan, "'Chilling Effect' Feared, College Officials Attack Scholarship Ban," *Washington Post*, December 14, 1990, p. A1.
37. Kenneth J. Cooper, "Scholarships Based on Race Prohibited, Groups Challenge Education Dept. Ruling," *New York Times*, December 13, 1990, p. A1.
38. Ann Devroy and Dan Balx, "Bush Stands Neutral While Aides Debate Scholarship Policy," *Washington Post*, December 15, 1990, p. A4.
39. Ann Devroy, "White House Backs Off on Scholarships, Education Dept. Told to Retreat on Policy Barring Race-Based Grants," *Washington Post*, December 18, 1990, p. A1; "Dept. Issues Policy Statement on Race-Exclusive Scholarships," *United States Dept. of Ed. News Release*, December 18, 1990, p. A20.

The revised statement claimed that universities could distribute race-exclusive scholarships if such scholarships were funded entirely by a private entity and if eligibility restrictions were devised by the private donor. This statement was perceived as a political maneuver rather than a legal reconsideration, and was criticized for drawing a distinction rendered illegitimate by the Civil Rights Restoration Act of 1987. According to this act, Title VI provisions apply to any operation or subdivision of a university or college. Therefore a federally funded institution cannot administer privately earmarked funds that the school itself would be prohibited from providing. 20 U.S.C. §1687 (1988).

40. Both the House Committee on Education and Labor and the House Committee on Government Operations opposed Williams's actions. U.S. Congress, House of Representatives, Committee on Education and Labor, *The Department for Education, Office of Civil Rights Policy on Student Financial Assistance*, Hearing, 103d Cong., 2d sess., December 19, 1990 (Washington, D.C.: U.S. Government Printing Office, 1991) (hereafter cited as *Education and Labor Hearing*); U.S. Congress, House of Representatives, Committee on Government Operations, *The Fiesta Bowl Fiasco: Department of Education's Attempt to Ban Minority Scholarships*, 102d Cong., 1st sess., H.R. 102-411(Washington, D.C.: U.S. Government Printing Office, December 4, 1991) (hereafter cited as *The Fiesta Bowl Fiasco*).

41. Letter from Michael L. Williams, Assistant Secretary of the U.S. Department of Ed. Office for Civil Rights to Mr. John Junker, Executive Director, Fiesta Bowl, December 4, 1990. Nonexempt federal regulatory procedures must comply with the Administrative Procedure Act (APA), which requires that all rules be published in the Federal Registrar before they are made final. Williams was criticized for ignoring these procedures and "lurching from policy by press release to policy by press conference." Honorable Augustus F. Hawkins, "Opening Statement," *Education and Labor Hearing*, p. 5.

42. Carol Inerst, "Alexander Vows to Unravel Minority Scholarship Issue," *Washington Times*, February 7, 1991.

43. To supplement the various surveys conducted by education and civil rights groups, Alexander published a notice of proposed policy guidance in the Federal Register and requested public comment from educators and other interested parties. 56 Fed. Reg. 24, 383 (1991). One problem with the data is that surveys and reports tend to use different terminology. The U.S. General Accounting Office (GAO) issued a report on "minority-targeted" scholarships, but this includes scholarships based on race or ethnicity, sex, religion, disability, age, and national origin. United States General Accounting Office, *Higher Education: Information on Minority-Targeted Scholarships* (Washington, D.C.: GAO, January 14,1994) (hereafter cited as *GAO Report*). Other reports use undefined terms such as "race-conscious," "race-based," "minority-specific," and "minority-exclusive." This chapter cites numbers from those surveys that seem relatively clear about the types of programs included.

44. 20 U.S.C. §1134d-f; 42 U.S.C. §7141(d).

45. Mark Pitch, "Colleges Offer Data to Assess Scholarship Policy's Impact," *Education Week*, January 9, 1991.

46. Rev. Proc. 1975-50, 1975-2 C.B. 589.

47. U.S. Department of Education, Office of Higher Education Programs, *Higher Education Opportunities for Minorities and Women--Annotated Selections* (Washington, D.C.: U.S. Dept. of Education, 1994), p. 18.

48. Id., p. 19.

49. Ibid.
50. Id., p. 20.
51. "College Board Releases Data on Minority-Specific Scholarships," *News from the College Board,* December 1990.
52. Ibid.
53. Carol Inerst, "Scholarship Review Has Simon Skeptical," *Washington Times*, June 5, 1991. These are OCR figures, derived from surveys conducted by the American Association of State Colleges and Universities, the National Institute of Independent Colleges and Universities, the College Board, and ACE.
54. Ibid.
55. "What Color Is Your Scholarship?" *Washington Times*, December 9, 1991, p. E2.
56. Ibid.; "Few Colleges Offer Minority Scholarships, Study Finds," *Education Daily*, April 3, 1991, p. 1.
57. "Few Colleges Offer Minority Scholarships, Study Finds," p. 1.
58. National Institute of Independent Colleges and Universities, *Preliminary Results of NIICU Survey on Minority Scholarships at Independent Colleges and Universities* (Washington, D.C.: NIICU, 1991). Of the remaining portion of the funding, 8 percent come from federal sources, 4.4 percent from the state, and 9.9 percent from other sources.
59. National Association of Student Financial Aid Administrators, *NASFAA Mini-Survey on Designated Minority Scholarships* (Washington, D.C.: NASFAA, 1991), p. 2. At public four-year institutions about 69 percent of minority aid is designated by the school; at private four-year institutions, about 93 percent is designated by the school.
60. Dinesh D'Souza, *Illiberal Education: The Politics of Race and Sex on Campus* (New York: Free Press, 1991), p. 4.
61. Thomas J. DeLoughry, "At Penn State: Polarization of the Campus Persists amid Struggles to Ease Tensions," *Chronicle of Higher Education*, April 26, 1989, p. 30.
62. Ibid.
63. *NASFAA Mini-Survey on Designated Minority Scholarships*, p. 2.
64. Ibid.
65. *Higher Education Opportunities for Minorities and Women--Annotated Selections*, p. 21.
66. Fox Butterfield, "Colleges Luring Black Students with Incentives," *New York Times*, February 28, 1993, p. A30.
67. Ibid.
68. 59 Fed. Reg. 36, 8757-8764 (1994).
69. Ibid.
70. Ibid.
71. Id., at 8757.
72. Ibid.

73. Carol Inerst, "Education Dept. Endorses Grants Based on Race," *Washington Times*, January 13, 1994, p. A3.
74. "Scholarships for Racial Justice," *Sacramento Observer*, August 8, 1993, p. C1.
75. William John Shepherd, "Unconscionable," *Washington Times*, March 30, 1993, p. F3.
76. Previously, federal affirmative action had been subjected to an intermediate level of scrutiny.
77. Linda Greenhouse, "The Supreme Court: Affirmative Action; Justices, 5 to 4, Cast Doubt on U.S. Programs That Give Preferences Based on Race," *New York Times*, June 13, 1995, p. A1.
78. *Poberesky v. Kirwin*, 38 F. 3d 147 (1994).
79. Kimberly J. McLarin, "Impact of Court Ruling on Black Scholarships," *New York Times*, November 2, 1994, p. 23. In 1993-94, 139 African-American students were receiving Banneker scholarships from a program budget of $1.26 million.
80. J. Joseph Currean and Andrew H. Baida, *Brief of Apellees: Poberesky v. Kirwin*, Attorney General's Office, Baltimore, September 13, 1991, p. 2.
81. *Poberesky*, at 3. The University of Maryland was not open to African-American students until 1954, and is still under court-ordered desegregation plans. The Banneker program was part of the university's desegregation plan approved by OCR. Janell M. Beard, David M. Hecker, and Norman J. Chachkin, *Amicus Curiae Brief: Poberesky v. Kirwin*, NAACP Legal Defense and Educational Fund, New York, September 16, 1991, p. 38.
82. *Poberesky*, at 12-13.
83. Id., at 15-16 (citations omitted).
84. Id., at 19-20.
85. Id., at 25.
86. Id., at 27.
87. Id., at 28.
88. Id., at 36.
89. "Mississippi Mellows on Issue of Bias in State Universities," *New York Times*, March 13, 1993, p. A14.
90. Ibid.
91. Barbara Astone and Elsa Nuñez-Wormack, *Pursuing Diversity: Recruiting College Minority Students* (Washington, D.C.: School of Education and Human Development, George Washington University, 1990), p. iii.
92. "Testimony of Robert H. Atwell, President, American Council on Education," in U.S. Congress, Committee on Labor and Human Resources, Subcommittee on Education, Arts and Humanities, *Minority Participation and Retention in Higher Education*, Hearing, 103rd Congress, 2nd sess., May 17, 1994.
93. Astone and Nuñez-Wormack, *Pursuing Diversity*, p. 16.

94. Id., pp. 16, 2.
95. William B. Johnson and Arnold H. Packer, *Workforce 2000: Work and Workers for the 21st Century* (Indianapolis: Hudson Institute, 1987), p. 98. In 1987, 42 percent of all jobs required one or more years of college. Of all new jobs, 52 percent required at least one year of college and 30 percent required four or more years of college.
96. Carol Frances and Associates, "Trends in College-Going Rate by Age, Race, and Gender 1976-1989," report prepared for the Association of Urban Universities (Warrenton, VA.: Carol Frances and Associates, 1990), in *Education and Labor Hearings*, p. 30.
97. Ibid.
98. Paper presented by Earl S. Richardson, president, Morgan State University, Baltimore, and chairman, National Association for Equal Opportunity in Higher Education, in *Minority Participation and Retention in Higher Education*, p. 25. In 1982, the college-going rate for African Americans between the ages of eighteen and twenty-four was 28 percent, compared with 33.1 percent for whites. In 1992, the rate for African Americans was 33.8 percent compared with 42.2 percent for whites. This sort of gap exists for all age and gender groups except women aged sixteen to seventeen, for whom the black college-going rate has surpassed the rate for whites. Carol Frances and Associates, "Trends in College-Going Rates," p. 2.
99. Paul W. Kingston, "The Pursuit of Inclusion: Recent Trends in Minority Enrollments in Higher Education," *Education Policy* 6 (1992): 382. The proportion of African-American freshmen remained relatively steady at two-year colleges (public and private) and public universities. While the proportion of African Americans at public colleges increased slightly, it decreased slightly at private colleges and decreased substantially at private universities. Private institutions report an increase in minority representation because of large influxes of Asian Americans and a greater enrollment of Hispanic students.

    It should be noted that the enrollment figures for African Americans are not evenly distributed amongst institutions because an increasing percentage of African Americans are enrolling in historically black colleges and universities (HBCUs). In 1981-82, 37.5 percent of African-American freshmen chose to attend HBCUs and in 1989-90 the percentage was 41%. Id., pp. 381-382, 390-392.
100. "Testimony of Robert H. Atwell, President, American Council on Education," in *Minority Participation and Retention in Higher Education*, p. 41.
101. Ibid., citing NCAA Division I graduation rates and High School and Beyond (HSB) statistics.
102. Johnston and Packer, *Workforce 2000*, p. 89. In 1970, nonwhites formed 11.1 percent of the labor force, in 1985 this number was 13.1 percent, and in the year 2000 it is expected to be 15.5 percent.

103. Id., p. 6.
104. DeLoughry, "At Penn State," p. 33; Butterfield, "Colleges," p. 30, quoting Eric Widmer, dean of admission and financial aid at Brown University.
105. Reginald C. Govan and William L. Taylor, eds., *One Nation Indivisible: The Civil Rights Challenge for the 1990's* (Washington, D.C.: Citizens' Commission on Civil Rights), p. 149.
106. Alexander W. Astin and Carolyn J. Inouve, "How Public Policy at the State Level Affects Private Higher Education Institutions," *Economics of Education Review* 7 (1988): p. 47.
107. Gary Orfield, "Money, Equity, and College Access," *Harvard Educational Review* 62 (Fall 1992): 361.
108. Id., p. 340. See also Michael S. McPherson and Morton Owen Schapiro, *Keeping College Affordable* (Washington, D.C.: Brookings Institution, 1991), pp. 75-105, finding "a strong link between 'choice' and income."
109. A. Stephen Higgins, "Student Financial Aid and Equal Opportunity in Higher Education," *College and University* 58 (Summer 1983): 343. There is general agreement that the greatest educational problems lie in our primary and secondary schools, but higher-education equality for minorities cannot await public school reform. Govan and Taylor, eds., *One Nation Indivisible*, p. 147.
110. Amaury Nora and Fran Horvath, "Financial Assistance: Minority Enrollments and Persistence," *Education and Urban Society* 21 (1989): 305. See also "Statement of Cornelia M. Blanchette, Associate Director, Education and Employment Issues, Health, Education, and Human Services," in *Minority Participation and Retention in Higher Education*, p. 44.
111. Nora and Horvath, "Financial Assistance," p. 305.
112. Orfield, "Money, Equity, and College Access," p. 341.
113. McPherson and Shapiro, *Keeping College Affordable* p. 51. See for example, Larry L. Leslie and Paul T. Brinkman, "Student Price Response in Higher Education: The Student Demand Studies," *Journal of Higher Education* 58 (1988): 181-204; Charles F. Manski and David A. Wise, *College Choice in America* (Cambridge, Mass.: Harvard University Press, 1983); Eric L. Jensen, "Financial Aid and Educational Outcomes: A Review," *College and University* (Spring 1983): 287-302.
114. Orfield, "Money, Equity, and College Access," p. 341.
115. Jomills Henry Braddock II, "The Perpetuation of Segregation across Levels of Education," *Sociology of Education* 53 (1980): 183. After college cost, high school GPA and racial composition of one's high school were the most effective factors.
116. The supply of high-achieving African-American students falls way below the demand. In 1992 only 1,403 African-American students scored at least 600 out of 800 on the SAT verbal, compared with 55,224 white students. On the SAT math section, only 3,404 African-American students

scored 600 or above, compared with 132,846 white students. Butterfield, "Colleges," p. 30.

117. Robert A. Sevier, "Recruiting African-American Undergraduates," *College and University* 68 (Fall 1992/Winter 1993): 48.

118. Id., p. 49. Almost 72 percent of the respondents came from two-parent families and rated their parents as their most important advisors in their college decision. "I enjoy doing things with my family" was the broad attitudinal statement most agreed upon, and 78.5 percent claimed that raising a family was an important or very important life goal.

119. Id., p. 49.

120. Rhonda Richards, "The Race for Black Students, Who's Winning?" *YSB*, November 1993, p. 54.

121. Butterfield, "Colleges," p. A30.

122. In 1990 the median income for an African-American family with related children was $19,359, compared with $34,230 for whites. That year, 32.9 percent of African Americans between the ages of sixteen and twenty-one lived below the poverty line, compared with 13 percent for whites. U.S. Bureau of the Census, *Statistical Abstracts of the United States* (Washington, D.C., 1992), pp. 451, 457.

123. Orfield, "Money, Equity, and College Access," p. 347; "Testimony of Robert H. Atwell, President, American Council on Education," in *Minority Participation and Retention in Higher Education*, p. 41. Between 1980 and 1990, the average tuition for in-state students at four-year public colleges rose 138 percent, from $840 to $2,006. The average tuition at four-year private colleges rose 173 percent, from $3,811 to $10,400. *Statistical Abstracts of the United States*, p. 169.

Pell Grants are need-based aid available to undergraduate students who attend at least half time. No student can receive an award exceeding 60 percent of the cost of attendance at his or her institution. In 1990 the maximum award was $2,300. That year, about 3,276,000 students received an average award of $1,438. McPherson and Shapiro, *Keeping College Affordable*, pp. 4-5; *Statistical Abstracts of the United States*, p. 168.

124. "Statement of Cornelia M. Blanchette, Associate Director, Education and Employment Issues, Health, Education, and Human Services," in *Minority Participation and Retention in Higher Education*, p. 44.

125. For student loans, the federal government insures banks against default risk and subsidizes students' interest payments. Stafford Loans are only available to students who attend at least half time and have "demonstrated need," as evidenced by their family's resources and the cost of tuition at their chosen college. In 1992, about 4,4140,000 students received an average Stafford Loan of $2,826. *Statistical Abstracts of the United States*, p. 168. If families do not qualify for or have reached the limit for Stafford Loans, they are eligible for Parent Loans to Undergraduate Students (PLUS) and Supplemental Loans to Students (SLS). These loans are guaranteed and their interest rates are regulated, but there is no subsidy

for the interest, and interest rates may fluctuate. McPherson and Shapiro, *Keeping College Affordable*, p. 5.

126. Orfield, "Money, Equity, and College Access," p. 348.

127. Govan and Taylor, *"One Nation Indivisible*, p. 150.

128. Nora and Horvath, "Financial Assistance," p. 306.

129. Orfield, "Money, Equity, and College Access," p. 357. Work-study is a program whereby the federal government pays colleges 70 percent of the cost of providing jobs to students who show some financial need. In 1992, there were 752,000 work-study recipients earning an average of $945 per year. *Statistical Abstracts of the United States*, p. 168.

130. Orfield, "Money, Equity, and College Access," p. 170.

131. One result has been the overrepresentation of African Americans in low-cost, two-year undergraduate institutions. The percentage of African-American undergraduates enrolled in two-year institutions is 43.1 percent compared with 36 percent for whites. Astone and Nuñez-Wormack, "Pursuing Diversity," pp.17-19.

132. Nora and Horvath, "Financial Assistance," p. 302; Orfield, "Money, Equity, and College Access," pp. 360-361.

133. Orfield, "Money, Equity, and College Access," p. 360.

134. Id., p. 361.

135. Ibid.

136. Ibid.

137. Thomas A. Flint, "Early Awareness of College Financial Aid: Does It Expand Choice?" *Review of Higher Education* 16 (Spring 1993): 322.

138. Orfield, "Money, Equity, and College Access," p. 361.

139. Supra, at notes 123-139.

140. Richards, "The Race for Black Students," p. 57.

141. Ibid.

142. William G. Bowen and Neil L. Rudenstine, "Colleges Must Have the Flexibility to Designate Financial Aid for Members of Minority Groups," *Chronicle of Higher Education*, January 9, 1991, p. B3.

143. D'Souza, *Illiberal Education*, p. 5.

144. *GAO Report*, p. 69.

145. See generally, id.

146. Ibid.

147. *OCR Report*, p. 93.

148. D'Souza, *Illiberal Education*, p. 5.

149. Astone and Nuñez-Wormack, "Pursuing Diversity," p. 53.

150. Richards, "The Race for Black Students," p. 54.

151. Katherine S. Mangan, "At Texas: An Undercurrent of Hostility amid Efforts to Promote Multiculturalism," *Chronicle of Higher Education*, April 26, 1989, p. 29. See also DeLoughry, "At Penn State," p. A30.

152. Ibid.

153. Carol Inerst, "College Whites Fight 'Favoritism,'" *Washington Times*, April 26, 1990, p. A1.

154. Ibid.
155. Ibid.
156. Ibid.
157. National Association of Scholars, "The Wrong Way to Reduce Campus Tensions," *Chronicle of Higher Education*, April 24, 1991, p. A15.
158. Letter from Michael L. Williams, Assistant Secretary, of the U.S. Dept. of Ed. Office for Civil Rights, to Mr. John Junker, Executive Director, Fiesta Bowl; Ward, "Race Exclusive Scholarships," at 101.
159. This recommendation excludes private monies distributed by private donators to individual students because the fourteenth amendment, and therefore Title VI, "erects no shield against merely private conduct, however discriminatory or wrongful." *Shelly v. Kramer*, 334 U.S. 1, 13 (1947). However, a college or university may be perceived as acquiescing in discriminatory conduct if it facilitates or profits from such activities. As the Supreme Court established in *Crosen*, a school receiving government funds "may not induce, encourage or promote private persons to do what it is constitutionally forbidden to accomplish." Jay. B. Howd, "Race-Exclusive Scholarships in Federally-Assisted Colleges and Universities—Will They Survive?" 16 *Southern Illinois University Law Journal* 451 (1992), at 477.
160. Howd, "Race-Exclusive Scholarships," p. 476.
161. Although it seems intuitive, several prominent scholars dispute the idea that increases in federal aid will have a positive effect on the African-American college-going rate. These conclusions, however, are generally based on recent student aid increases that primarily benefited middle-class students who would have gone to college anyway. Orfield, "Money, Equity, and College Access," pp. 344-343. See Also Nora and Horvath, "Financial Assistance," pp. 300-301.
162. McPherson and Schapiro, *Keeping College Affordable*, pp. 212-213. The value of a "needs-based" Pell grant is determined by family resources and cost of attendance at desired institution. However, the maximum grant is determined by the family's resources. In 1989-90 the maximum grant for a student with no resources was $2,300. Thus a low-income student's grant will not be increased if she chooses to attend a more expensive college.
163. Flint, "Early Awareness of College Financial Aid," p. 323.
164. Astone and Nuñez-Wormack, *Pursuing Diversity*, p. 93.
165. Id., p. 3.
166. Id., p. 48.
167. Otis T. Griffin, "The Impacts of Academic and Social Integration for Black Students in Higher Education," in Marvel Lang and Clinita A. Ford, eds., *Strategies for Retaining Minority Students in Higher Education* (Springfield, Ill.: Charles C. Thomas, 1992), pp. 26-27.
168. See for example, Marvel and Lang, "Strategies for Retaining Minority Students"; Astone and Nuñez-Wormack, *Pursuing Diversity*; Alexander

W. Astin, *Minorities in American Higher Education* (San Francisco: Jossey-Bass, 1982); Harold L. Hodgkinson, ed., *Higher Education: Diversity Is Our Middle Name* (Washington, D.C.: National Institute of Independent Colleges and Universities, 1986).

References

Books

Astone, Barbara and Elsa Nuñez-Wormack. *Pursuing Diversity: Recruiting College Minority Students*. Washington, D.C.: School of Education and Human Development, George Washington University, 1990.

Crossland, Fred E. *Minority Access to College*. New York: Schocken Books, 1971.

D'Souza, Dinesh. *Illiberal Education: The Politics of Race and Sex on Campus*. New York: Free Press, 1991.

Govan, Reginald C., and William L. Taylor, eds. *One Nation Indivisible: The Civil Rights Challenge for the 1990s*. Washington, D.C.: Citizens' Commission on Civil Rights, 1990.

Graham, Hugh Davis. *The Civil Rights Era*. Oxford: Oxford University Press, 1990.

Johnson, William B., and Arnold H. Packer. *Workforce 2000: Work and Workers for the 21st Century*. Indianapolis: Hudson Institute, 1987.

Lang, Marvel, and Clinita A. Ford, eds. *Strategies for Retaining Minority Students in Higher Education*. Springfield, Ill.: Charles C. Thomas, 1992.

McPherson, Michael S., and Morton Owen Schapiro. *Keeping College Affordable: Government and Educational Opportunity*. Washington, D.C.: Brookings Institution, 1991.

Preer, J. L. *Minority Access to Higher Education*. Washington, D.C.: American Association of Higher Education, 1981.

Steele, Shelby. *The Content of Our Character: A New Vision of Race in America*. New York: St. Martin's Press, 1990.

Law Review Articles

Baida, Andrew H. "Not All Minority Scholarships Are Created Equal: Why Some May Be More Constitutional Than Others," 18 *Journal of College and University Law* 333 (1991).

Bistline, Andrea L. "Preferential Admissions Policies and Single-Minority Scholarships: The Legal Implications of Race-Preference in Higher Education." 97 *Dickenson Law Review* 283 (1993).

Howd, Jay B. "Race-Exclusive Scholarships in Federally Assisted Colleges and Universities--will they survive?" 16 *Southern Illinois University Law Journal* 451 (1992).

Milkulak, Brian. "Classism and Equal Opportunity: A Proposal for Affirmative Action in Education Based on Social Class." 33 *Howard Law Journal* 113 (1990).

Olivas, Michael A. "Federal Law and Scholarship Policy: An Essay on the Office for Civil Rights, Title VI, and Racial Restrictions." 18 *Journal of College and University Law* 21(1991).

Spector, Rachel. "Minority Scholarships: A New Battle in the War on Affirmative Action." 77 *Iowa Law Review* 307 (1991).

Taylor, Kimberly Paap. "Affirmative Action for the Poor: A Proposal for Affirmative Action in Higher Education Based on Economics, Not Race." 20 *Hastings Constitutional Law Quarterly* 805(1993).

Ward, John A. "Race Exclusive Scholarships: Do They Violate the Constitution and Title VI of the Civil Rights Act of 1964?" 18 *Journal of College and University Law* 73 (1991).

Journal Articles

Allen, Walter R. "The Color of Success : African-American College Students at Predominantly White and Historically Black Public Colleges and Universities." *Harvard Educational Review* 62 (1992): 26-44.

Astin, Alexander W., and Carolyn J. Inouve. "How Public Policy at the State Level Affects Private Higher Education Institutions." *Economics of Education Review* 7 (1988): 47-65.

Baum, Sandra R., and Saul Schwartz. "Merit Aid to College Students." *Economics of Education Review* 7 (1988): 127-133.

Braddock, Jomills Henry II. "The Perpetuation of Segregation Across Levels of Education: A Behavioral Assessment of the Contact-Hypothesis." *Sociology of Education* 53 (1990): 178-186.

Edlin, Aaron S. "Is College Financial Aid Equitable and Efficient?" *Journal of Economic Perspectives* 7 (1993): 143-157.

Feagin, Joe R. "The Continuing Significance of Racism: Discrimination against Black Students on White College Campuses." *Journal of Black Studies* 22 (June 1992): 546-578.

Flint, Thomas A. "Early Awareness of College Financial Aid: Does It Expand Choice?" *Review of Higher Education* 16 (Spring 1993): 309-327.

Higgins, A. Stephen. "Student Financial Aid and Equal Opportunity in Higher Education." *College and University* 58 (Summer 1983): 341-361.

James, Estelle. "Student Aid and College Attendance: Where Are We Now and Where Do We Go from Here?" *Economics of Education Review* 7 (1988): 1-15.

Kane, John, and Lawrence M. Spitzman. "Race, Financial Aid Awards, and College Attendance: Parents and Geography Matter." *American Journal of Economics and Sociology* 53 (1994): 85- 97.

Kingston, Paul W. "The Pursuit of Inclusion: Recent Trends in Minority Enrollments in Higher Education." *Educational Policy* 6 (1992): 377-396.

Knapp, Laura Greene, and Terry G. Seaks. "An Analysis of the Probability of Default on Federally Guaranteed Student Loans." *Review of Economics and Statistics* (1992): 404-411.

Kobrak, Peter. "Black Student Retention in Predominantly White Regional Universities." *Journal of Negro Education* 61 (1992): 509-530.

Lang, Marvel. "Barriers to Blacks' Educational Achievement in Higher Education." *Journal of Black Studies* 22 (June 1992): 510-522.

McPherson, Michael S., and Morton Owen Schapiro. "Does Student Aid Affect College Enrollment? New Evidence on a Persistent Controversy." *American Economic Review* 81 (March 1991): 309-318.

Moore, Robert L. et al. "The Effect of the Financial Aid Package on the Choice of a Selective College." *Economics of Education Review* 10 (1991): 311-321.

Nora, Amaury, and Fran Horvath. "Financial Assistance: Minority Enrollments and Persistence." *Education and Urban Society* 21 (1989): 299-311.

Orfield, Gary. "Money, Equity, and College Access." *Harvard Educational Review* 62 (Fall 1992): 337-372.

Sevier, Robert A. "Recruiting African-American Undergraduates: A National Survey of the Factors That Affect Institutional Choice." *College and University* (Fall 1992/Winter 1993): 48-50.

Smith, Stephanie, and Tom Matthews. "How Do Students Choose a Particular College? A Survey of Admitted Students: 1990." *College Student Journal* (1990): 482-488.

Stampen, J. O., and Alberto F. Cabrera. "Exploring the Effects of Student Aid on Attrition." *Journal of Student Financial Aid* 16 (1986): 28-40.

Stampen, J. O., and Alberto F. Cabrera. "The Targeting and Packaging of Student Aid and Its Effect on Attrition." *Economics of Education Review* 7 (1988): 29-46.

Newspaper and Magazine Articles

"Administration Supports Race-Based Scholarships." *Seminole Tribune*, May 28, 1993, 7.

"An Appeals Court with Blinders, "*New York Times*, Editorial Desk, November 3, 1994, A30.

Bowen, William G., and Neil L. Rudenstine. "Colleges Must Have the Flexibility to Designate Financial Aid for Members of Minority Groups." *Chronicle of Higher Education*, January 9, 1991, B1.

Butterfield, Fox. "Colleges Luring Black Students with Incentives." *New York Times*, February 28, 1993, A1.

"College Board Releases Data on Minority-Specific Scholarships." *News from the College Board*, December 1990.

"Court Bars Race-Based Scholarship Programs." *St. Petersburg Times*, October 29, 1994, A1.

DeLoughry, Thomas J. "At Penn State: Polarization of the Campus Persists amid Struggles to Ease Tensions." *Chronicle of Higher Education*, April 26, 1989, 30.

"Few Colleges Offer Minority Scholarships, Study Finds." *Education Daily*, April 3, 1991, 1.

Greene, Elizabeth. "At Oberlin: Liberal Traditions, Intentions Are No Guarantee of Racial Harmony." *Chronicle of Higher Education*, April 26, 1989, A31.

Greenhouse, Linda. "The Supreme Court: Affirmative Action; Justices, 5 to 4, Cast Doubt on U.S. Programs That Give Preferences Based on Race." *New York Times*, June 13, 1995, A1.

Holmes, Steven A. "Minority Scholarship Plans Are Dealt Setback by Court." *New York Times*, May 23, 1995, 9.

Inerst, Carol. "Alexander Vows to Unravel Minority Scholarship Issue." *Washington Times*, February 7, 1991, A4.

Inerst, Carol. "College Whites Fight 'Favoritism.'" *Washington Times*, April 26, 1990, A1.

Inerst, Carol. "Education Dept. Endorses Grants Based on Race." *Washington Times*, January 13, 1994, A3.

Inerst, Carol. "Panel Remark 'Racist,' Education Official Says." *Washington Times*, March 22, 1991, A1.

Inerst, Carol. "Scholarship Review Has Simon Skeptical." *Washington Times*, June 5, 1991, A4.

Inerst, Carol. "Williams Hits 'Confused' Policies." *Washington Times*, November 11, 1991, A6.

Inerst, Carol, and Carleton R. Bryant. "Colleges Vow to Circumvent Civil Rights Rule." *Washington Times*, December 13, 1990.

Inerst, Carol, and Carleton R. Bryant. "Grants Based on Race OK by Kemp." *Washington Times*, December, 17, 1990, A3.

Kneller, Susan R. "Supreme Court Hears Arguments on Racial Preference Programs." *U.S. Law Week*, January 20, 1995.

Labaton, Stephen. "Appeals Court Ruling Alarms Educators, University of Maryland Decision on Black Scholarship Program." *Dallas Morning News*, November 6, 1994, 4A.

Lowery, Mark. "The War on Equal Opportunity." *Black Enterprise*, February 1995, 148.

Magner, Denise K. "Blacks and Whites on the Campuses: Behind Ugly Racist Incidents, Student Isolation and Insensitivity. " *Chronicle of Higher Education*, April 26, 1989, A1.

Mangan, Katherine S. "At Texas: An Undercurrent of Hostility Amid Efforts to Promote Multiculturalism." *Chronicle of Higher Education*, April 26, 1989, A29.

Mauro, Tony. "Civil Rights Lawyers Keep Warry Watch on Supreme Court; Justices Will Hear Challenge to Race-Conscious Programs." *Recorder*, January 9, 1995, 1.

McLarin, Kimberly J. "Impact of Court Ruling on Black Scholarships." *New York Times*, November 2, 1994, D23.

"Minority College Enrollments Rise; Graduation Rates Remain Low." *Precinct Reporter*, March 10, 1994, A2.

National Association of Scholars. "The Wrong Way to Reduce Campus Tensions." *Chronicle of Higher Education*, April 24, 1991, A15.

Pitch, Mark. "Colleges Offer Data to Assess Scholarship Policy's Impact." *Education Week*, January 9, 1991, 26.

Purdum, Todd S. "President Shows Fervent Support for Goals of Affirmative Action." *New York Times*, July 20, 1995, A1.

Rhonda, Richards. "The Race for Black Students: Who's Winning?" *YSB*, November 1993, 54.

Roberts, Paul Craig. ". . . Biased Bidding," *Washington Times*, December 18, 1990, G1.

"Scholarships for Racial Justice." *Sacramento Observer*, August 8, 1993, C1.

Shepherd, William John. "Unconscionable." *Washington Times*, March 30, 1993, F2.

"Students Rally for Minority Scholarship Funding." *Portland Scanner*, April 1, 1992, 7.

Taylor, Stuart, Jr. "Race: The Most Divisive Issue." *New Jersey Law Journal*, August 23, 1993, 10.

"What Color is Your Scholarship?" *Washington Times*, December 9, 1991, E2.

Will, George F. "Negative Action; Race-based College Aid is a Form of Discrimination." *Pittsburgh Post-Gazette*, November 3, 1994, B3.

Yang, Catherine, Maria Mallory, and Ali Cuneo. "A 'Race-Neutral' Helping Hand?" *Business Week*, February 27, 1995, 120.

Additional Sources

Advisory Committee on Student Financial Assistance. *Ensuring Access: Challenges in Student Aid in the 1990's.* Washington, D.C.: Advisory Committee on Student Financial Assistance, July 1990.

Beard, Janell M., David M. Hecker, and Norman J. Chachkin. *Amicus Curiae Brief: Poberesky v. Kirwin.* New York: NAACP Legal Defense and Educational Fund, September 16, 1991.

Currean, J. Joseph, Jr., and Andrew H. Baida. *Brief of Apellees: Poberesky v. Kirwin.* Baltimore: Attorney General's Office, September 13, 1991.

National Association of Student Financial Aid Administers. *NASFAA Mini-Survey on Designated Minority Scholarships*. Washington, D.C.: NASFAA, 1991.

National Institute of Independent Colleges and Universities. *Preliminary Results of NIICU Survey on Minority Scholarships at Independent Colleges and Universities*. Washington, D. C.: NIICU, 1991.

U.S. Congress, House of Representatives, Committee on Education and Labor. *Hearing on the Department for Education, Office of Civil Rights Policy on Student Financial Assistance*, 101st Cong., 2d sess., December 19, 1990. Washington, D.C.: U.S. Government Printing Office, 1991. [Includes prepared testimonies, OCR records, and several newspaper articles cited in this text.]

U.S. Congress, House of Representatives, Committee on Government Operation. *The Fiesta Bowl Fiasco: Department of Education's Attempt to Ban Minority Scholarships*, H. R. 102-411, 102d Cong., 1st Sess., December 4, 1991. Washington, D.C.: U.S. Government Printing Office, 1991.

U.S. Congress, Senate, Committee on Labor and Human Resources, Subcommittee on Education, Arts and Humanities. *Minority Participation and Retention in Higher Education*, Hearing, 103d Cong., 1st sess., May 17, 1994. Washington, D.C.: U.S. Government Printing Office, 1994.

U.S. Department of Commerce, Economics and Statistics Administration, Bureau of the Census. *Statistical Abstracts of the United States*. Washington, D.C.: Bureau of the Census, 1992.

U.S. Department of Education, Office of Higher Education Programs. *Higher Education Opportunities for Minorities and Women--Annotated Selections*. Washington, D.C.: U.S. Department of Education, 1994).

U.S. General Accounting Office. *Higher Education: Information on Minority Targeted Scholarships*, Report to Congressional Requesters. Washington, D.C.: GAO, January 14, 1994.

Chapter 7

Fresh Start:
Redefining Affirmative Action to
Include Socioeconomic Class

Jonathan Goldman

A ffirmative action is defined by the *American Heritage Dictionary* as "action taken to provide equal opportunity, as in admissions or employment, for minority groups." Much of the controversy surrounding the issue is due to confusion concerning just what type of "action" is involved. Randall Kennedy suggests that there are four degrees of affirmative action, ranging from least to most extreme: (1) encouraging minorities to "enter the race"[1] with regard to jobs and college admissions; (2) using race as criteria for a "tie breaker" when faced with two candidates with essentially the same qualifications; (3) giving preference to a candidate on the basis of his or her minority status; and (4) assigning quotas of acceptance or hiring for different minority groups.[2]

Many people believe that affirmative action is a responsible policy only in the first two cases. Individuals should be hired for jobs or admitted to universities on the basis of merit. To give preference to candidates because of their minority status or to hire a fixed quota of minorities is to make qualifications second to goals of diversity. This seems unjust. No candidate (if he or she is underqualified) should receive preference over a more qualified candidate. A quota exists when employers or admissions officers agree to accept a fixed number of minority applicants or women (even if the last person's qualifications are substantially below those of other nonminority candidates). For this reason, quotas are repugnant to the philosophies of many, and have been declared illegal by the Civil Rights Act of 1964.

Using minority status as a criterion for making a decision between two similarly qualified candidates, however, is not only appropriate but necessary to achieve justice. This policy works on the assumption that the minority applicant has had to undergo setbacks and hardships beyond those of the other candidates because of his or her race or gender, to reach the same level of qualification. In a just system of affirmative action, minority candidates should and must be compensated for the extra hardships that they have had to endure.

Many critics of affirmative action argue that it is a form of "reverse racism," in which white males are victimized. Minority and female applicants are given preference solely on the basis of the color of their skin or their gender. Opponents argue that slavery is long past and that affirmative action amounts to antiwhite racism. They add that minority groups other than African Americans have never been subjected to institutionalized slavery, and women are not even a numerical minority in this country. On these grounds, many call for the end of affirmative action.

These concerns may or may not be valid. Racism and sexism, however, remain woven into the fabric of society. Racist and sexist beliefs and stereotypes are passed down from parent to child, from generation to generation, both knowingly and unknowingly. Slavery may be over, but the effects of racism are still felt by all minorities. Should not people be compensated for this discrimination? If so, when should racial and gender-based affirmative action end? The answer to this question is found by examining the effect of affirmative action policies to this point, particularly as they relate to the issue of socioeconomic class.

The Element of Class

A distinct division currently exists within the African-American community. This rift has been caused by, and is consistently reinforced by, affirmative action. It is a division of socioeconomic class. In 1992, 43 percent of black families fit into the lowest quintile of income distribution, while only 8 percent fit into the highest quintile. (This compares with 17 percent in the lowest quintile and 22 percent in the highest for whites).[3]

At one end of the scale are the lower class, the working poor, and the unemployed. This is the group of African Americans that is most often depicted by the media. In 1992, 31 percent of blacks lived below the poverty level.[4] According to William Julius Wilson, these lower-class African Americans are not helped by affirmative action. In his book *The Truly Disadvantaged*, Wilson writes: "Indeed, it would not be unreasonable to contend that the race-specific policies emanating from the civil rights revolution . . . do little for those who are truly disadvantaged."[5]

At the other end of the scale exists a smaller group of middle- and upper-class blacks. These African Americans are educated and successful. Either they have managed to make up the setbacks of discrimination on their own, or they have already benefited from affirmative action directly or through their parents. Yet here lies the problem of affirmative action as currently constituted. Having helped a group of minorities during its first and second generations, the program doomed itself to failure.

Because affirmative action is implemented solely on the basis of race, the children of these now middle-class and well-to-do African Americans are still eligible; the color of their skin has not changed. However, they have more money, and are better qualified for universities and jobs than their lower-class counterparts. They live in cities and suburbs with better public school systems, or their parents can afford to send them to private schools. Unlike many African Americans, they are not encumbered by the mental, social, and physical hardships of poverty. It is this better-qualified 20 percent of middle- and upper-class blacks in the upper two income quintiles[6] who tend to be chosen for universities and jobs over the lower class—the disadvantaged blacks who truly need the benefits of affirmative action. The result is that middle- and upper-class African Americans continue to benefit from a comparatively less-needed advantage because of the color of their skin alone, while lower-class blacks who suffer from both racial discrimination and economic disadvantage benefit very little from affirmative action. As the upper echelons of African-American society continue to climb the social ladder while the majority of African Americans do not, the rift in their community widens.[7]

Wilson notes the agreement of Glenn Loury, who writes: "A broad array of evidence suggests, at least to this observer, that better placed blacks [due to socioeconomic advantages] have simply been able to take more advantage of the opportunities created in the last twenty years than have those mired in the underclass."[8] This phenomenon is evidenced by the competition among top-notch colleges to attract middle- and upper-class African Americans from private schools, and the competitive minority recruitment by companies and firms of these same students after they have graduated. If many of these private school and Ivy League graduates have already benefited from affirmative action through their parents or through scholarships and aid before job recruitment begins, it is questionable whether they should continue to receive the special consideration of affirmative action programs in quite the same way. They have already been afforded the best possible education. Other, more disadvantaged candidates seem more deserving of priority in granting benefits.

Wilson notes that while the deteriorating condition of the black lower class may be associated with the upward mobility of advantaged blacks who benefit from affirmative action, the crucial point is that "[affirmative action] programs are mistakenly presumed to be the most appropriate solution to the problems of all blacks regardless of economic class."[9] Regarding affirmative action's current effects on the African-American community, he concludes:

> With the . . . authorization of affirmative action programs the government has helped clear the path for more privileged blacks, who have the requisite education and training to enter the mainstream of American occupations. However, such government programs do not confront the impersonal economic barriers confronting members of the black underclass, who have been effectively screened out of the corporate and government industries.... Such programs as affirmative action have had the unintentional effect of contributing to the growing economic class divisions within the black community.[10]

This phenomenon should also exist within other minority communities. In the large conglomeration of minority groups denoted as "Asian," for example, a wide disparity of socioeconomic and educational levels exists. Karen Nagasaki of the National Asian Pacific American Legal Consortium notes that Japanese Americans tend to be wealthier and better educated because they have generally been in this country for more generations; Vietnamese Americans tend to have immigrated more recently and are poorer and less educated. One must assume, therefore, that if companies or universities are seeking to hire or admit an "Asian,"[11] that Japanese Americans will generally have a socioeconomic advantage over Americans of Vietnamese descent. In this way Japanese Americans, who presumably do not need affirmative action as much as Vietnamese Americans, will tend to benefit both more often and at the expense of Vietnamese Americans. This situation is analogous to the class division within the African-American community.

Among Hispanics, Cubans tend to be wealthier, better educated, and therefore not so much in need of affirmative action as Mexican Americans and others. Again, this makes Cubans, in general, more appealing to hire and admit than other Hispanics. This may explain the fact that the Cuban unemployment rate, 8 percent, is significantly below the unemployment rate for other Hispanic groups—11 percent for Mexican Americans, for example, and 13 percent for Puerto Ricans.[12] For this reason, Cubans are excluded from many affirmative action programs.

Throughout society, members of minority groups in lower socioeconomic classes face further hardships. In addition to racial and gender discrimination, the "discrimination" of socioeconomic disadvantage is a powerful force. Even independent of minority and gender groupings, lower-class white males, for example, face setbacks due to economic and educational disadvantage. Such class-influenced deficits are particularly evident in the area of education; in poor areas, schools are of a lesser quality and drop-out rates are higher. This "educational class discrimination" is a serious problem; education is the avenue through which people gain the "human capital" they need to lift themselves out of poverty.

If the goal of affirmative action is to allow everyone to begin on the same starting line--or at least not to penalize individuals for characteristics such as race or gender—economic disadvantage must be considered in the equation. People have no more control over the socioeconomic status of their parents than they do over their skin color or gender. Compensation for the economic and educational deprivation, and for the social stigma and mental hardship of being disadvantaged, is warranted.

This proposal assumes that in addition to minorities and women, lower-class whites need affirmative action. Essentially, I propose to give those in the lower economic classes a boost in order that they might obtain the education they need to better compete in society. To achieve affirmative action's goal of an equal starting line, white Americans who have been denied the resources needed to achieve a good education deserve help just as if they had been discriminated against.   One must ask who has suffered more society-imposed disadvantage, the wealthy, private school educated African American, or the poor, disadvantaged white who was unable to receive an adequate education because of his or her socioeconomic position in society.

The prospect of need-based affirmative action worries some African Americans and members of other minority groups. If we grant affirmative action benefits on a socioeconomic basis to the bottom section of society, some fear that America will suddenly "discover" the white lower class. These critics argue that if a lower-class black and a lower-class white, both of equal merit, apply for a job or a position at a university, and each is entitled to affirmative action on the basis of his or her class, the white applicant will be hired over the black applicant because of racial discrimination. These skeptics harbor valid concerns: in a purely class-based affirmative action program, there would be no safeguards against racial discrimination.

Cornel West seems to agree with this sentiment in his discussion of black conservatives' rejection of affirmative action:

> Affirmative action policies were political responses to the pervasive refusal of most white Americans to judge black Americans by the quality of their skills rather than the color of their skin.

> . . . The new black conservatives assume that without affirmative action programs [that take race into account] white Americans will make meritorious choices rather than race-based ones. Yet they have adduced absolutely no evidence for this.[13]

Although wealthy and educated African Americans, Japanese Americans, Cuban Americans, and other minorities might not need the assistance of affirmative action as much as their less wealthy or educated counterparts in their racial and ethnic groups, they have still experienced the effects of racism.   Even though a minority may be wealthy and educated, he or she is still a minority. Money or education does not allow one to entirely escape racism's evils. Compensation on the basis of race and gender thus continues to be warranted.

Socioeconomic class transcends and complicates all racial and gender categories. Disproportionate numbers of minorities are members of the lower class.[14] The percentage of African Americans living below the poverty line has been hovering steadily around 30 percent since 1974. For Hispanics, this rate has been about 25 percent, and for whites the rate has been only around 9 percent.[15] These numbers are not changing. We have a cycle of poverty in this country from which it is difficult to escape. Although class considerations further magnify the existing ill-effects of racial discrimination, socioeconomic differences exist independently from race and gender. For this reason, discrimination on the basis of class and discrimination on the basis of race and gender must be dealt with separately.

Fresh Start: The Philosophy

The solution that I propose is called "Fresh Start."[16] This policy will incorporate considerations of race, gender, and socioeconomic class to grant affirmative action benefits to deserving students who are most in need. This class-, race- and gender-based system would never need to be changed, as it will adjust itself consistently to enable the "bottom" of society to lift itself to a higher level. Under the Fresh Start system, those who need affirmative action will change from generation to generation. In this way, middle- and upper-class minorities will not continually benefit from affirmative action at the expense of their lower-class counterparts.

Fresh Start will be different from current affirmative action in that it will apply only to education. Any educational institution that accepts students by application will be obliged to use Fresh Start in making its final admittance decisions. Compliance with the policy will be achieved by the same methods that are currently used to reinforce affirmative action policies. Neither Fresh Start nor any other system of affirmative action will be used in the work force. Instead, existing antidiscrimination policies will be more strictly reinforced with increased random spot-checks and investigations by the Equal Employment Opportunities Commission (EEOC). This will necessitate additional funding and reorganization, as the EEOC is already backlogged.[17] Hiring in the work force should be based solely on merit without regard to class, race, or gender.

This decision to limit Fresh Start to the educational arena is based on my assumption that education is the key out of poverty. We can equalize and thereby eradicate the societal distortions of discrimination and disadvantage by allowing everyone fair and equal access to quality education. This will bring everyone up to the same starting line. In this way, individuals will be able to achieve the full potential of their natural abilities without being either hindered or advanced by the distorting discriminations of society. The "fair and equal access" to which I refer is access corrected for socioeconomic disadvantage and racial and gender discrimination by means of Fresh Start. Through education, one acquires the skills employers seek.

Although it does exist, discrimination in the workplace is economically foolish, whereas in educational admissions there is no natural or economic deterrent to discrimination. Employers who reject better-qualified black candidatse in favor of lesser-qualified white males will receive less return on their investment than they could have. By contrast, a rival employer who hires on the basis of merit alone will benefit in the market. In the words of Wilbur Hicks, Princeton University ombudsperson, "People come in many different colors, but for businesses the most important color is green."[18]   In the realm of education, however, tuition payments are equal regardless of race or gender. The only incentives for educational facilities to admit on the basis of merit are the abstract notions of reputation (the school wants to be well represented by its graduates) and fund raising (if graduates are more successful, they may donate more money to their alma mater). A good education, however, produces worthy graduates with increased earning power. For this reason Fresh Start will not be detrimental to educational bodies.

Fresh Start is built around the theory that one should rank all citizens on the basis of socioeconomic status alone, from the richest to the single most destitute soul in the country. Then one must adjust the list to take into account the extra hardships that persons face on account of race and gender. This will require assigning some quantitative value to the amounts of discrimination experienced by different minorities. In this way, all minorities will receive their "thirty acres and a mule" which blacks were promised upon their release from slavery. Some will receive more benefit, and some less benefit according to the amount of discrimination and economic disadvantage that they have endured.

For example, if we determine that upper-class white males are statistically 10 percent higher on the socioeconomic ladder--they are granted a 10 percent lead in the analogous foot race--as compared with equally skilled, middle-class black males, then positions on the list for black males of the middle class will be augmented by 10 percent. Similarly, if Latino females are statistically 20 percent lower on the ladder than equally skilled, upper-class white males, then their positions on the list will be increased by 20 percent. These "corrected" positions represent the societal rung on which a person would be placed were it not for societal discrimination and socioeconomic disadvantage.

But people would not be granted admission into schools solely on the basis of their position on this adjusted, theoretical list. Admissions and hiring should be based on merit but adjusted in the final stages according to the list ranking. If two candidates for an admission slot are determined to be essentially equal in merit, then the one higher on the list should receive the position.

For example, if a middle-class Latino female and an equally qualified white male of the upper class were vying for a university's last opening, the Latino female should get the placement over the white male. This is evident because, on the basis of the hypothetical numbers above, the Latino female would be rated 20 percent higher than the white male. This is fair, because the middle-class Latino female will have had to overcome statistically 20 percent more hardship in society in order to reach the same position of education, talent, and merit as the upper-class white male. This 20 percent includes compensation for racial and gender discrimination and also compensation for socioeconomic disadvantage.

This system would also have effects within racial and gender groups. If variables of race and gender were held constant, Fresh Start would still take into account differences in social class. For example, if a lower-class black male and an equally talented upper-class black male were both applying to a college that only had room to admit one of the candidates, the lower-class candidate would be offered admission. This is fair, because the lower-class black male has had to overcome more socioeconomic disadvantage in reaching the same point as his upper-class counterpart. The lower-class male has worked harder to get to the same point and, therefore, is more deserving of admission. Fresh Start will not hurt middle-class minority gains, however, because members of this group will still have rightly deserved advantages over whites and individuals of the upper-middle and upper classes.

Question: If an upper-class African-American female and a lower-class white male, both of equal talent, were competing against each other for the same admissions spot, who gets the acceptance?

Answer: It depends on who has quantitatively had to overcome more discrimination and socioeconomic disadvantage in order to make it to the same point.

How can one really quantify discrimination or socioeconomic disadvantage? Is this program feasible? The answer is yes.

How it Works

In order for Fresh Start to work, a National Fresh Start matrix must be devised using data from the United States working population (see Table 1). This matrix will establish two independent ratios based on hourly wages.[19] With two independent ratios, one can isolate the effects of race and gender discrimination from those of socioeconomic disadvantage. When these ratios are averaged, each category of class, race, and gender will be compared to the upper-class white male with regard to discrimination and disadvantage.

Table 1
National Fresh Start Matrix Using White Male with Graduate Degree Standard, Based on Total Hourly Wages for Eighteen to Twenty-Four Year Olds

Educational Class:

Characteristic	(1) Not a High School Graduate[1]	(2) High School Graduate or GED	(3) Some College	(4) Bachelor's Degree	(5) Graduate Degree
White, male	.757	.785*	.806*	.903	1.00
White, female	.671	.811*	.837*	.889	.915
Black, male	.747	.770	.801	.914	.954
Black, female	.717	.743	.768	.884	.901

[1]Ninth to twelfth grade.
*Calculated using estimates of wages based on comparative trends in data, in the absence of available data.

The Fresh Start matrix can be expanded to account for an infinite number of different types of discrimination if society finds such expansions necessary. For example, we could easily calculate Fresh Start numbers taking into account veteran status, handicap, or sexual orientation. Such calculations can be done easily by computers as long as the data are available. In this case, the calculation of compensation factors becomes more "long" than difficult. For example, to add the consideration of sexual orientation to a Fresh Start matrix that takes into account only gender and black/white discrimination, one would have to consider the following categories: white/male/straight, white/male/gay, white/female/straight, white/female/gay, black/male/straight, black/male/gay, black/female/straight, and black/female/gay. For simplicity, the rest of this essay will take into account only gender and black/white racial differences. However, bear in mind that this paradigm can be easily expanded to include Asian Americans, Hispanics, Native Americans, and other groups.

Two statistics will be used to calculate Fresh Start numbers. First, *class numbers* will compare average hourly wages for specific minorities across class groups. This will provide a measure of socioeconomic disadvantage. Second, *compensation factors* will compare hourly wages for different racial and gender combinations within specific class groups. This calculation will compensate for racial and gender discrimination; it will not take socioeconomic disadvantage into account. Finally, these two factors will be averaged together to produce a *Fresh Start number*. This number will compare the total amount of unfair hardship faced for any given combination of socioeconomic class, race, and gender with that of the upper-class white male. The lower the number, the further away that category of person is from the upper-class white male and the more discrimination and disadvantage that person has faced.

Applicants for universities and schools will be placed into this National Fresh Start matrix according to their own personal data. Admissions officers will not have to do any calculating, but rather will look up their candidate on the National Fresh Start matrix using information about their race, gender, and parents' education. In this way, one will be able to determine the relative amount of discrimination that a candidate for admission has had to overcome in order to reach the desired level of achievement.

This information will be factored into a candidate's admissions decision only if he or she is at the margin of rejection. That is to say,

Fresh Start data will only be used to distinguish among a more or less equally qualified group of candidates, all of whom cannot be accepted owing to space qualifications. Fresh Start will thus avoid the problem of stigmatization from which current affirmative action suffers. Any candidate from this group of applicants who is accepted on the basis of his or her Fresh Start number is equally qualified with the other accepted candidates. In a sense, this person is even more qualified in that he or she has worked harder to get to the same level of qualification. Nonetheless, this information will be kept in the utmost confidence by the school or university.

Class Numbers

First, in a class-based system, one must have a standardized method of dividing the candidates on the basis of social class. These divisions should not be based on income. Noreen Goldman and Sara McLanahan suggest that parental education should be the primary consideration. Because education and income are correlated, an estimate of the average parental education will also be correlated to average parental income. Furthermore, because the education of parents is correlated with the education of their children, one can use estimates of average parental education as indicators of the social class of the candidates. For this reason, estimates of average parental education can be used as indicators of the social class of the candidates.[20]   Although many other factors are also important in determining the social class of individuals, McLanahan warns against using criteria that will affect people's behavior. She notes:

> [One should not] use total family income as a criteria because that discriminates against families with two working parents. You don't want to encourage parents to split up so that their children qualify for special treatment. . . . The point is that [one should not] choose measures that themselves might change parents' behavior--such as number of parents in the household or total hours of parents' work.[21]

By the same token a candidate's region is a particularly important indicator of socioeconomic class, but it should probably not be a factor. Although differences in the cost of living and huge variances in the quality of school systems exist in different parts of the country and in urban, suburban, and rural areas, one does not want to incite an influx of migration to the inner cities, for example. Hypothetically, this could happen if people moved to the cities in the hopes that their children would benefit more from Fresh Start.

As part of Fresh Start, when one applies for a position to a school or university, the section of the application that asks for one's race or gender will be expanded. Because of discrimination laws, this part of the application must be optional. In addition to race, it will ask questions about the level of education obtained by the applicant's parents. The applicant will have the option of marking "not a high school graduate," "high school graduate only," "some college, no degree," "completed college, obtained bachelor's degree," "completed graduate school, obtained graduate or professional degree" (see Figure 1).

Figure 1

This section of the application is optional. Please mark "not applicable" if the denoted parent did not raise you while you were growing up.

I. Race

[ ] African-American   [ ] Asian American
[ ] Caucasian   [ ] Hispanic
[ ] Native American   [ ] other

II. Gender

[ ] male   [ ] female

III. Mother's education: [check the last that applies].

[ ] not a high school graduate
[ ] high school graduate only (includes GED)
[ ] some college
[ ] completed college
[ ] completed graduate school
[ ] not applicable

IV. Father's education: [check the last that applies].

   [   ] not a high school graduate
   [   ] high school graduate only (includes GED)
   [   ] some college
   [   ] completed college
   [   ] completed graduate school
   [   ] not applicable

   The information gained about parental education can be used to estimate a candidate's potential earnings capacity (that is, socioeconomic class) in the job market. This statistic will be based on an average of the education of the candidate's mother and father. For the purpose of averaging the education of the candidate's parents, the various degrees of education will receive numbers. "Not a high school graduate" will be 1; "high school graduate only" will be 2; "some college," will be 3; "completed college," will be 4; and "completed graduate school," will be 6 (a rating of 6 rather than 5 is given because this is really an increase of two levels of education, as there is no category for "some graduate school, no degree").[22] If the applicant has only a single parent, then only the information from that parent will be used to determine the earnings capacity of the candidate. Using these numbers as estimates for earnings capacity, each candidate will be placed in one of five socioeconomic classes: lower, lower-middle, middle, upper-middle, or upper class.

   Each class group will receive a class number. This number is a ratio based on average parental education for a specific racial, gender, and class group, relative to the average parental education of the same racial and gender group in the upper-class group. Because education is correlated with hourly wage, one can find the average hourly wage for a person of a specific racial and gender combination in each of the five socioeconomic groups. By dividing each of these five values by the average hourly wage of the upper-class group for the same race and gender, one can find this ratio. In short, the class number will express hourly wages relative to the upper class while holding specific racial and gender categories constant. Class numbers will be calculated on a yearly basis by the Internal Revenue Service (See Table 2.)

Table 2

***Class Numbers Using a Graduate Degree Standard and
Education to Approximate Class, Based on Total Hourly
Wages for Eighteen to Twenty-Four Year Olds***

Educational Class:					
Characteristic	*(1)* *Not a High School Graduate*[1]	*(2)* *High School Graduate or GED*	*(3)* *Some College*	*(4)* *Bachelor's Degree*	*(5)* *Graduate Degree*
White, male	.514	.569*	.611*	.805	1.00
White, female	.513	.660*	.708*	.875	1.00
Black, male	.540	.593	.644	.859	1.00
Black, female	.560	.617	.664	.886	1.00

[1]Ninth to twelfth grade.
*Calculated using estimates of wages based on comparative trends in data, in the absence of available data.

Although some of this difference in wages is due to class discrimination, those who worked harder to achieve a greater depth of education deserve most of the additional wages that generally follow. However, among the candidates who are applying--the children of these differently educated parents--these differences in parental education do amount to discrimination and unfair disadvantage of a sort. Differences in the education of parents results in arbitrary differences in the education and socioeconomic class of their children. This partially justified inequity among parental wages ruins any possibility of equality of opportunity among their children.

Compensation Factors

At this point, the groundwork for the class base of the Fresh Start program is set. Now we must add race and gender to the equation before putting the plan into action. This step involves calculating "compensation factors" within each class bracket on the basis of race and gender distinctions. This calculation will isolate per-hour wage discrimination on the basis of race and gender within each class group. These compensation factors will be calculated using the white male wage as the standard.[23] The results will presumably always be one or less, unless some minority group is earning more per hour than white males in any of the five class categories.

Racial and gender-based wage discrimination unfairly influences the class groupings in society. Compensation factors will be calculated often--possibly on an annual or biannual basis. This will allow people to see both the progress that is being made and the discrimination that is still left to overcome. These statistics can be tabulated by the Internal Revenue Service on the basis of payroll and social security taxes. (See Table 3.)

Table 3
Compensation Factors Using a White Male Standard and Education to Approximate Class, Based on Total Hourly Wages for Eighteen to Twenty-Four Year Olds

Educational Class:					
Characteristic	(1) Not a High School Graduate[1]	(2) High School Graduate or GED	(3) Some College	(4) Bachelor's Degree	(5) Graduate Degree
White, male	1.00	1.00*	1.00*	1.00	1.00
White, female	.829	.962*	.965*	.902	.830
Black, male	.954	.947	.957	.968	.908
Black, female	.874	.869	.871	.882	.801

[1]Ninth to twelfth grade.
*Calculated using estimates of wages based on comparative trends in data, in the absence of available data.

One reads Table 3 as follows: in class group 1, white females make 83 percent of white male wages; black males make 95 percent of white male wages; and so on. These ratios of relative intraclass group racial and gender discrimination differ among the socioeconomic class groups: that is to say, there is an interaction between the variables of race, class, and gender. Within some socioeconomic class groups, different races and genders are discriminated against more than in others; patterns of racial and gender discrimination are not the same for each class. For example, in the lower-class group, white females face the most setbacks, while in the other four class groups, it is the black female who is lowest on the ladder. On the basis of these data, the relative amounts of racial and gender discrimination within each class group can be determined. (See Table 4.)

Table 4
Relative degree of racial amd gender discrimination
[1 = suffers most discrimination < ----------- >
5 = suffers least discrimination]

Educational Class:					
Characteristic	(1) Not a High School Graduate[1]	(2) High School Graduate or GED	(3) Some College	(4) Bachelor's Degree	(5) Graduate Degree
White, male	5	5*	5*	5	5
White, female	1	3*	3*	2	2
Black, male	3	2	2	3	3
Black, female	2	1	1	1	1

[1]Ninth to twelth grade.
*Calculated using estimates of wages based on comparative trends in data, in the absence of available data.

Fresh Start Numbers

At this point, one must combine class considerations with considerations of race and gender to find the quantitative effects of discrimination and disadvantage. To do this, the class group number must be averaged with the compensation factor for each minority and class group. This results in the Fresh Start number. The Fresh Start number is a relation of the amount of discrimination for every combination of class, race, and ethnicity as compared with the upper-class white male. The more discrimination and disadvantage due to class, race, and gender, the lower the number. (See Table 1.)

Because these numbers are statistically based estimates of the amount of total discrimination and disadvantage that a person has faced on the basis of class, race, and gender, they will be used to help make some of the difficult choices of admittance to schools. When an admissions committee has narrowed its candidate pool to a group of people who are all qualified for admission but are similar in nature, it will plug the candidates' statistics in to the Fresh Start table. Those candidates who have lower Fresh Start numbers (that is, those who have overcome more discrimination and disadvantage in order to reach the same level of qualification) will get offers of admission.

For example, if persons of each combination of black/white race, gender, and socioeconomic class group were essentially equally qualified, and each was applying for the last opening at a university or other educational institution, the Fresh Start matrix would decide the order of acceptance (that is, the order of most hardship endured) in the following manner:

Race: W = white   B = black
Gender: M = male   F = female
Class: 1 = lower class   2 = lower-middle class
             3 = middle class   4 = upper-middle class
             5 = upper class

1) WF1	5) WM1	9) BM3	13) BF4	17) BM4
2) BF1	6) BF3	10) WM3	14) WF4	18) WF5
3) BF2	7) BM2	11) WF2	15) BF5	19) BM5
4) BM1	8) WM2	12) WF3	16) WM4	20) WM5

These results are not necessarily intuitive, and yet they are based on an even combination of the two measurements that compensate for race and gender discrimination and class-based disadvantage.

Corollary Programs

Although this program does not immediately solve the social ills that are caused by discrimination, it does compensate for them in the realm of education in order that they might be overcome in subsequent generations. Furthermore, as a corollary program, the government should work to improve the overall quality of education in this country--particularly in the inner cities. Such measures will allow Fresh Start to work more swiftly. Fresh Start works easily in the private school, college, and graduate school arenas. It also works when students are asked to apply to so-called magnet schools for elementary and high school. If students are not applying to a school, however there is no vehicle through which Fresh Start can work.

Much of the classist, racist, and gender-based discrimination and disadvantage in this country is manifested through variations in the quality of education that is obtained before the point of application to college. The public schools that are located in lower-class and minority school districts tend to be of a lesser quality than schools in other areas. Significant educational damage will have already occurred before it is time for these students to apply to college. If disadvantaged students have not managed to overcome adversity sufficiently to meet minimum educational standards for entry into a school, Fresh Start cannot help them. Furthermore, many of those groups who are hit hardest by the lack of quality education will never even apply to college. These students, a disproportionate number of whom are members of the underclass and minorities, may be passed over by Fresh Start.

Nonetheless, I stop short of recommending that all educational institutions at all levels accept students by application. If such a program were instituted, qualified students who were accepted into the better elementary, junior high, and high schools would essentially have to be "bussed" to schools that would not necessarily be in their school district. Better schools in wealthier districts would remain superior, and certain schools might not be improved. This sort of program would be grossly unpopular. In any case, ensuring both quality and equality of education from the beginning is of the utmost importance. Programs such as Head Start have already been effective in doing this, and should be expanded and improved.[24] If the quality of public schooling continues to remain as low as it is, particularly in the inner cities, the socioeconomic and racial differences in education will only widen further and be even harder to overcome.

Notes

1. Martin Luther King, Jr., uses the analogy of a foot race in his book *Why We Can't Wait* (New York: Penguin Books, 1963):

   Whenever the issue of compensatory or preferential treatment for the Negro is raised, some of our friends recoil in horror. The Negro should be granted equality, they agree; but he should ask nothing more. On the surface, this appears reasonable, but it is not realistic. For it is obvious that if a man entered at the starting line in a race three hundred yards after another man, the first would have to perform some impossible feat in order to catch up with his fellow runner. (p. 134)

2. Randall Kennedy, lecture, Woodrow Wilson School of Public and International Affairs, Princeton University, March 30, 1995.
3. *Statistical Abstract of the United States*, (1993), no. 717.
4. *Statistical Abstract*, no. 737.
5. William Julius Wilson, *The Truly Disadvantaged: The Inner City, the Underclass, and Public Policy*; (Chicago: University of Chicago Press), p. 110.
6. *Statistical Abstract*, no. 717.
7. Wilson, *The Truly Disadvantaged*, p. 109.
8. Ibid. p. 111.
9. Ibid.
10. William Julius Wilson, *The Declining Significance of Race* (Chicago: University of Chicago Press), p. 19.
11. Although this is not the way affirmative action is supposed to work, the policy often mutates into a quotalike system of admittance or hiring. This is particularly evident in university admissions.
12. *Statistical Abstract* no. 622.
13. Cornel West, *Prophetic Fragments* (Trenton, N.J.: Africa World Press, 1988), p. 57.
14. *Statistical Abstract*, no. 49, 50, 53.
15. *Statistical Abstract*, no. 737.
16. I am grateful to Brian A. Goldman for the name Fresh Start.
17. Carol Swain suggests that owing to internal problems, perhaps the EEOC should be disbanded to create an entirely new organization to reinforce existing civil rights laws. This is also a viable solution in the absence of affirmative action in the workplace.
18. Wilbur Hicks, presentation to Woodrow Wilson School policy task force, Princeton, University, March 23, 1995.
19. By being based on hourly wage statistics, these ratios become more representative of the actual racial and gender-based wage discrimination and socioeconomic disadvantage that exists in the workplace. (Women,

for example, are more likely to work part-time jobs than men. For this reason, if averages of monthly or annual earnings were used, women would be overcompensated) Noreen Goldman, professor, Woodrow Wilson School, April 11, 1995.

20. Noreen Goldman, meeting, April 11, 1995.
21. Sara McLanahan, professor, Woodrow Wilson School, March 27, 1995.
22. In the case that a candidate's parents average education numbers do not work out to a whole number, the candidate's eventual Fresh Start number will be figured by averaging the Fresh Start numbers for the two appropriate classes.
23. This "white male standard" is an arbitrary one. These rankings could be just as easily adjusted to be expressed in Latino female terms or Native American male units. The white male seems to be the current standard, however, and I will continue to use it as such.
24. See chapter by Priya Rajan.

Chapter 8

Residential Segregation, Racial Discrimination, and the Road to Reform

Cindy Kam

Many Americans are tempted to dismiss discrimination and segregation as phenomena that plagued ignorant, elitist societies of earlier times. As a whole, we profess to believe in equality and equal opportunity for all human beings. Yet our individual actions do not necessarily conform to this noble mold. On the contrary, injustices and prejudice still exist; hate crimes and stereotyping continue to arise; equality and freedom of choice do not reign free in American society.

The federal government has recognized the existence and survival of racism and discrimination in many sectors of American society. Employment, education, and housing, have been the areas of worst repute, where racial discrimination has most glaringly limited the opportunities and, some would argue, the life chances of racial minorities. Antidiscrimination laws and affirmative action policies were intended to ensure equal opportunity for all Americans. Whether they have accomplished this goal and whether they have been accepted by the American public are subjects that have elicited much debate.

The affirmative action policies that have received the most attention (and the most notoriety) have been those involving employment and education which are intended to guarantee equal opportunity and to compensate for past cases of discrimination. Although most affirmative action policies have focused on jobs and schools, another aspect of life plays an important role in determining education and employment opportunities—housing. Place of residence influences both the choice (or lack thereof) of schools one might attend and the employment opportunities one might pursue. The legacy of past housing discrimination, in addition to the hardship of current housing discrimination, continue to affect the opportunities that avail themselves to minorities.

Section 1982 of the Civil Rights Act of 1866, President Kennedy's Executive Order No. 11063 in 1962, Title VI of the Civil Rights Act of 1964, and the Fair Housing Act of 1968 were all enacted to curb housing discrimination. These antidiscriminatory measures were designed to help individuals assert their right to equal treatment and, later, to work with the government to identify perpetrators of discrimination. Yet a glance at America's cities and suburbs leads one to question whether these laws have succeeded.

This chapter examines the state of fair housing in this country to assess whether antidiscrimination laws suffice in curbing discriminatory activity. It aims to answer three broad questions. How serious is residential segregation by race? Is racial segregation the result of discrimination? What government policies, if any, will temper and eventually eliminate discrimination in the housing market?

I argue that conventional antidiscrimination laws are not sufficient. Such legislation means nothing without adequate enforcement, and its reactive nature hampers its effectiveness. The firmly rooted nature of housing discrimination demands an affirmative, future-oriented stance toward fair housing and integration. Segregation by race is enforced in this country—by government programs, by local zoning laws, by the real estate and construction industries, and by prejudiced or ignorant individuals. These unpunished and even unnoticed discriminatory acts reinforce stereotypes, misconceptions, and discrimination. As segregation continues, people learn less and care less about one another; the gulf between different groups of people widens, and injustices multiply.

Because housing is inextricably tied to education and employment, the effects of residential segregation are long-standing and pervasive. Enforced residential segregation can lead to de facto school segregation and limited employment opportunities. With integration, by contrast, blacks and whites can begin to relate personally as neighbors and co-workers, to share community resources, and to support the same schools. This sustained interaction can decrease the influence of stereotypes and prejudice, thereby addressing more systemic problems of discrimination that are related to housing.

The focus here on blacks is not meant to imply that discrimination against other minorities, such as Latinos, Asians, and Native Americans does not exist. Rather, the documented evidence of discrimination against blacks indicates that blacks are more segregated in American society than any other ethnic group and are more frequently the victims of discrimination.[1] The remedies that will be addressed fall under the rubric of affirmative action housing policies. This term applies to actions that attempt to redress discriminatory actions and to work toward an integrated society that, in itself, will prevent additional discrimination. In essence, affirmative action housing policies are antidiscriminatory measures that step beyond merely reacting to past complaints and instead incorporate necessary elements for preventing future discrimination. Such affirmative action policies have included mandates that public housing developments be located in low-minority populated areas, that housing developers who receive public funds advertise especially to minorities, and that townships ensure that a certain proportion of housing units be affordable to low-income households. Other strategies include outreach support services, metropolitan rather than city-limited housing consultations, and economic incentives to move to increase heterogeneity within a community.

The Early Roots of Fair Housing Policies

As unlikely as it sounds, in the last decades of the nineteenth century, blacks and whites "lived side by side in American cities" (Massey and Denton, 1993, p. 17). Despite the disadvantages that blacks faced, urban residential segregation was not a prevalent phenomenon during this era. Blacks and whites "moved in a common social world, spoke a common language, shared a common culture, and interacted personally on a regular basis" (ibid., p. 18). Notably, though, blacks did not constitute the majority of the population within cities; prior to the twentieth century, more than 80 percent of blacks continued to confront unfair and unequal treatment as sharecroppers in the rural South (ibid.). With the advent of industrialization and the corresponding migration of blacks from rural to urban areas (especially to northern urban areas), urban whites witnessed an influx of poor and uneducated blacks who had ventured out of the rural South in search of better opportunities. Whites, threatened by this "invasion," and convinced by Social Darwinism that blacks were inherently inferior, insisted upon a system of residential segregation (Farley and Frey, 1994, p. 22).

By the 1940s some movement to the outer limits of cities had occurred, as whites opted for new forms of transportation, such as urban rail systems and cars, to escape working-class slums. At times segregation was legally enforced; in other instances it was a well-understood social norm that governed individual preferences as well as real estate practices. For the most part, the law, the housing market, and the white majority supported racial segregation. Richard Wright's acclaimed 1940 novel, *Native Son*, describes the effects of these racist housing policies. White businessmen profited from discriminating against blacks. Real estate agents refused to offer options to blacks in white areas; furthermore, with increased immigration to certain black areas (i.e., northern cities such as New York, Detroit, and Chicago), white profiteers forced blacks to pay higher rents for usually poorer-quality housing units in crowded ghettos. A dialogue from *Native Son* illustrates the relationship between white businessmen and black renters.

> "Isn't it true that you *refuse* to rent houses to Negroes if those are in [non-Negro] areas of the city?"
> "Why, yes . . . it's an old custom," Mr. Dalton said.
> "Mr. Dalton, doesn't this policy of your company tend to keep Negroes on the South Side, in one area?"
> "Well, it works that way." (Wright, 1940, p. 303)

Real estate agents and landlords took advantage of white America's explicit disdain for living near black people. Private individuals who sold their homes, real estate agents, and lenders conspired to keep blacks out of all-white areas. Sellers and realtors effectively steered blacks away from all-white areas, confining black residential options to existing minority areas. Similarly, private lending institutions ensured that blacks would not receive the financial support necessary to move into all-white neighborhoods. Local and state legislatures passed laws that mandated segregation and upheld restrictive covenants (Sander, 1988, p. 878). On the same note, public housing remained largely segregated; when local housing authorities attempted to integrate housing developments, riots and violence ensued. To appease local (white) constituencies, housing authorities built public housing complexes (intended for blacks) in all-black areas. In Chicago, in particular, the housing authority's objective was to maintain the geographic gulf between white and black Chicago (Lemann, 1991, pp. 72-73).

Federal government policies failed to condemn disreputable practices such as blockbusting,[2] restrictive racial covenants, and redlining; in fact, the Federal Housing Administration (FHA) itself perpetrated discriminatory acts. Although the federal government had pledged to help Americans achieve the American Dream of homeownership, from 1934 to 1968, the FHA mortgage program widened suburban housing options for white Americans only. FHA mortgages and Veterans Administration (VA) mortgages, along with a huge investment in the interstate highway system, triggered suburbanization and new home construction. Black Americans were excluded from these plans. The FHA sanctioned local authorities' practices of redlining; local authorities drew lines around supposedly "economically unsound" (minority or integrated) neighborhoods that would pose "bad" credit risks for these federal mortgage loans. These authorities either refused financial support for mortgages to these areas or presented more demanding conditions of support (Kushner, 1983, p. 282). Leonard Rubinowitz and Elizabeth Trosman note, "The FHA actively practiced racial discrimination in the administration of its programs (before the 1960s)" (1979, p. 495). These racist policies largely confined black Americans to degenerating central cities. The federal loans system leaned heavily toward new housing construction, more than unit rehabilitation, which contributed even more to the decay of the existing urban housing stock. Finally, the Department of Housing and Urban Development (HUD) turned a blind eye to the blatantly racist policies of local housing authorities that crammed poor blacks into isolated, already crowded, ghettos.

Although federal courts on several occasions struck down the legitimacy of segregation laws and restrictive covenants, federal agencies dismissed these decisions and continued to ignore and even to promote racist policies.[3] The Civil Rights Act of 1866, Section 1982, maintained that blacks could not be discriminated against in public and private property transactions (Kushner, 1983, p. 4). Its provisions were largely ignored, although the Supreme Court cases that upheld it expressly condemned discrimination. It was not until 1962 that the federal government took a definitive stance against housing discrimination; President Kennedy's Executive Order No. 11063 banned racial discrimination in "housing that is owned, operated, or assisted by the federal government" (ibid., p. 6). The order also vested agencies with the responsibility of taking "all action necessary and appropriate to prevent discrimination."[4] Kennedy's order proved, at best, a symbolic step toward a fair housing approach; its coverage was limited in that it applied prospectively, it did not assign enforcement responsibilities to any federal agency, and it excluded the bulk of federal housing—FHA and VA dwelling units.

Although Kennedy's Executive Order only applied to one percent of the existing housing stock and was relatively ineffective, it did mark the beginning of legislative activity on behalf of fair housing. State and local governments began to strike down their segregation laws in favor of antidiscrimination and even "experimental" integration policies (Sander, 1988, p. 880). In 1964, Title VI of the Civil Rights Act declared that no one, "on the ground of race, color, or national origin," should be discriminated against under any federally assisted program.[5] This provision covered federally subsidized units and urban revitalization programs. It did nothing, however, to address the private housing market, which constitutes the bulk of the American housing stock.

After four years of congressional quarreling and foot-dragging, President Johnson signed the Fair Housing Act of 1968, also known as Title VIII. Title VIII condemned discriminatory practices that individuals, realtors, and the government itself perpetrated. It banned discrimination in almost all of the national housing stock, with exceptions such as owner-occupied homes sold by the owner, and designed a process through which individuals could sue for damages (Graham, 1990, p. 271). It also prohibited racist practices among lenders and realtors, specifically banning preferences in advertising, blockbusting, and racial steering.[6] Title VIII signified a marked departure from "business as usual," because it legitimized the government's role in the private as well as the public housing market.

The Fair Housing Act also designed a program for the federal government; it vested the federal government with the responsibility for "'affirmatively' promoting fair housing" (Sander, 1988, p. 880). Previous measures had held no single agency or individual responsible for enforcement. Title VIII, however, designated the secretary of housing and urban development to investigate complaints and the attorney general to charge those guilty of a "pattern or practice" of discrimination. Hugh Graham comments: "While the enforcement machinery of the 1968 open housing law [has] been ineffective, the law . . . nevertheless made open housing a national policy, and discrimination in most of the nation's housing a crime" (1990, p. 275).

For most Americans and legislators, the passage of the Fair Housing Act meant that the government could now redirect its energies to education and job training programs, with the issues of open housing established, if only in name. Yet even if the laws had been fully enforced, "contemporary authorities . . . cautioned that such laws were unlikely to bring about rapid change in patterns of racial segregation" (Graham, 1990, pp. 275-276).

Residential Patterns Since the Fair Housing Act

It was not until the 1960s that racial segregation began to fade, when segregation laws were struck down and housing discrimination became illegal. With these legal barriers lifted and with the protection of the Fair Housing Act, blacks were to have access to housing options previously denied to them. Blacks would no longer be confined to minority areas; they would have choices about where they lived.

After the passage of Title VIII, some blacks did indeed take advantage of these new housing options; however, at the same time, many others remained locked in highly concentrated black areas, including the ghettos of Chicago, Detroit, New York, and St. Louis. From 1940 to 1970 residential segregation stayed at a constant level, either through local regulations or through overt discrimination by real estate agents, lenders, and neighborhood residents; through the Fair Housing Act, these obstacles were somehow expected to disappear.

Whether black-white segregation continues to exist, in and of itself, has proved to be a highly debatable subject. Some authors claim that segregation has decreased in American cities; therefore, there is no basis for the claim that discrimination still exists. Other authors have pointed to residential patterns in large metropolises to maintain that blacks and whites are still segregated. Even the optimistic authors who note decreased levels of segregation in certain areas admit that intense racial segregation in America's largest cities, where most blacks live, still exists.

Residential segregation is typically measured with the index of dissimilarity, which ranges from 0 to 100, with 100 signifying complete apartheid and 0 perfect integration.[7] Chicago heads the list as the most segregated metropolis, with a segregation index of 91 (1960 and 1970) and of 88 (1980) (Farley, 1991, p. 276). Reynolds Farley and William Frey find a broad, though modest, degree of desegregation in which the average index score fell four points in the 1980s, from 69 to 65. Attempting to prove that racial segregation has decreased, they note that the most significant strides toward integration have been made in smaller, newer metropolises (Farley and Frey, 1994, pp. 30, 40).

Less optimistic than Farley and Frey, Douglas Massey and Nancy Denton attribute the decreases in segregation in smaller, newer cities to "unusual instability in housing patterns . . . rather than to an ongoing process of neighborhood racial integration" (Massey and Denton, 1993, p. 63). In addition, these low segregation scores may simply signify that blacks compose a tiny proportion of the population, period—not that they are necessarily integrated into the community.[8] Massey claims that housing segregation has not decreased; residential patterns have remained stable in the ghettos. Cities such as New York and Newark have become even more segregated; "levels of racial segregation in large urban areas are high and show little sign of decline" (Massey, 1990, p. 330).

Blacks continue to live apart from whites; of all minorities, blacks are most segregated from whites. They are also more segregated from whites than any other ethnic group has ever been segregated (Farley and Frey, 1994, p. 32). The most well-off blacks find themselves more segregated than even the poorest Hispanics (Massey and Denton, 1993, p. 87).

As census data reveal, blacks currently make up between 12 and 13 percent of the national population. They compose 24 percent of the total population inside central cities; 56 percent of blacks live in central cities, while only 23 percent of whites do (Bennett, 1995, pp. 1-4). Nine out of ten suburban householders are white; half of all whites live in suburbs. Suburbanization, the heralded solution toward integration, has not worked; "many of the suburbs entered by blacks became extensions of inner-city ghettoes, and comparatively few suburbs were truly integrated" (Sander, 1988, p. 884). Many suburban blacks live in older areas adjacent to the central cities. These are unappealing to whites and often become black areas themselves. For example, the "suburb" of Camden, New Jersey, is even more of a ghetto than the city of Philadelphia, with higher poverty, crime, and delinquency rates; "in many ways, black suburbs replicate the problems of the inner city" (Massey and Denton, 1993, p. 69). It is a game of catch-up as whites flee black encroachment and blacks pick up the slack in the housing market. Suburbanization has not solved the problems of segregation.

The statistics are startling. Only 5.8 percent of white households (4.3 million) live in poverty areas; 55.6 percent of black households (3.9 million) live in poverty areas (Woodward, 1994, pp. 4, 42). Blacks, for the most part, are concentrated in America's central cities; furthermore, a large portion are confined to poor, black inner-city neighborhoods—the ghettos. Those who escape central cities have populated suburban ghettos. In 1995, twenty-seven years after the passage of the Fair Housing Act, whites and blacks for the most part continue to reside in separate areas, to participate in separate communities, and to live in separate societies.

Factors in Residential Patterns

Several factors determine where individuals live. Personal preferences, economic factors, and discriminatory practices are some of the internal and external elements that may determine black and white residential patterns. An examination of these factors is necessary when analyzing racial segregation, for residential separation does not necessarily connote discrimination. If blacks and whites simply prefer to live separately, perhaps policymakers ought not to intervene in these voluntary decisions. If differences in income and possibly inequality in compensation cause residential segregation, however, then the existing wage structure and the mechanisms for financing home ownership and renting may be the focus of reform. If discriminatory practices limit the residential options of individuals, then this unequal treatment also must be challenged.

Self-Segregation Theory

Many Americans assume that the current patterns of residential segregation are voluntary; individuals prefer homogeneous neighborhoods and are satisfied with their residential housing choices. Jai Poong Ryu notes that this self-selection theory holds that it is a biological instinct to be attracted to the similar and repelled by the foreign; in this view "segregation of blacks is natural" (Ryu, 1983, p. 17). Peter Mieszkowski also describes the voluntary segregation theory, which states that blacks and whites compete for territory; reciprocal prejudice leads to all-white and all-black neighborhoods (Mieszkowski, 1980, p. 9).

If these theories are true, the subject of housing segregation would not be an issue that a liberal democratic government would address; individuals would simply be exercising their own residential preferences. Indeed, politicians rally to maintain their all-black districts, black nationalists clamor for black unity, and black students even demand segregated dormitories. Yet despite these publicized events, most blacks do not seem to advocate voluntary segregation. Numerous surveys have demonstrated that blacks prefer desegregation to strict segregation, believe in integration, and support legislation to work toward these ideals. Whites too believe in the principles of integration and fair housing, although they are less likely to abide by them in practice (Massey and Denton, 1993, p. 88).

In 1969 Pettigrew's study demonstrated that 75 percent of black respondents preferred integration; only one-sixth preferred segregation (Farley, Bianchi, and Colasanto, 1979, p. 101). In 1976 and 1992, the Detroit Area Survey gauged black and white respondents' preferences regarding the racial makeup of their neighborhoods. Respondents viewed pictures of hypothetical neighborhoods with varying levels of segregation/integration. In 1976, 63 percent of blacks ranked a 50/50 composition as their first choice; 20 percent chose this mix as their second choice. Of the white respondents, 24 percent indicated that they would feel uncomfortable in a neighborhood that was 7 percent black; the discomfort level increased as the black share increased. The results in 1992 show that whites have become slightly more tolerant of blacks. Black respondents least preferred the all-white and all-black neighborhoods; this finding conflicts with the theory of voluntary segregation (Farley and Frey, 1994, p. 28).

Yet the fact that blacks and whites live in separate areas might still be proof enough to some that a certain degree of self-segregation is occurring. Blacks may segregate themselves because they do not want to be the first, or only, black family in a white neighborhood, as the Detroit Area Survey indicates. They may fear the violence, intimidation, and hostility that may confront the first black family to infiltrate a white monolith. The issue hinges not upon the case of voluntary self-segregation, but upon coerced self-segregation. Coercion disrupts freedom of choice in housing.

The theory of self-segregation also assumes that blacks have free choice to compete with whites in the housing market. The existence of this "equal playing field" can be disputed, however.

Class Differences Theory

In both the private and the public housing markets, income plays a large role in determining residence. The class differences argument maintains that those who earn more and are willing to pay more will live in wealthier areas that have better municipal services, lower crime rates, lower rates of poverty, and more affluent residents. If it is the case that blacks earn less and hence live in poorer areas, an economist would probably dismiss perceived racial segregation as merely a de facto result of the free market and no cause for alarm. Yet if this economic theory does not apply to blacks as well as to whites, then further investigation must be undertaken to deduce where the economic model decomposes.

With the Fair Housing Act of 1968, upwardly mobile blacks legally had new access to previously forbidden areas, yet movements toward integration were limited. Continued racial segregation in inner-city areas might be construed as the result of more widespread black poverty: in 1993, the median income for blacks was $21,550; for whites, the median income was $39,310. Since 1969 blacks have experienced a slight dip in earnings, while whites have benefited from a real increase. The ratio of black to white income has decreased from .61 in 1969 to .55 in 1993 (Bennett, 1995, pp. 1-2). These figures hint that, on the whole, blacks are materially worse off than whites. Economic differentiation would be expected; racial segregation could be an unsurprising outgrowth of these economic disparities.

Richard Sander writes that this economic theory "is more wrong than right" because it ignores intra-community economic diversity. He finds that "although the *median* income for blacks is much lower than the white median, the distribution of incomes for the two races largely overlaps." Dismissing this "crude economic theory," he writes that "income differences only explain from ten percent to thirty-five percent of the racial segregation actually observed" (Sander, 1988, p. 886). Income differentials barely explain racial segregation.

Farley also maintains that the effects of racial segregation are more severe than those of class segregation. Although some middle-class blacks have forged their way into suburbs, their new location does not guarantee middle-class integration. On the contrary, their white neighbors often fear that the area will soon be "taken over" by blacks; they begin to leave the area in a panic. Whites sell their units and blacks take advantage of the new supply of housing. The increased supply makes the units more accessible to lower-income blacks. As a result, suburbanization does not necessarily lead to integration between blacks and whites of similar classes (Farley, 1991, p. 288).

In a similar vein, when Massey and Denton explore the issue of class as a potential factor in segregation, they write, "the argument is easily and forcefully settled: race clearly predominates" (1993, p. 85). Even high- and middle-income blacks experience a high degree of segregation; it is not that these more affluent blacks are unaware of housing options outside the ghetto.

Discrimination Theory

The Fair Housing Act signified the national government's most definitive approach toward ensuring open housing for all Americans. Unlike previous measures, Title VIII designated an enforcement agency and applied to almost all of the nation's housing stock. Most Americans and legislators believed, and probably continue to believe, that the Fair Housing Act effectively resolved the issues of discriminatory housing practices.

Despite such optimism, integration has not occurred, and as previously discussed, the self-segregation and economic theories cannot account for much of the continuing segregation. The Fair Housing Act has not completely fulfilled its goals. Nathan Glazer comments: "Discriminatory practices seem substantially more widespread in the sale and rental of housing than in employment or education, though it is impossible to quantify this proportion in any of these areas" (1987, p. 134). Blacks hence face a limited range of choices, and this limit infringes upon blacks' rights—rights that Title VIII purported to ensure.

Narrowing the residential options for blacks occurs in both subtle and overt ways. Individuals can use violence to intimidate minorities. Real estate agents can manipulate the apparent supply of housing. Lenders can identify areas or even people as "bad risks" and refuse financial support. Local councils can use zoning ordinances to restrict entry into the area. Racial discrimination continues to fuel racial segregation.

Mechanisms for Maintaining and Fostering Discrimination

What factors in individual decision making, the housing and lending market, and government policy have permitted, and even contributed to, the survival of discrimination? Factors such as lax enforcement on the part of the federal government, white disinterest in and even hostility toward black civil rights, misconceptions and stereotypes among blacks and whites, white opposition to potential black neighbors, and loopholes in "affirmative" legislation are among of the elements that have stymied attempts to uproot racial discrimination in housing. Although this discrimination is less blatant than that of the era before 1968, its effects are no less pernicious.

Personal and Group Prejudice

Polls, surveys, and everyday discourse demonstrate that in the 1990s, most Americans have fully accepted the principle of racial equality. They believe that people of any race ought to have equal opportunities in employment, education, and housing. To some analysts, such results demonstrate that Americans are becoming more tolerant of others and more accepting of the rights of racial and ethnic minorities. Others would maintain that the American people have not become less racist; they have merely become better at concealing racist tendencies.

The issue of open housing is one that has gained acceptance in theory; as Paul Sniderman and Thomas Piazza write, "the *principle* of equal treatment has been accepted . . . the legitimacy of official segregation . . . has evaporated. This represents a sea change in American public life" (1993, p. 33). Americans are more likely than ever to accept the fact that minorities have the right to choose their residence. But acceptance of broad principles does not necessarily translate into approval of specific policies aimed at realizing those principles.

The Detroit Area Survey of 1976 has been the most widely cited assessment of the different preferences of whites and blacks in racial residential makeup. In 1992, when the survey was performed again, whites were more tolerant of blacks. The percentage of whites who would feel uncomfortable in an area that was 7 percent black decreased from 24 percent to 16 percent. Likewise, the percentage of whites who would leave an area where one-third of the households were black dropped from 41 percent in 1976 to 29 percent in 1992. The Detroit Area Survey demonstrates that while white tolerance of black neighbors has increased over time, whites still prefer areas with fewer blacks. Whites are hesitant about moving into mostly black areas and feel uncomfortable as the number of blacks in their neighborhoods increases; a majority would move if black households composed 57 percent of the neighborhood, thereby outnumbering white households (Farley and Frey, 1994, pp. 28-29). Blacks and whites both may claim to accept racial integration to an extent; their differences lie in the degree to which they will accept racial mixing.

As Sander observes, it is not racial integration that whites oppose; rather, it is racial resegregation that they fear. Whites may be willing to live in stably integrated areas, especially with blacks of similar socioeconomic status; yet whites become wary when the black population begins to increase. Blacks and whites have different measures of integration; blacks feel most comfortable in neighborhoods with 30-60 percent black households, while whites prefer neighborhoods that are 20 percent black (Sander, 1988, p. 896). These different conceptions of integration are one cause of racial turnover.

The classic theory of housing discrimination states that white neighborhoods prefer to remain primarily white, while blacks prefer to live in integrated areas. A small proportion of blacks may be acceptable to local whites in a certain number of areas; black demand for entrance into these areas exceeds the supply. Whites will accept this integration until the "tipping point" is reached. At this tipping point, whites begin to leave the area—usually in large numbers—out of fear that the area will become resegregated; this sudden departure of whites—not the arrival of blacks—causes the market prices in the area to fall. As whites move out, blacks move in because (1) blacks are more willing to live in areas with increasing black populations, and (2) the market obstacles are removed (the price is lower and realtors and lenders permit the entry of black homeseekers). White demand thus "drops off sooner than does black demand, and the prophecy of resegregation comes to pass" (Sander, 1988, p. 897). Sander contends that the obstacles to racial integration are found not in white individuals' personal rejection of blacks as individuals, but in whites' rejection of blacks as a group.

Massey and his colleagues note that the "tipping point" model accepts the fact that whites have a white enclave to which they can flee; "given black preferences for racially mixed neighborhoods, however, such enclaves can only be maintained through discriminatory actions" (Massey, Gross, and Shibuya, 1994, p. 442). These discriminatory actions, on the individual, noninstitutionalized level, manifest themselves in hostility and outright violence as well as more manipulative means, such as outbidding a prospective minority homeseeker. When whites feel threatened by resegregation they leave the area, fearing economic and social problems such as lowered values of their homes, increased crime, increased social disorder, and decreased neighborhood prosperity. They head for "protected areas" that, supposedly, will not be vulnerable to infiltration and takeover. These areas are protected by the predispositions and misconceptions of the individual residents, the operation of the housing and lending market, the misuse of local zoning regulations, and the lax enforcement of Title VIII.

The Housing and Lending Markets

The housing and lending markets, both private and public, have also shaped the racial composition of neighborhoods. Those who present, offer, and sell housing as well as those who finance housing have a subtle yet powerful ability to influence where homeseekers reside.

As recently as 1991, HUD conducted a Housing Discrimination Study (HDS) to determine the extent of discrimination in the housing rental and sales market.[9] The study evaluates the incidence of "unfavorable treatment" given to blacks and Hispanics seeking homes in urban areas. The HDS notes that discrimination can occur in any of three stages: "Housing Availability," "Contributions to Completing a

Transaction," and "Steering." The black and Hispanic auditors in the study represented not an average homeseeker, but one "qualified to rent or buy the average housing unit advertised in a major metropolitan newspaper" (Turner, Struyk, and Yinger, 1991, p. vii). No one can argue that economic disadvantage is the cause of the unfavorable treatment. The study finds that blacks receive unfavorable treatment in all three stages; renters have a 46 percent probability and buyers have a 50 percent probability of encountering unfavorable treatment (ibid., 1991, p. 36).

In stage one, the real estate agent may withhold information from the homeseeker. HDS auditors were responding to advertisements in large metropolitan newspapers that were supposedly open to all individuals. When approached by blacks, however, real estate and rental agents refused to grant appointments or lied about unit availability. In terms of the "severity of discrimination," blacks are likely to be shown or recommended 25 percent fewer units in the rental market and 21 percent fewer units in the sales market; "without complete information about available units, minority homeseekers cannot participate equally in the housing market" (Turner, Struyk, and Yinger, 1991, pp. 13, 16-17). The problem is information failure in the "regulated" housing market.

In stage two, minority homeseekers may experience unfavorable treatment in attempting to complete their housing transactions; they may be presented with less appealing conditions, such as higher rents, mandatory security deposits, application fees, and shoddier amenities. Whites were often given incentive discounts. The HDS notes: "Rental agents made a greater effort to do business with majority customers than with minorities. The overall index of unfavorable treatment is 41 percent for blacks." The HDS further finds that "agents are more likely to ask minority buyers about their qualifications and less likely to ask about their housing needs" (Turner, Struyk, and Yinger, 1991, p. 23).

In the third stage of the home search, minorities may confront racial steering. Although steering is difficult to document, it can certainly influence the housing choices of homeseekers. HDS finds that in 21 percent of audits, black homeseekers are shown homes in areas with a higher minority population than are white auditors.

Through incomplete information, misleading service, and steering, blacks are precluded from fully participating in the housing market. In analyzing why discrimination in housing occurs, Yinger provides two possibilities: the "customer-prejudice hypothesis" and the "agent-prejudice hypothesis." In the former, realtors and sellers cater to the preferences of their valued customers, who are prejudiced whites. In the latter, realtors and sellers themselves are prejudiced (Yinger, 1987, p. 45).

Besides confronting these barriers in searching for a home, blacks also face formidable obstacles in financing their units. The self-perpetuating discriminatory practices in real estate interplay with similar practices in the lending business; real estate brokers may discriminate "to obtain cooperation from discriminating lenders" (Yinger, 1987, p. 46). Several studies of the banking industry have confirmed that residents or potential residents of racially mixed or all-black neighborhoods receive unfavorable treatment. These neighborhoods, when compared with white neighborhoods of similar socioeconomic status, receive less private credit, less mortgage funding, and fewer loans for home improvements. Current research demonstrates that income alone cannot account for differentials in loan rejection rates between blacks and whites; "high-income blacks were rejected more often than low-income whites in thirty-five metropolitan areas" (Massey and Denton, 1993, pp. 106-108). There appears to be a strong case for racial discrimination in financial spheres.

Despite this type of discrimination, whereby blacks receive less financial support than whites, residents of integrated areas fare worst of all. Banks are more reluctant to support integrated areas than all-white or all-black areas, for fear of potential instability or resegregation. The fact that banks do not back integrated areas "institutionally restricts white demand for racially mixed neighborhoods and builds resegregation structurally into urban housing markets" (Massey and Denton, 1993, p. 107). Until racial integration disentangles itself from racial resegregation, the "takeover" theory, the odds are stacked against steps toward integrated residential patterns.

The Role of the Government

Federal, state, and local governments have the ability to condone and to condemn certain moral principles. Activities on each level of government have contributed to continued housing discrimination. Title VIII gave HUD the bulk of the responsibility for overseeing the law. The Justice Department was also closely involved in prosecuting brokers and lenders who had a history of discrimination. In addition state and local governments found subtle ways of manipulating zoning ordinances to exclude blacks and other minorities.

The Department of Housing and Urban Development

Title VIII gave HUD the power to investigate and mediate in complaints about discrimination. HUD had an "affirmative mandate" not only to refrain from discrimination in its own programs and to respond to individual complaints but also to make strides toward achieving "fair housing throughout the United States" (Rubinowitz and Trosman, 1979, p. 493). The Fair Housing Act was a symbolic gesture that lacked pragmatic punch; hindered by other arms of government, its own programmatic decisions, and Title VIII's provisions, HUD has received attention not for its initiative but, rather, for its inaction.

From HUD's first appropriation in FY 1969, the department's enforcement prerogative was ignored. Congress appropriated only $2 million of the requested $11 million necessary for the deployment of 850 enforcement officers. This short shrift indicates the low priority that Congress assigned to the protection of fair housing.

To its further detriment, HUD has been victim of the changing winds of politics; the streak of conservative administrations, broken only by President Carter in 1976 and President Clinton in 1992, did not bode well for Title VIII enforcement. Under Presidents Nixon and Ford, HUD received little support for its duties. The Carter administration pushed HUD more than the two previous administrations had, while HUD drafted regulations that would specifically define and prohibit discriminatory practices such as steering and redlining. President Reagan's moratorium on new regulations, however, blocked these initiatives. Reagan's administration also dismantled mechanisms for open housing. Under President Bush, HUD again received little attention. The Clinton administration, in contrast, has openly supported the efforts of HUD Secretary Henry Cisneros, who has pushed for new initiatives that would open housing opportunities for low-income Americans. As a result, Cisneros has "done more for fair housing than any secretary in the history of the agency" (Gallagher, 1994, p. 12). But Cisneros has encountered opposition from the 104th Congress, which has severely cut the funds available to HUD for all programs, including that of fair housing enforcement.

Political limitations aside, HUD has also failed to uproot discrimination in its own procedures and programs. Title VIII declared that HUD must consider the race of occupants and the racial composition of areas chosen for HUD-assisted housing. Yet despite this race-conscious, affirmative mandate, HUD "typically settled for less than full compliance with the law and generally did not conduct follow-up investigations. . . . Perhaps the worst indictment of HUD's enforcement efforts has been its failure to prevent racial steering by realtors and lenders who use HUD-insured loans to finance the very transactions that result from steering" (Sander, 1988, p. 889). Through several of its programs, instead of consciously providing opportunities to integrate communities, HUD has maintained race-neutral policies that overlook and uphold residential segregation.

Through its Section 235 program from 1969 to 1972, HUD provided low-income families with attainable home ownership opportunities that promised low-cost financing. This large-scale program, however, acceded to private market forces that steered whites into new suburban homes and blacks into decrepit, inner-city units. With Section 235, HUD ignored race and the pervasive forces at work among brokers, developers, lenders, and community groups that perpetuated discrimination. HUD did not require local HUD offices to take action toward expanding the housing options for minorities, nor did it ensure that applicants were cognizant of the duties of home ownership. HUD could also have counseled white and black families about possibilities in integrated areas. But HUD did not fulfill any of its affirmative action responsibilities; hence, the typical patterns of residential segregation continued.

Similarly, HUD has also taken race-blind approaches with respect to public housing placement and tenancy. The federal Section 8 Housing Assistance Program basically gives low-income applicants a voucher to be used in the private housing market, subject to the agreement of the private landlord. Section 8 had the potential to widen housing options for holders of the vouchers; no longer would their choices be limited to public housing projects. But because HUD has not actively supported black families, blacks confine themselves to black areas, for fear of white hostility or market discrimination. When voucher-holders receive counseling and assistance, housing patterns have become more desegregated (Lief and Goering, 1987, pp. 242-249). The Section 8 program is another demonstration of HUD's failure to fulfill its affirmative mandate.

HUD's greatest area of influence has been in the public housing projects. For the construction of public housing projects, local housing authorities have turned to HUD for funding; as funder, HUD has had a direct responsibility to ensure that the programs upheld the concept of fair housing. HUD instituted a "first-come, first-served" rule that mandated that local authorities give tenants the first vacancies available, rather than allow tenants to be generally funneled into homogeneous housing projects, as they had been before. This new rule, however, had so many exceptions that local authorities could still capriciously assign tenants. HUD turned a blind eye, moreover, to local authorities who constructed housing projects for blacks in all-black areas. It was not until the Supreme Court in 1975 ordered HUD to change its policies that it had to take an active stance toward desegregation within public housing projects.[10]

The department's many mistakes in program administration, in addition to its organizational limitations, have stymied HUD's compliance with its mandate. In 1969 HUD limited its duties to reacting to the complaints of individuals. Instead of initiating investigations of discrimination, HUD staff had to rely upon the gumption of the few individuals keen enough to detect discrimination and brave, patient, and determined enough to file a complaint. The major criticism of HUD rests in its failure to properly exercise its enforcement responsibilities. As Massey and Denton cynically note, "Although the country had its fair housing law, it was intentionally designed so that it would not and could not work" (1993, p. 195).

HUD's role under Title VIII was one of informal arbiter and intermediary. It could neither enforce compliance nor file criminal charges against those who broke the law. The other structural limit to Title VIII was its reliance upon individuals to file suit against a particular person, agency, or organization; yet individuals themselves are often unaware of discrimination. This emphasis on individual remedies as opposed to broader-based solutions confined HUD's duties to merely reacting to past cases of discrimination rather than pursuing farther-reaching solutions.

The 1988 Fair Housing Amendments attempted to remedy these deficiencies in enforcement and prosecution. The amendments facilitated the process of filing a complaint by extending the time to file a complaint by four-fold (to two years), by streamlining the hearing process, and by giving administrative judges the power to order full redress for grievances, with additional fines of $10,000 for the first breach and $50,000 for the third. HUD now had to complete investigations within a hundred days or else inform the involved parties of the reasons for the delay. In addition, the punitive punishment for a history of discrimination was increased to $50,000 for the first conviction. And HUD finally received the power to initiate investigations unprompted by private complaints; any findings were required to be tried before an administrative judge.

The intentions and the mechanisms are currently in place for HUD to attempt to eliminate housing discrimination. Nevertheless, problems continue. As a result of the 1988 amendments, more complaints have been filed, yet few investigations have been initiated by the secretary of HUD. HUD suffers from inadequate resources and "has been plagued by persistent and debilitating backlogs at the investigation and conciliation stage of the process. . . . At times this backlog has threatened to undermine the federal government's entire enforcement effort." For example, in FY 1992, HUD received 11 percent more complaints than it had in FY 1991. Yet of the 6,352 complaints it received, by the end of the fiscal year, 2,522 complaints were still pending, uncompleted (Relman, statement to U.S. Congress, 1994). Despite the fact that the amendments might have facilitated filing complaints, HUD itself is understaffed and unprepared to handle such a load.

HUD has also been hurt by political turmoil, with its existence put into jeopardy by the 104th Congress. Vociferous attacks have deemphasized HUD's enforcement responsibilities while discrediting its operations as an agency. Continued cuts to HUD's budget make the future and the priority of enforcement funding uncertain.

The Department of Justice

Although Title VIII gives HUD most of the authority for overseeing fair housing, the Department of Justice plays an important role in upholding fair housing. The attorney general has the duty to file suit against the "institutional actors in the housing market" who have a history of discrimination. Although the Justice Department has boasted a better record of enforcing fair housing than HUD has, it too has suffered from limited resources. Attorney employment reached a maximum of twenty during the Carter administration; but during the Reagan years, cutbacks in funding resulted in cutbacks in action. Litigated cases dropped from thirty to zero in the first year of the Reagan administration (Sander, 1988, pp. 889-890). This elimination stemmed not only from lack of financial support but from hostile leadership in the administration. Under the Clinton administration, the Department of Justice has received more attention and praise for its efficiency in processing cases.

Local Housing Authorities

On the local level, many municipal governments and community groups have instituted and relied upon exclusionary zoning ordinances to screen out low-income homeseekers and, by implication, minorities. Municipal zoning ordinances, originally designed to protect the public health, are used to regulate lot size and unit type. For example, some communities set minimum lot requirements and rule out multifamily units.

In implementing federal (HUD) programs, local housing authorities have often failed to abide by the tenets of Title VIII. As previously mentioned, some have been guilty of consciously separating blacks and whites. Local authorities such as the Chicago Housing Authority have steered blacks into all-black public housing projects.

The current means of recognizing and rectifying housing discrimination rests upon individuals' complaints. Yet the nature of discrimination in the housing and lending market often prevents the individual homeseeker from realizing that he or she is the victim of discrimination. Hence much of the discrimination that occurs goes unrecorded and unpunished.

Measures for Reform

Individual decision making, the housing market, and the government have combined to thwart efforts toward open housing in America. What has been, can, and should be done to ensure fair housing for all Americans? Both successful and less successful methods of combating discrimination in the housing market are considered here. Effective reform involves several factors: program objectives, necessary components, obstacles to implementation, and assessment of success in accordance with goals. Policy recommendations will follow in the next section.

Benign Discrimination, a.k.a. Benign Quotas

It is hard to imagine that benign discrimination would be socially acceptable or politically feasible; as the old maxim states, "Two wrongs don't make a right." Proponents of benign discrimination, however, believe it can redress past discrimination. Sander describes benign discrimination as "lessening racial barriers through a form of social engineering. In contrast, 'invidious discrimination' intends to create racial barriers." Areas that are most prone to influxes of minorities because of their proximity to central cities have instituted benign quotas in an attempt to maintain a desirable racial balance in a community. Suburban strategies that overtly attempt to balance racial composition through separate waiting lists violate Title VIII and the Constitution's equal protection clause (Sander, 1988, pp. 907, 927).

Public housing developments may also use benign discrimination. Starrett City, a housing development in New York City, used separate, race-based waiting lists—one white and one black--in an attempt to maintain a 64 percent white, 22 percent black, 8 percent Hispanic population. For Starrett City, situated in a predominantly black area, black demand far exceeded white demand, which meant that blacks had to wait much longer than whites for units. The district and circuit courts both struck the Starrett City quotas down as illegal and in violation of Title VIII (Sander, 1988, pp. 907-912).

Starrett City is only one of many housing developments and suburbs that seem to have violated the very principle of nondiscrimination that they were attempting to carry out. Although the courts have emphasized the importance of integration, they have overturned benign quotas as illegal.

Affirmative Marketing

Affirmative marketing, a counter to racial steering of the past, suggests to blacks and whites alike that they explore new residential options; this measure shows blacks homes in mostly white areas and vice versa, unveiling new, previously unconsidered housing choices. Affirmative marketing is also known as benign steering and can be administered through in-depth housing counseling and outreach programs.

Since 1972 HUD has required that agencies and developers involved in the department's subsidized and unsubsidized programs develop affirmative fair housing marketing plans (AFHMs). The plans require that units be publicized to minorities using advertisements that clearly display an "equal opportunity slogan or logo," that minority media be used, that agencies comply with nondiscriminatory regulations in hiring, and that agents receive training—oral and written—on nondiscriminatory practices. Although the AFHM regulations are limited in application (there are a series of exceptions to the regulations), and although they have been barely enforced or monitored, they do provide a model for examining affirmative marketing techniques.

Communities have also attempted managed integration by themselves advertising for a certain type of homeseeker in order to maintain a certain racial balance. Affirmative marketing may also include site tours and counseling. Unlike detrimental steering practices, affirmative marketing "is supported by law, results in an integrative move, and expands housing choice. Steering is against the law, results in a segregative move, and restricts housing choice" (Saltman, 1991, p. 430).

Shaker Heights, Ohio, is one example of an extremely integrated community that stems from affirmative marketing. The Shaker Heights program targets racial groups whose numbers are low in the community; "it is a conscious effort to maintain racial integration and stability in that community of some 32,000 people." The affirmative marketing program gives tours, distributes information regarding schools, businesses, and real estate, and encompasses a regional market. The housing values in Shaker Heights have risen 45 percent in six years. A regional effort, the Shaker Heights program cooperates with the governments and school systems of nearby suburbs (Saltman, 1991, p. 432).

Expanding Information

Congress has made small steps toward furthering open housing; the Home Mortgage Disclosure Act (HMDA), passed and amended in the 1970s, required that "federally chartered fiscal institutions" disclose the locations, incomes, and race of those granted and denied loans. In addition, the 1977 Community Reinvestment Act required that federal banking institutions address the needs of communities as a whole; they must not exclude low-income areas. Although these changes have made possible studies of the relationship between race and lending, the reporting might, in turn, convince lenders that subtle discrimination can be found.

In the 1980s, the goal of fair housing was aided when the Supreme Court held that audits of real estate agencies and lending institutions were legally admissible evidence of discrimination. This liberal interpretation of Title VIII has strengthened fair housing organizations' ability to challenge discrimination through the courts. Testers, who investigate realtors' and lenders' fair housing practices by posing as home buyers, can now themselves sue agencies for discrimination. The widespread use of testing may force real estate agencies and lending institutions to be aware of the possibilities of getting caught in an unflattering situation.   The fact that HUD and private fair housing organizations regularly conduct audits not only facilitates the detection of discriminatory practices (testers are more aware than the average person of what can be construed as discriminatory treatment), but also expedites the process of filing a complaint, since fair housing organizations are conversant with the procedures involved. As of 1986, HUD has granted funding to fair housing organizations (both public and private) to conduct audits and to implement education and outreach programs.   Testing programs can help discourage discrimination as well as encourage minorities to venture into new areas.

Antisnob Zoning: The Class-Based Approach

Because of the extensive interplay between race and class, some reformers have suggested a class-based rather than a race-based approach, believing that it might be more politically feasible.   The premise is that a class-based approach will implicitly improve the lives of many blacks, for they will presumably be involved in a class-based initiative aimed at tearing down the economic barriers to certain communities. Under class-based zoning initiatives, communities are required to provide a minimum level of low-income housing; thus low-income families and individuals would have more housing options. The concentration of poor people in central-city ghettos might also begin to decrease, as the poor are dispersed in neighboring communities.

As already noted, many local municipalities have abused zoning ordinances under the guise of maintaining the integrity of an area. Suburbanites contend that multifamily units may cause overcrowding, that small lot sizes will disturb the traffic patterns, and so on. In New Jersey and Massachusetts, antisnob laws have been implemented to open up these previously closed communities.

In New Jersey, for example, affluent municipalities had long manipulated zoning ordinances to screen out the poor and, by implication, minorities.[11]   The Mount Laurel I, II, and III decisions, which spanned the late 1970s and early 1980s, mandated that each community ensure that a certain proportion of low-income housing exist within its boundaries, thereby reversing this exclusionary zoning. These decisions rested upon a clause in the New Jersey state constitution, which gave the state authority to regulate property use for the "general welfare." *Mt. Laurel I* (1975) terminated the capricious and calculated authority of local municipalities; municipalities had to provide their "fair share of the regional need for low and moderate-income housing" (Lamar, Mallach, and Payne, 1989, p. 1199). The state supreme court handed down the decision rather naively, however, expecting voluntary compliance. With no guidelines to follow and no penalties to avoid, municipalities ignored the ruling.

Mount Laurel returned to the courts in 1983 as a result of this inaction. In *Mount Laurel II* (1983), a more detailed set of stipulations focused not only on removing barriers to low- and middle-income homeseekers, but also on providing a realistic opportunity for low- and middle-income families to find housing in the area. The court opinion suggested that municipalities provide incentives to developers to construct low-cost housing; additionally, each municipality's fair share would be precisely calculated. Enforcement mechanisms were also specific; three judges would oversee *Mount Laurel* cases, and they would commission experts to advise municipalities. *Mount Laurel III* affirmed the jurisdiction of the new Council of Affordable Housing (COAH), established in 1985, over *Mount Laurel* cases.

The success of *Mount Laurel I, II*, and *III* has been mixed. On the positive side, 31,000 units, as of 1994, have been constructed; in light of decreased federal support for construction, *Mount Laurel* housing has contributed significantly to the affordable housing stock. Private developers have constructed the bulk of the new housing units. A survey demonstrated that this process of building improved people's attitudes about affordable housing; survey respondents believed that the housing posed a social benefit to the community (Lamar, Mallach, and Payne, 1989, p. 1260).

Implementing the *Mount Laurel* decisions has met obstacles, however. Municipalities attempted to set aside half of all of the required units for individuals who already either lived or worked in the community. In 1993 the state public advocate filed suit against six municipalities that had adopted this occupancy preference, on the grounds that the current minority population was disproportionately small in relation to the housing region and that such preferences constituted a discriminatory standard. The state supreme court supported the conclusions of the public advocate, noting that "a facially neutral law or policy will be held to be a prima facie violation of Title VIII if it results in a discriminatory impact on the sale or rental of housing, even though there is no evidence of discriminatory intent" (Grieder, 1993, p. 33).

Under a loophole in the *Mount Laurel* decisions, moreover, municipalities were provided with a mechanism through which they could basically pay poorer townships to absorb their fair share of affordable housing. These Regional Contribution Agreements (RCAs) contradict the spirit of the *Mount Laurel* decisions.

In addition, reliance upon the private market hinders the *Mount Laurel* decisions; although steps have been taken towards increasing the housing stock, the private market has still not addressed the housing options for all families in need. Marketing for *Mount Laurel* units has also limited the decisions' ability to address regional housing needs; marketing has been concentrated in local areas, via word of mouth and other informal methods. Outreach programs to market housing opportunities to those from inner-city areas have barely been initiated.

In terms of alleviating the problems of racial segregation and housing discrimination, the class-based approach New Jersey has taken has achieved limited success. Some maintain that class-based opposition to integration is loosely disguised racial prejudice at work. The organization and implementation of the *Mount Laurel* decisions have failed in affirmatively reaching out to populations in urban areas, which are mainly black areas. The compliance with the law and the actual construction of units has been a slow, tedious process, hampered by local opposition. The *Mount Laurel* model, nevertheless, does provide a tentative scheme of how to try to integrate communities—economically and, by implication, racially—through low-income housing schemes.

The Metropolitan Solution: The Gautreaux Program

As a result of the 1975 Supreme Court decision in *Gautreaux v. Hills*,[12] the Chicago Housing Authority (CHA) and HUD have collaborated on a race-based remedy to redress years of discriminatory practices that segregated public housing developments. The Court-ordered remedy was a scattered-site construction plan, in which new public housing projects had to conform to a set of guidelines concerning the height, density, size, and placement of the units. The new public housing units would be scattered in nonblack areas and designed to blend into the existing housing fabric of the area. Yet for years after the ruling, nothing was done to implement the scattered-site element. CHA officials shied away from the unpopular notion of building public housing, and it was not until 1987 that the Court designated a private developer, the Habitat Company, as the "Receiver," responsible for implementing the scattered-site program.

Habitat's success has been limited by varying degrees of community opposition to public housing construction and by the high land prices that have effectively blocked Habitat's efforts to build. Nevertheless, it has constructed over one thousand units in seven years (Cunniff, 1994).

The other arm of the *Gautreaux* remedy is the much-celebrated Section 8 housing assistance program. This program operates through a private fair housing organization, the Leadership Council for Metropolitan Open Communities (LCMOC). LCMOC has designed a comprehensive program to help families move out of Chicago's public housing and into nearby suburban communities. The Gautreaux Program takes a holistic approach to the problems of those living in Chicago's public housing. Moving families to the suburbs not only provides them with job opportunities, improved schools, and safe communities, but also exposes them to cultural norms of hard work, diligence, and respect.

Because the *Gautreaux* consent decree was based upon race, the Gautreaux Program helps black families. These families receive intensive training in homeseeking and home duties as well as counseling on responsibility, motivation, and confidence. A counselor keeps tabs on the family throughout the process of searching for a home. Because this arm of the *Gautreaux* remedies is based on a family-by-family approach, little community opposition has arisen. James Rosenbaum and Susan Popkin (1990) compared the Gautreaux Program Section 8 families with CHA Section 8 families. In both groups, the families came from CHA public housing projects and were primarily female-headed. CHA Section 8 families typically stayed within the city, in minority areas, and did not receive any benefits besides the voucher itself. Rosenbaum and Popkin found that families in the Gautreaux Program withstood more hostile neighborhoods, tougher schools, and transportation barriers, since public transportation in these areas is less developed than in the city of Chicago. Yet despite these obstacles, the Gautreaux Program families had higher rates of employment (surprisingly, since the LCMOC neither encouraged nor discouraged seeking employment), improved school performance, and higher satisfaction levels with their communities and schools. Those who really moved to the suburbs were also more likely to be friends with whites and had as many friends as they did in their old neighborhoods.

The success of the Gautreaux Program suggests many policy possibilities. Small, family-by-family initiatives do not elicit as vociferous a public outcry as larger-scale movements to construct public housing in the suburbs. Being in the suburban milieu seems unequivocally better for these families, who feel better about their own safety, self-actualization, and ambitions. Role models play a part in inspiring them to work. "The results indicate that neighborhoods make a great difference in their quality of life" (Rosenbaum and Popkin, 1990, pp. 1-4).

The *Gautreaux* and *Mount Laurel* models highlight the necessity for comprehensive programs that encompass outreach services, affirmative marketing, and full compliance. At the same time, they stimulate fears of "gutting the ghetto" of those individuals who have the most initiative, leadership skills, and hope. Programs that attempt to move people—be it through low-income set-asides, affirmative marketing, or metropolitan referrals-must also address the issues confronting ghetto neighborhoods in transition. Metropolitan programs must not only draw people out of the central cities but also enhance the quality of life within them in order to stimulate economic and racial integration in cities as well as in their surrounding communities.

Policy Recommendations

The programs discussed here are only a sampling of the many experiments currently taking place in communities across America. Many of them have succeeded, in one way or another, in achieving nondiscrimination and integration. What more general and specific recommendations should be considered as community organizations, nonprofits, local municipalities, and the federal government attempt to uproot housing discrimination?

1. The federal government must commit itself not only to curtailing discriminatory practices in its own programs and procedures, but also to promoting race-conscious remedies to compensate for and to undo the damages from decades of promoting and permitting racist policies.

- Public position-taking. To help prioritize the elimination of housing discrimination, public figures need to endorse the enforcement and actions of HUD and fair housing agencies. Extensive media campaigns must educate the public and public officials on the pervasiveness of discrimination. Legislators must also recognize the problem of housing discrimination so that they will support and enact programs that strike at the roots of housing discrimination.

- Active investigation. HUD must actively investigate now that it has the power to do so. Even with Secretary Henry Cisneros's aggressive leadership, secretary-initiated investigations have been disappointingly low. Active investigations must become an institutionalized expectation of the secretary of HUD.

- More efficient, more thorough investigation. HUD needs more resources to reduce and eventually eliminate the backlog of cases currently pending. HUD closes many cases prematurely, without adequate investigation, because it lacks the personnel support to carry out full investigations (Relman, statement to U.S. Congress, 1994). Such lax and incomplete enforcement discredits the agency's potential threat to violators of Title VIII.

- Adequate resources to HUD. HUD still suffers from understaffing and inadequate resources. Enforcement composes a minuscule portion of HUD's budget as in FY 1993, civil rights enforcement received $65 million out of the annual spending of $26 billion (less than half of 1 percent of annual spending). The FY 1995 budget proposes cuts of $150 million, which in itself is more than twice the budget for enforcement.

- More demanding standards for federal programs. All federally assisted housing programs and grants (including Community Development Block Grants) should adopt an affirmative stance toward eliminating housing and lending discrimination. Potential recipients of grants should be investigated prior to the grant for potential violations of Title VIII and Title VI of the 1964 Civil Rights Act.

- Increased support to state and local bodies. HUD has shifted much of the responsibility for enforcement to state and local agencies; in doing so, it must ensure that these agencies are properly monitored, trained, and staffed. State and local agencies should be regularly monitored in program and organizational matters, and they should be intensively trained in cultural sensitivity, legal recourses for discrimination, and the subtle ways in which discrimination is played out in government, the housing and lending markets, and individual decisions. State and local agencies must also receive adequate funding to cope with the huge caseloads that deluge their offices.

- Tougher penalties. The Fair Housing Amendments of 1988 increased punitive measures against those individuals found guilty of an isolated incident of discrimination as well as those convicted of a pattern and practice of discrimination. Another possibility to be considered is the criminalization of discrimination.

2. Change the incentives for real estate and lending institutions by altering the norms of the industry—focusing on disrupting the networks that perpetuate discrimination.

- Incentives for housing and lending institutions. If housing and lending institutions operate on a for-profit basis, and if there is a premium for segregated communities, the institutions themselves may benefit from yielding to consumer demand. The government must increase the risks of getting caught, getting prosecuted, and getting punished to increase the costs of discrimination.
- More stringent monitoring and review. Random auditing coupled with zealous antidiscrimination enforcement in the rental, sales, and lending industries can offset the premium for segregation. Consequently, such actions can disrupt the self-reinforcing networks that maintain racial segregation.
- Incriminating information. The Home Mortgage Disclosure Act has provided valuable information in determining the extent of racial bias in lending institutions. We should continue to press for the release of information relevant to detecting discrimination. This data will facilitate finding violators and will force institutions to

reexamine their own practices and consider the risks of prosecution.

- Symbolic steps and agreements. Currently, Cisneros has an agreement with the country's largest mortgage organization, the Mortgage Bankers Association of America, that lenders will try to take affirmative steps toward hiring and serving minorities through setting goals and timetables. Such symbolic agreements help to spread awareness and to impose an element of pressure upon the relevant institutions.

- Increased emphasis on lending. Very few lending cases are prosecuted and investigated, despite the strong link between discrimination in lending and in the real estate markets. In FY 1992 fair lending complaints amounted to 271, only 4 percent of total complaints. Because oversight of lending institutions falls under the jurisdiction of the Federal Trade Commission, the Department of Justice, and HUD (via funding for local auditing and secretary-initiated investigations), responsibility for prosecution may be difficult to determine. The necessary enforcement mechanisms and the designated enforcement agency must be more clearly identified. The prosecution and investigation of lending institutions, especially mortgage brokers and department store mortgage offices, depend crucially upon secretary-initiated investigations.

- Training. While testing is important for ferreting out violators, training sessions are necessary for spelling out the law. Training sessions should be mandated for institutions that are involved with HUD-supported programs. These training sessions discuss affirmative marketing techniques, nondiscrimination laws, affirmative program mandates, and penalties to discrimination. Local training should also be available for interested lending and real estate institutions, whether through a local fair housing organization or through the local housing authority.

3. Expand the housing options for homeseekers through coordinating information networks and outreach programs. Educate homeseekers and current residents about the real, not rumored, effects of housing integration.

- Education. Homeseekers should learn to identify what practices can be construed as discrimination and what legal redress will protect their rights. Such education should occur through local fair housing organizations or through the local housing authority.
- Mandated multiple listing services. Because most housing and lending agencies are small by nature, information regarding other nearby localities is limited. Multiple listing services would eliminate the opportunities for withholding information regarding available housing. At the same time, they would also broaden the scope of housing for all homeseekers.[13]
- Increased funding for affirmative programs. More funding is needed for block grants to organizations to conduct pro-integration programs, such as race relations seminars, to provide extra maintenance as neighborhoods change. These programs help to stabilize neighborhoods and to improve community relations.
- Regional outreach programs. To complement mandated multiple listing services, local housing authorities should also join with neighboring authorities and fair housing organizations to create a program of outreach and support services. The program would encourage homeseekers to consider previously unlikely areas; its services should include offering statistics on neighborhood change, regional and local information concerning employment and schools, site-visit tours, and homeseeking counseling.
- Metropolitan referrals in public assistance. Holders of federal Section 8 housing subsidies should receive housing referrals that encompass regional housing options, in accordance with the government's responsibility to reverse decades of discriminatory practices. Local housing authorities must also provide these homeseekers with support services such as counseling and site visits.

The practice of strict antidiscrimination, including the prosecution of those who have discriminated, has not existed in the United States. As a result, misconceptions, stereotypes, and segregation have survived. Bias in individual decisions, the housing and lending markets, and government programs, moreover, is often so insidious that it is undetectable, and so firmly rooted that it is impervious to straightforward antidiscrimination policies. There are many responsibilities of the federal government in the realm of housing discrimination. Most important among these is its duty to compensate for the discriminatory practices it formerly condoned and for the detrimental segregation that has resulted. This compensation can take the form of antidiscrimination measures, but they must go beyond merely reacting to complaints of past discrimination. The only way that the government can combat housing discrimination is through a comprehensive, past-present-*and*-future-oriented program that affirmatively ensures real housing choices for all Americans. Antidiscrimination, then, shifts from being merely past-reactive to incorporating present-corrective and future-preventative components.

The most effective affirmative programs will share several characteristics. They will attempt to provide more information to all homeseekers to expand the range of housing choices. They will confront the rumors about the pitfalls of integration with the truth of its triumphs to enlighten homeseekers as well as local residents. They will force lending and housing institutions to abandon their covert and overt networks of discrimination. And they will recognize that the issue of fair housing is one that affects not just one neighborhood or one community, but entire metropolitan communities. Suburbs and cities must work together to attack the problems of racial discrimination and housing segregation—and these efforts will aid in addressing the issues of equal opportunity in education and employment. Only collaborative, comprehensive, forward-looking reforms have the power and potential to eliminate racial discrimination in the housing market and to temper the continuing effects of racial injustice in this country.

Notes

1. The reader interested in the effects of housing discrimination on other minorities may refer to Michael Davis, *City of Quarts* (New York: Verso Press, 1990).
2. "Blockbusting" is the practice in which real estate brokers induce a panic in white neighborhoods so that whites will be forced to sell their homes at discounted prices in their anxiousness to avoid a black "takeover." Brokers then sell the units at market prices to blacks.
3. The 1948 Supreme Court case *Shelley v. Kramer* invalidated racially restrictive covenants. However, Lemann writes that this merely "increased the level of panic in white neighborhoods that now had no legal means of preventing integration" (Lemann, 1991, p. 72).
4. Exec. Order No. 11,063, 27 Fed. Reg. 11, 527 (1962)—see Rubinowitz and Trosman (1979), p. 516.
5. 42 USC § 2000d.
6. "Steering" is the practice in which brokers will, usually subtly, maintain the racial composition of neighborhoods by presenting limited housing options to homeseekers.
7. The index of dissimilarity describes how many blacks would have to move to a different area to achieve accurate representation by population in the area. For example, a city that is x percent black would have an even pattern over x percent black per neighborhood (or, more commonly used, per census tract). When there is overrepresentation, then, an index of, say, 80 would signify that 80 percent of blacks would have to relocate to achieve even representation in the city. Persistently high numbers indicate that minority ghettos are firmly rooted in particular areas.
8. A single census tract may appear to be integrated because it has a 50 percent black and 50 percent white population. However, the tract itself might be divided into separate black and white regions, and the index would not detect such continuing segregation. Sander (1988), p. 883, corresponding notes.
9. The HDS is one example of the use of testers to determine unfavorable treatment. During testing, or auditing, auditors report to the same agencies, banks, or residential units. The auditors have created identical qualifications and characteristics, with the only difference being their races. The purpose of the audit is to compare the disparities in treatment of identically qualified candidates of different races.
10. This case, *Gautreaux v. Hills*, will be addressed in the next section.
11. For more about the efficacy of Massachusetts' statute, see the brief article by Peter S. Canellos, "After 20 Years, Anti-snob Zoning Found Ineffective," *Boston Globe*, January 1, 1989.
12. *Hills v. Gautreaux*, 425 U.S. 284 (1976).
13. For more information on multiple listing services, see John Yinger, "Closed Doors, Lost Opportunities," chap. 11, p. 45.

References

Ball, Joanne. 1988. "Yonkers Isn't Alone in Resisting Desegregation." *Boston Globe*, September 18.

Bennett, Claudette E. 1995. *The Black Population in the United States, March 1994 and 1993*. U.S. Bureau of the Census, Current Population Report, P20-480. Washington, D.C.: U.S. Government Printing Office.

Canellos, Peter S. 1989. "After 20 Years, Anti-snob Zoning Found Ineffective." *Boston Globe*, January 1.

Carmines, Edward G., and Richard A. Champagne, 1990. "The Changing Content of American Racial Attitudes: A Fifty-Year Portrait." *Research in Micropolitics* 3: 187-208.

Cunniff, Bill. 1994. "New Look Is Invigorating Scattered Public Housing." *Chicago Sun-Times*, July 15.

Farley, Reynolds. 1991. "Residential Segregation of Social and Economic Groups among Blacks, 1970-1980." In Christopher Jencks and Paul E. Petersen, eds., *The Urban Underclass*. Washington, D.C.: Brookings Institution.

Farley, Reynolds, Suzanne Bianchi, and Diane Colasanto. 1979. "Barriers to the Racial Integration of Neighborhoods: The Detroit Case." In Wade Clark Roof, ed., *Race and Residence in American Cities*. Philadelphia: American Academy of Political and Social Sciences.

Farley, Reynolds, and William H. Frey. 1994. "Changes in the Segregation of Whites from Blacks during the 1980s: Small Steps toward a More Integrated Society." *American Sociological Review* 59 (February): 23-45.

Gallagher, Mary Lou. 1994. "HUD's Geography of Opportunity." *Planning* 60 (July).

Glazer, Nathan. 1987. *Affirmative Discrimination: Ethnic Inequality and Public Policy*. Cambridge, Mass.: Harvard University Press.

Graham, Hugh Davis. 1990. *The Civil Rights Era: Origins and Development of National Policy*. New York: Oxford University Press.

Grieder, John G. 1993. "Fair Housing Act: Local Occupancy Preferences Violate Goal of Fair Housing Act." *New Jersey Lawyer*, April 12.

Kushner, James A. 1990. *Fair Housing: Discrimination in Real Estate, Community Development, and Revitalization*. Colorado Springs: McGraw-Hill.

Lamar, Martha, Alan Mallach, and John M. Payne. 1989. "Mount Laurel at Work: Affordable Housing in New Jersey, 1983-1988." 41 *Rutgers Law Review* 1197, 1199-1280.

Lemann, Nicholas. 1991. *The Promised Land: The Great Migration and How It Changed America*. New York: Vintage Books.

Lief, Beth J., and Susan Goering. 1987. "The Implementation of the Federal Mandate for Fair Housing." In Gary A. Tobin, ed., *Divided Neighborhoods: Changing Patterns of Racial Segregation*, vol. 32, *Urban Affairs Annual Reviews*. New York: Sage Publications.

Massey, Douglas S. 1990. "American Apartheid: Segregation and the Making of the Underclass." In *American Journal of Sociology* 96 (September): 329-357.

Massey, Douglas S., and Nancy A. Denton. 1993. *American Apartheid: Segregation and the Making of the Underclass.* Cambridge, Mass. Harvard University Press.

Massey, Douglas S., Andrew B. Gross, and Kumiko Shibuya. 1994. "Migration, Segregation, and the Geographic Concentration of Poverty." In *American Sociological Review*, 59 (June): 425-445.

Mieszkowski, Peter. 1990. *Studies of Prejudice and Discrimination in Urban Housing Markets.* Boston: Federal Reserve Bank of Boston.

Pennick, Aurie. Interview, March 30, 1995.

Rosenbaum, James E., and Susan J. Popkin. 1990. "The Gautreaux Program: An Experiment in Racial and Economic Integration." *The Center Report: Current Policy Issues at the Center for Urban Affairs and Policy Research* 2 (Spring): 1-4.

Rubinowitz, Leonard S., and Elizabeth Trosman. 1979. "Affirmative Action and the American Dream: Implementing Fair Housing Policies in Federal Homeownership Programs." 4 *Northwestern Law Review* 74: 491-616.

Ryu, Jai Poong. 1983. *Residential Segregation of Blacks in Metropolitan America.* Seoul: American Studies Institute.

Saltman, Juliet. 1991. "Maintaining Racially Diverse Neighborhoods." *Urban Affairs Quarterly* 26 (March): 416-439.

Sander, Richard. 1988. "Individual Rights and Demographic Realities: The Problem of Fair Housing." 3 *Northwestern Law Review* 82: 874-938.

Sniderman, Paul M., and Thomas Piazza. 1993. *The Scar of Race.* Cambridge, Mass.: Harvard University Press.

Stanfield, Rochelle L. 1994. "The Split Society." *National Journal*, April 2, p. 762.

Turner, Margery Austin, Raymond J. Struyk, and John Yinger. 1991. *Housing Discrimination Survey: Synthesis.* U.S. Department of HUD, HD-5811. Urban Institute and Syracuse University Contract, August.

U.S. Congress, House Committee on Education and Labor, Subcommittee on Select Education and Civil Rights. 1994. 103rd Cong., 2nd sess., July 28 (Federal News Service). Prepared Statement of John P. Relman, Director of the Fair Housing Project at the Washington Lawyers' Committee for Civil Rights and Urban Affairs.

Williams, Kale. Interview, July 1994.

Woodward, Jeanne M. 1994. *America's Racial and Ethnic Groups: Their Housing in the Early Nineties.* U.S. Bureau of the Census, Current Housing Reports, H121/94-3. Washington, D.C.: U.S. Government Printing Office.

Wright, Richard. 1940. *Native Son.* New York: Harper & Row.

Yinger, John. N.D. "Closed Doors, Lost Opportunities: The Causes, Consequences and Crises for Racial and Ethnic Discrimination in Housing." Manuscript.

Yinger, John. 1987. "The Racial Dimension of Urban Housing Markets in the 1980s." In Gary A. Tobin, ed., *Divided Neighborhoods: Changing Patterns of Racial Segregation*, vol. 32, *Urban Affairs Annual Reviews* New York: Sage Publications.

Chapter 9

The Head Start Program: Constructive Affirmative Action

Priya V. Rajan

Since the first mention of the phrase, affirmative action has sparked intense public emotion and controversy, reaching a climax in the current heated debate in Congress. The doubtful future of affirmative action programs has prompted a search for alternative ideas to accomplish the "level playing field" that affirmative action originally intended to achieve. One such governmental program that in effect is moving toward this ideal already exists, having begun thirty years ago as part of President Johnson's War on Poverty. Among the many components of his plan was Head Start, an outreach program intended to improve the academic and developmental conditions of poor children. Over the past three decades it has weathered significant economic and political change.

Head Start attempts to provide disadvantaged preschool-aged youngsters with the self-confidence and skills necessary to defy their impoverished surroundings. In 1989, 47 percent of blacks and 40 percent of Hispanics under the age of eighteen were living in poverty, as compared with 14 percent of non-Hispanic whites.[1] As a result, the majority of participants in outreach programs are minorities. Of those enrolled in Head Start, 67 percent are nonwhite.[2] This strong correlation between race and poverty indicates that while this child outreach program, which specifically targets disadvantaged students, falls outside the traditional understanding of affirmative action programs, it targets much of the same population. President Clinton has pledged his support to Head Start, and has suggested further that the government reevaluate its existing race and gender preferences in order to emphasize similar programs that help all poor people.[3] How does Head Start, which selects its participants on the basis of income, achieve for disadvantaged groups some of the goals of affirmative action? The fact that Head Start has survived multiple administrations attests to the strength of the program and suggests that it deserves a place of prominence in the current affirmative action debate, particularly as a more politically palatable alternative to race-based affirmative action programs.

Description

Head Start is a $3.5 billion comprehensive preschool program directed by the federal government's Administration for Children, Youth and Families within the Department of Health and Human Services. Along with academics, it offers balanced meals, immunizations, and other basic health services that affect a child's development. Head Start differs from ordinary child-care agencies both in its comprehensive nature and in its more community-oriented agenda. Preschool children whose family income falls within certain guidelines are eligible for the program.[4] Currently 740,493 preschoolers attend Head Start. They, however, constitute only 40 percent of those eligible for entry into the program.[5] Head Start has ten regional offices, each of which is responsible for a certain section of the country. These offices oversee the grantees, or the organizations that operate the Head Start programs.

By the mid-sixties, an abundance of research had confirmed the importance of guidance in a child's formative years, leading the government to conclude that many poor children lacked the focused attention and instruction at home that most middle- and upper-class children received. Children suffered both short- and long-term effects when their parents did not have the resources, skills, or time to adequately provide for them.

> Millions of . . . children are essentially victims of mental malnutrition. They don't get enough appropriate learning opportunities for their brain to develop optimally. And they reach the school years not only deprived of the background experiences their more fortunate peers have, but also with a brain permanently less capable of learning.[6]

Swayed by these findings, President Johnson persuaded Congress to pass legislation establishing Head Start in 1965.

Head Start is the only preschool option available to many children. The majority of Head Start participants are three or four years old, though participants range from under three to five years of age. Experts fear that even this intervention may be too late to truly help children; they believe that the ideal program would begin with prenatal care for mothers and continue from there. For those it serves, Head Start provides a positive environment and an arena for encouraging social development to take place.

Since Head Start is a federal program, grantees receive most of their funds directly from the federal government. The government pays $4,343 per child. This figure does not reflect the full expenditure on Head Start, however. For every four federal dollars, the grantee must generate one dollar in funding, which can be in the form of cash, volunteer time, or in-kind donations such as the use of school facilities. This figure also does not include the money the Department of Agriculture provides for specific services such as school lunches. Eighty percent of the funds go toward salaries and benefits for Head Start teachers and other personnel; the rest pays for supplies and equipment, transportation, and facilities.

At present, the Head Start program is not fully funded, meaning it does not have enough money to enroll every child eligible. As a result, every grantee must limit the number of children it can accommodate. Every Head Start center is currently full and has a waiting list of families who want to enroll. This list is required so that grantees can quickly place children in any spots that may open. Grantees have some discretion in choosing their participants, but they are required to have an explicitly documented recruiting procedure. According to Craig Turner, chief of the Project Management Operations Branch in the Head Start Bureau, each grantee, on the basis of its assessment of the community, determines what factors to use when making judgments about whom to enroll.[7] Some give priority to the poorest families, some to single mothers, and others to children in families where substance or child abuse might be occurring. Ultimately Head Start would like to expand to include all those who are eligible.

Although more parents want to participate than are currently being served, because Head Start is a voluntary program there is no guarantee that all eligible parents would enroll their children even if it were to receive full funding. When parents are incapable of taking the necessary steps to participate, however, often a neighbor, grandparent, or other concerned party will contact the local Head Start agency. In these situations, Head Start pursues the issue and tries to reach the needy family. Turner emphasizes, "We do try to do community outreach. There still needs to be someone precipitating the involvement, but not necessarily the mother."[8]

How Effective is Head Start?

Early studies showed significant gains in the cognitive ability of Head Start youngsters. Later longitudinal studies, however, indicated that these benefits "fade out" after the first two years of schooling, and that afterward little difference exists between Head Start alumni and their peers. Numerous investigations have cited these later data. In their controversial book *The Bell Curve*, Charles Murray and Richard J. Herrnstein comment, "There is no reason to think that any realistically improved version of Head Start, with its thousands of centers and millions of participants, can add much to cognitive functioning."[9] This purported "fade-out" has caused many analysts to question the value of Head Start.

Head Start advocates offer numerous responses to these criticisms. Even if one accepts that "fade-out" of academic gains occurs, the case for continuing funding for Head Start remains strong. The Head Start program has far broader objectives than solely long-term cognitive gains. Head Start excels at its primary purpose—to provide a nurturing haven for poor children to gain self-confidence, good health, and preparation for entry into elementary school. Its importance lies in providing these children with a healthy lifestyle and a stronger foundation for their development. With respect to these goals, Head Start can claim resounding success. More specifically, it has improved the quality of life for numerous three- and four-year-olds who might have otherwise suffered from poor nutrition and from illnesses that could have been prevented through proper immunizations. The preschool component of Head Start provides its participants with the opportunity to interact with other children and develop the social skills necessary in elementary school. Few will contest the claim that Head Start children begin school with a greater motivation and ability to learn. One Head Start director states, "Head Start cannot erase all the effects of poverty. But it does allow children to enter school knowing colors and shapes and having social skills necessary to learn. . . . That's an important accomplishment, especially in the case of minority children."[10]

There is also evidence that Head Start provides long-term social benefits. An examination of one Head Start-like program, the High/ Scope Perry Preschool Study, found that for every dollar invested in the Perry Preschool Program, $7.16 was saved in terms of social costs. The study identified 123 African-American children living in poverty and placed 58 of them in the Perry Preschool Program while the other 65 served as a control group. Researchers collected data on both groups at intervals throughout their growth.[11] It found that program participants needed special education and repeated grades less often, completed higher levels of schooling, had a lesser tendency to be involved in crimes, and had higher incomes. The preschool program thus saved money in terms of the costs of special educational services, the criminal justice system, welfare assistance, and damages to potential crime victims, and generated higher taxes paid owing to higher earnings. Although this program was an expensive prototype not concerned with cost-effectiveness, it "shows what programs for young children living in poverty can achieve if they are done right."[12] According to the study, if Head Start could increase the amount spent per child to $5,500 in order to improve program quality, raise staff salaries, and increase program supervision, the potential for similar success would dramatically increase. Similar evidence exists from studies of Head Start as well, but the data are limited. An analysis by the United States Department of Health and Human Services states, "The studies available suggest that Head Start children may develop the desired social competence to adapt more readily to their school environment and achieve more 'real life' academic successes than their non-Head Start peers."[13]

Head Start supporters also argue that critics may be expecting too much from a program that covers such a brief period in a child's life. Because numerous factors affect children's development, experiences at age four may not be traceable in everyone. Although good preschool experiences are essential, they cannot define a child's future. Advocates assert that Head Start should be judged on the basis of its value for children while they are enrolled, because there is no way of accounting for the trials they may have to endure later on. According to one authority, the arguments opposing Head Start "[are] like saying why bother trying if this isn't going to turn every kid into a CEO."[14]

Proponents of Head Start also suggest that the fade-out effect may be due to the conditions of the public schools. They claim that when children leave Head Start they are ready to learn, and that it is the educational system which is not working properly. Children lose their advantage only after entering public schools that undermine everything that Head Start attempted to instill. One study found that part of the fade-out could be attributed to the fact that the poorest children, the ones most in need of a strong educational environment, were going into the worst public schools. The researchers wrote, "Federal, state, and local policies . . . systematically undo with one hand something to which we devote substantial resources with the other."[15] Part of the discouraging reality is that "many alert and curious minority youngsters arrive in kindergarten eager to learn, yet are channeled into school structures that sap their curiosity and numb their minds."[16]

The program also engenders achievements in parties other than the children enrolled. In addition to directing families to other social service providers, such as Medicaid, so that older siblings can receive assistance, Head Start places a strong emphasis on parental involvement. It helps parents to understand both the need to work with teachers and the appropriate way to do so to ensure their children's educational growth. Each grantee also establishes a policy council that includes parents of Head Start participants. This council votes on decisions relating to the center. Jim Kalb, of the Head Start Bureau, comments: "There is real involvement of parents in shaping their child's lives as related to Head Start. It is a source of empowerment. It brings parents into a more active role regarding their child's development."[17] Numerous parents whose lives have improved after enrolling their children in Head Start testify to its worth. "In a very real way, Head Start was able to turn [that family] around," says Turner.[18] Head Start not only benefits individual families but also helps the community. It has raised public awareness about the needs for early intervention programs and their importance in the development of youth. Head Start's inclusive approach has encouraged the schools within its communities to focus more on fostering parental involvement in the learning processes of children.

Political Stance

Head Start seems to have led a charmed life in terms of public and political support, in part because few dispute the legitimacy of improving the lives of disadvantaged children. It is hard to oppose a program that takes innocent, eager three- and four-year-old children out of potentially destructive environments for a few hours every day and provides them with games, snacks, and hands-on learning. Even Charles Murray, who expressed doubt regarding academic gains from Head Start in *The Bell Curve*, has said, "I think that if you can put children, particularly children who have very little stimulation, who are coming from very bad homes, in a pleasant, well-run, affectionate, stimulating environment, that is a good thing to do."[19] The program's family-based approach to remedying social problems also appeals to many citizens concerned with the changing status of the American family.

Head Start's distinction from controversial welfare programs has worked to its advantage. Because it is not an entitlement program, it is not as susceptible to claims that it creates an adverse incentive for families to stay poor. Once a child is enrolled in Head Start, he or she is eligible for the next two years, thus alleviating any fears parents may have that their child may be dismissed from the program because of a rise in family income.

Child advocacy groups such as the Children's Defense Fund and the Quality Education for Minorities Project have expressed their support for Head Start because it has proven to be an effective program. In addition educators and analysts have advocated expansion of the program as part of the effort to alleviate the weaknesses of urban education.

Head Start's political support also extends beyond people whose only interest is children. Deemed "America's favorite anti-poverty program,"[20] it has retained bipartisan congressional support since its creation. The amount of recognition it has received, coupled with its popularity among the American public, has expanded its backing. Congress almost universally favors Head Start, particularly because it is one of the few antipoverty programs that has exhibited any measure of success. According to Rebecca Jones of the Senate Committee for Labor and Human Resources, Head Start receives much of its endorsement from longer-term senators, regardless of their party affiliation, because they have a better idea of what the program does and the battles it has fought.[21]

When the government liberally funded and heavily endorsed Head Start and other early childhood programs during the 1970s, the reading scores of minority children improved substantially. The gap between white and minority scores, though it did not disappear, lessened as a result of these increases. Head Start received its most serious blow when the Reagan administration squeezed funds allocated to it and other educational programs aimed at helping poor youths. After the cutbacks, many Head Start programs were severely scaled down or completely eliminated. These programmatic cutbacks had a significantly detrimental impact on low-income children, as evidenced by the results of a test conducted by the Educational Testing Service. In recent years, presidents have been more enthusiastic. President Bush authorized increased funding for Head Start during his term of office as evidence of his commitment to education. During this time, Head Start received its greatest increases in funding, and its budget more than doubled from $1.3 billion to $3.3 billion. The Bush administration focused on increasing the number of children served by Head Start. President Clinton requested from Congress a $700 million increase in Head Start's budget to expand it into summer programs and other innovations. Although he received only $210 million, the reasons for the lower increase rested primarily on the financial constraints faced by Congress. Head Start was one of the few programs to receive any increase, rather than being cut or level funded as most others were. It also survived an attempt to include it in a recision bill that would have revoked $42 million dollars from its FY 1995 appropriation.

Head Start Evaluation and the 1994 Reauthorization Act

Although Head Start's benefits attest to its value, the program has developed a number of problems. In 1993 the government set up an advisory committee to evaluate Head Start and report its findings to Congress. The committee was composed of administrators from various governmental departments at both the state and the federal level, experts in the field of child development, and leaders of child advocacy groups. One of the committee's most serious findings was the disparate quality among grantees. Edward Zigler, one of the original architects of Project Head Start, has estimated that approximately 30 percent of the 1,300 existing Head Start centers deserve to be closed down.[22] Zigler attributes this unevenness to the desire to rapidly expand Head Start despite a serious lack of resources and insufficient planning. According to Zigler, "It would be better to serve fewer children and serve them well than what we are doing today, because the quality of Head Start in these 1300 centers around the country are heterogenous, some excellent, some mediocre, and some very marginal."[23]   Inefficiencies currently abound throughout the Head Start centers. All children are not receiving immunizations, the staff is poorly trained, and some programs have more money than they know what to do with while others have none. The average salary for a Head Start teacher is $16,700.[24] As a result, very few well-trained and qualified applicants apply for jobs as Head Start educators. The Advisory Committee reported that almost half of the grantees had difficulties in finding an adequate staff.[25]

Another serious problem found by the committee was the lack of support for participants once they leave the Head Start environment and enter public schools. Head Start has proved that it can produce remarkable gains, but something must be done to help sustain this progress. The director of one Head Start grantee commented, "When you use Head Start as your core or as your base and you spring all these other services out around, then children will not have the fade-out when they get to second or maybe third grade."[26]   The fade-out effect indicates the need for significant program changes, such as increased interaction with school systems, that will maintain achievments to a greater degree. Head Start must address this and other shortcomings to make it a more effective social plan.

The Advisory Committee provided numerous recommendations to Congress regarding improving the Head Start program.   These focused on improving quality, increasing expansion, and promoting community partnerships. Reforms to address the problem of quality included:

- increases in staff salaries and more training opportunities to address the problem of incompetent staff,
- demanding greater accountability from the programs to decrease the number of deficient grantees, and
- improving the efficiency in the financial and procedural management of the Head Start centers.

In response to Head Start's isolation from other services, particularly local school systems, the Advisory Committee recommended:

- continuing the Head Start Transition Project, which began in 1990,
- establishing communication between the Head Start agency and the Department of Education, and
- linking Head Start to welfare reform.

The Advisory Committee also suggested three plans for dealing with the changing nature of the family and accommodating the diverse needs of participants:

- expanding Head Start to reach rural areas and to combat the serious risks of areas with extremely high poverty concentrations,
- moving toward full-day and full year services, rather than the current half-day services which last the duration of the school year, and
- serving families with younger children.

The committee noted the limited number of longitudinal studies on Head Start participants and their families and the need for more research on policy issues regarding the way the program is run.[27]

Many of these proposals found their way into the Head Start Reauthorization Act of 1994, which Congress rapidly passed with bipartisan support. Among the act's most significant changes was the creation of a series of set-asides that mandated the way Head Start had to allocate some of its funds. Twenty-five percent of any increases in Head Start's appropriation must go toward improving quality, though each grantee can determine in which areas it most needs to improve. Congress further decided that $35 million be spent annually on the Head Start Transition Program to help children move from Head Start to public school. It also allocated 3 percent of Head Start's appropriation toward funding Early Head Start, a plan to broaden Head Start's scope and reach children under three years of age. This percentage will have increased to at least 5 percent in 1998. The set-asides ate up most of the $210 million increase that Head Start received in 1995 and curtailed expansion for this fiscal year. Jim Kolb stated that it would take approximately $400 to $500 million to get past the set-asides and focus on expansion.[28] Clinton has asked for a $400 million increase for Head Start in 1996, which will allow it to expand by 32,000 more children.[29]

The findings of the Advisory Committee have helped the Head Start Bureau make changes as well. It is in the process of correcting or dropping deficient grantees. Head Start is required to perform an on-site review every three years. It is also working on instituting collaborative agreements with other child-care providers in the community to make it possible for parents to drop their children off in the morning and pick them up after work. Head Start cannot provide complete day-care services because of their cost, but this sort of cooperation can provide parents with an appropriate place to send their children that is not all paid for with Head Start funds. One Head Start official explained, "It's a commingling of dollars so you can do more. It goes a long way toward making it possible for mom to stay in the work force."[30]

Associating Head Start and Affirmative Action

President Clinton has stated that "the cause of women and minorities in America is better served by broad-based programs based on economic need, rather than affirmative action efforts based on race and gender . . . because they work better and have a bigger impact and generate broader support."[31] Clinton's attitude seems to reflect the current trend in American thought. One analyst has commented:

> It's fine, the public says, to compensate for past discrimination by means of special training programs, Head Start efforts, [etc.] . . . "Help minorities compete," whites say, "but don't predetermine the results of the competition—no quotas, no preference for one race over another, no dual standards whereby whites and blacks are judged differently."[32]

Given the unstable future of policies specifically termed "affirmative action," it is important to explore other avenues that fit the theoretical framework of affirmative action programs in spirit and pursue them under the guise of less controversial plans. This "rhetoric retooling," as Randall Kennedy calls it,[33] makes programs that are essentially forms of affirmative action more palatable to politicians.

Outreach programs like Head Start lend themselves perfectly to this purpose. Persons with stricter conceptions of affirmative action may not agree with the equating of socioeconomic programs with race-specific ones. However, the undisputable relationship between economic and racial status makes the distinction rather negligible, particularly in the realms of economic and educational disparity. The percentage of certain minorities in Head Start programs is higher than these groups' rate of appearance in the general population. Furthermore, Head Start has helped focus attention on the concerns of minorities as well as low income-families. "As a result of Head Start activities, for the first time many school districts [have] revised curricula to place more emphasis on the needs of minorities; health institutions [have] changed services and schedules to serve the low-income more effectively."[34]

Because Head Start does not have the polemical undertones attached to it that policies specifically labeled as affirmative action have, it provides a more politically feasible mechanism to fulfill affirmative action goals.

In providing positive reinforcement, Head Start neutralizes the standard argument that affirmative action programs place a stigma on the minorities they purport to help. Head Start strives to unlock the abilities that its participants may already have but do not know how to exercise. This applies to both the children and the parents involved. Affirmative action has been likened to ensuring that everyone has the same starting line in a foot race. Head Start fits this assessment well, for it provides training for poor children comparable to what most children from higher-income families would have received prior to entry into school. It tries to increase the potential for future success in a group that otherwise may get trapped in a cycle of wasted opportunity. Kolb explains, "Head Start attempts to give poor children who start out with a couple of strikes against them an ability to succeed. It is a way of making sure kids are not punished for economic shortcomings of parents and have something resembling level playing fields."[35] Head Start is also an ideal form of affirmative action because charges of reverse discrimination, which often accompany preferential policies, do not apply. Its participants are chosen based on their financial situation, and Head Start focuses on leveling people of diverse socioeconomic circumstances rather than racial backgrounds.

The Next Step

Continue Current Support for Head Start

The comprehensive nature of Head Start's services has resulted in a multifaceted program that affects all aspects of its children's lives. While providing a preschool education as well as basic health services, Head Start cultivates its participants' social skills and self-confidence. Moreover, Head Start's family-centered approach solicits parental involvement and champions the needs of low-income families within the community. It is one of the few antipoverty programs able to provide these worthwhile benefits in a rewarding manner to low-income areas, and hence it merits continued financial and political patronage.

Some critics complain that Head Start costs more than it is worth. While cost-effectiveness is important, always focusing on aggregate statistics often ignores individual achievements. Along with dollar figures, stories about children and families who conquered their adversities through Head Start's influence and encouragement provide valid indicators of its success.

Head Start's future looks relatively secure right now. For the most part, both private citizens and government officials strongly back Head Start. It is important, however, to continue to strengthen and expand Head Start's support, particularly in times of fiscal crisis when Congress is looking for programs to cut.

Steps to Achieve Most of the Goals of the Advisory Committee

The Advisory Committee targeted several areas of the Head Start program that need improvement and offered suggestions for new initiatives to better integrate Head Start with individual families and the community. Although the Head Start Bureau and Congress have taken steps toward making some of the recommended changes, they should continue to focus efforts on achieving these goals and provide adequate support to ensure their proper execution.

Advanced programming such as the Head Start Transition Project and Early Head Start must be implemented gradually, so that they are not plagued with the same weaknesses with regard to quality that Head Start now has to deal with. By learning from past mistakes, the government can effectively broaden Head Start to include younger children and help its participants make the transition to elementary school.

Closely Analyze the Public School System

Politicians appear to believe that a comparatively modest early investment is sufficient to ensure that poor children have successful educational futures. However, while the Head Start experience is an excellent beginning, it cannot sustain children throughout their academic careers. The researchers who studied the impact of public school quality on Head Start "fade-out" question a public policy "which directs resources at the entry point of schooling while simultaneously allowing serious structural inequalities to obviate these early effects, however beneficial they may be."[36] The public school system needs to effect many of the same reforms Head Start is currently working on, such as providing quality instruction that will motivate students. An additional aim for urban schools should be to preserve the safe and productive environment that the Head Start program provides.

Some may question increasing monies for Head Start when the deficiencies in the public school system are innumerable. Head Start focuses on more than just education, however, and warrants separate funding. Moreover, the Department of Education already has the multibillion-dollar Chapter One program, which targets poor children once they are in school. Barbara Clark, a legislative analyst in the United States Office of Legislation, believes both programs should coexist. "It is not a battle of either/or. Head Start does not exist in a vacuum."[37] A sustained commitment to the quality of education throughout the nation will work in combination with Head Start programs to produce an educated, competent populace in which disparities among classes and race are diminished.

Perform More Longitudinal Studies and Analytical Research

Ascertaining exactly what Head Start accomplishes is complicated by the lack of regular longitudinal studies on its participants. The paucity of empirical data prevents an accurate assessment of current progress, thus increasing the difficulty in making functional changes. It should be noted that this research is not needed to determine the overall effectiveness of Head Start; it has already been established that the program is beneficial. Rather, studies are needed to ascertain ways in which the program could serve its participants more efficiently.

Each of the 1,300 Head Start grantees retains a great deal of flexibility in its procedures and the programs it provides. Because of this, it is difficult to obtain centralized information regarding Head Start programs. Numbers that should be easily available, such as the overall percentage of applicants to Head Start that receive spaces, are inaccessible. The federal government should consolidate and systematize data from each of the grantees and make its findings available. The information needed includes the kinds of programs each grantee offers, the techniques used to interact with the community, general sketches of the types of parents who enroll their children in Head Start, and so on. This sort of data is essential for ascertaining the demand for the program, for sharing strategies that have shown particular success, and for determining where attention needs to be focused.

Recognize the Affirmative Action Benefits Head Start Achieves

Legislators such as House Speaker Newt Gingrich and Senate Majority Leader Bob Dole have sought to eradicate affirmative action from the political agenda. Randall Kennedy notes, however, that the ambiguous nature of the phrase "affirmative action" in present political arenas broadens the range of policies and practices for which the term is applicable.[38] Identifying Head Start, which is widely accepted, as a form of affirmative action would make the concept much more palatable to politicians and would diffuse some of the current animosity toward it.

Head Start differs from more commonly acknowledged forms of affirmative action in that it offers a race-neutral method of accomplishing affirmative action goals. Yet to the extent that the majority of Head Start participants are nonwhite, it disproportionately affects minorities. Inculcating Head Start into the affirmative action agenda does not mean eradicating all other forms of affirmative action. Head Start cannot combat racism in its purest form, for example, but antidiscrimination laws exist to address that problem. In attacking one of the roots of the poverty dilemma, Head Start may succeed in creating more minorities with a level of competency high enough to compete with others in both higher education and employment.

Hold Realistic Expectations Regarding Head Start

Observers have exaggerated both the problems and the victories of Head Start. Although claiming that the program serves as a complete "anti-drug, anti-crime, pro-education strategy"[39] may increase its support, such a statement only heightens people's disillusionment when it turns out that the program is unable to live up to this description. Head Start never marketed itself as a panacea that would cure racial inequality, urban decay, and poverty in a single blow. Head Start is a worthy undertaking that offers noticeable benefits, but it cannot offset every negative factor that poor families face.

There are approximately 1,950,000 low-income three and four year old children in the United States. This overwhelming number of youth living in poverty provides statistically compelling evidence that society should assist them in improving their situation. Financial constraints deny many of these children some of the most basic resources and services their wealthier peers receive, thus denying them true equality of opportunity. The principal means for achieving this is to ensure quality educational development and growth opportunities for these children so that they may learn and develop intellectually and socially. The Head Start program has proved through its success that it is the first step along this path.

Notes

1. Richard J. Herrnstein and Charles Murray, *The Bell Curve* (New York: Free Press, 1994), pp. 333-334.
2. Project Head Start Fact Sheet, Administration for Children and Families, Administration on Children, Youth, and Families, February 1995.
3. John Aloysius Farrell, "Clinton Sees Rights Shift; 'Need' over Race, Gender," *Boston Globe*, March 4, 1995.
4. Eligible children must live in a family whose income falls below the poverty line. Ten percent can come from families with incomes over the poverty line and 10 percent of the enrollment is reserved for children with disabilities.
5. "Creating a 21st Century Head Start: Final Report of the Advisory Committee on Head Start Quality and Expansion," U.S. Department of Health and Human Services, December 1993, p. 2.
6. "Hope for Those Lagging Test Scores," *Chicago Tribune*, January 14, 1990.
7. Craig Turner, chief of Project Management Operations Branch, Head Start Bureau, interview, April 24, 1995.
8. Ibid.
9. Herrnstein and Murray, *The Bell Curve*, p. 415.
10. "And a Plus in Bush's Ledger," *Orlando Sentinel Tribune*, January 31, 1990.
11. Data were collected from the participants annually from ages three to eleven and then at ages fourteen, fifteen, nineteen, and twenty-seven.
12. Lawrence Schweinhart, "What the High/Scope Perry Preschool Study Reveals about Developmental Transitions and Contextual Challenges of Ethnic Males," High/Scope Educational Research Foundation, p. 3.
13. Barbara J. Barrett, Larry Condelli, Harriet Ganson, Catherine McConkey, Ruth Hubbell McKey, and Margaret Plantz, "Executive Summary: The Impact of Head Start on Children, Families, and Communities," prepared for the Head Start Bureau, June 1985, p. 20.
14. Rebecca Jones, adviser on child policy, Labor and Human Resources Committee, United States Senate, interviewed, April 24, 1995.
15. Valerie E. Lee and Susanna Loeb, "Where Do Head Start Attendees End Up? One Reason Why Preschool Effects Fade Out," January 1994, p. 16.
16. "Reading Skills Rise Slightly; Blacks' Stagnant Scores Blamed on Cuts in Head Start," *Chicago Tribune*, January 10, 1990.
17. Jim Kolb, Head Start Bureau, interview, April 18, 1995.
18. Craig Turner, chief of Project Management Operations Branch, Head Start Bureau, interview, April 20, 1995.
19. Carolyn Lochhead, "The Anti-Poverty Program Everyone Loves to Love," *Washington Times*, January 8, 1991.

20. Douglas Besharov, "Fresh Start: What Works with Head Start?" *New Republic*, June 14, 1993.

21. Rebecca Jones, adviser on child policy, United States Senate Committee for Labor and Human Resources, interview, April 24, 1995.

22. Jim Kolb, Head Start Bureau, placed the figure at around 10 percent in an interview on April 18, 1995.

23. Edward Zigler, Yale University, appearance on the MacNeil/Lehrer NewsHour, February 16, 1993.

24. Craig Turner, chief of Project Management Operations Branch, Head Start Bureau, interview, April 20, 1995.

25. "Creating a 21st Century Head Start: Final Report of the Advisory Committee on Head Start Quality and Expansion," U.S. Department of Health and Human Services, December 1993, p. 10.

26. Blanche Russ, director of Parent/Child, Inc., appearance on the MacNeil/Lehrer NewsHour, February 16, 1993.

27. All recommendations taken from U.S. Department of Health and Human Services, "Creating a 21st Century Head Start: Final Report of the Advisory Committee on Head Start Quality and Expansion," December 1993.

28. Jim Kolb, Head Start Bureau, interview April 18, 1995.

29. Craig Turner, chief of Project Management Operations Branch, Head Start Bureau, interview, April 18, 1995.

30. Craig Turner, chief of Project Management Operations Branch, Head Start Bureau, interview, April 24, 1995.

31. Farrell, "Clinton Sees Rights Shift."

32. William Schneider, CNN political analyst, appearance on *Inside Politics*, February 20, 1995.

33. Randall Kennedy, Harvard University, speech to the Woodrow Wilson School, Princeton University, March 30, 1995.

34. Administration for Children, Youth, and Families, "Head Start: A Child Development Program," p. 12.

35. Jim Kolb, Head Start Bureau, interview, April 18, 1995.

36. Lee and Loeb, "Where Do Head Start Attendees End Up?" p. 17.

37. Barbara Clark, legislative analyst, U.S. Office of Legislation, interview, April 24, 1995.

38. Randall Kennedy, Harvard University, speech to the Woodrow Wilson School, March 30, 1995.

39. Elizabeth Gilman, Sally J. Styfco, and Edward Zigler, "The National Head Start Program for Disadvantaged Preschoolers," in Sally Styfco and Edward Zigler, eds., *Head Start and Beyond* (New Haven, Conn.: Yale University Press, 1993), p. 18.

Index

Index

About the Contributors

Ricshawn S. Adkins graduated with high honors from Princeton University in June 1996 with a bachelor of arts degree. Her plans are to work as a policy consultant before attending graduate school.

April A. Chou graduated with honors from Princeton University in June 1996 with a bachelor of arts degree. Her plans are to work a while before attending graduate school.

Jonathan S. Goldman graduated from Princeton University in June 1996 with a bachelor of arts degree. For the next few years he plans to teach high school and pursue fine art photography. Eventually, he hopes to become a trial lawyer.

Cindy D. Kam graduated with highest honors from Princeton University in June 1996 with a bachelor of arts degree. Her plans are to enter the Ph.D. program in political science at the University of Michigan in September 1996.

Jessica Malman graduated with highest honors from Princeton University in June 1996 with a bachelor of arts degree. Her plans are to work a while before continuing her education.

Justin McCrary graduated with honors from Princeton University in June 1996 with a bachelor of arts degree. His plans are to work a while before attending graduate school in economics.

Priya V. Rajan graduated from Princeton University in June 1996 with a bachelor of sciences degree. Her plans are to attend medical school.

Carol M. Swain, Associate Professor of Politics and Public Affairs at the Woodrow Wilson School, Princeton University is the author of *Black Faces, Black Interests: The Representation of African Americans in Congress*. She earned her Ph.D at the University of North Carolina at Chapel Hill.

Fredrick Vars graduated with highest honors from Princeton University in June 1995 with a bachelor of arts degree. He plans to attend Yale Law School in September 1996.